PRAISE FOR JAN BONDESON'S
MURDER HOUSES OF LONDON

'A gripping tour of London's bloodiest buildings, the
particulars of which have been meticulously researched
and entertainingly presented.'
Adam Wood, Editor of *Ripperologist*

'I cannot recommend this book highly enough. It is a
definite must-have.'
Stewart P. Evans

'Jan Bondeson conducts us on a masterly mystery tour
of London's 'black plaque' houses, where murder has left
a bloodstained visiting card... Wherever Dr Bondeson
shines his torch into dark places, he sheds new light with
the application of his powerful logic.
Richard Whittington-Egan

'Jan Bondeson can be guaranteed to tell bizarre and
quirky real-life tales and to find stories that were thought
to be unfindable.'
Paul Begg

'Jan Bondeson delves into the clandestine corners of city
life to reveal stories that would probably have preferred
to have been left undiscovered. You'll never look at the
closed doors of London the same way again. A catalogue
of crime covering more than two centuries, Murder
Houses of London combined relentless research with
splendid story-telling to produce a book of unrivalled
interestingness.'
James Harkin, Head Researcher at *QI*

'Houses of Death: Chilling tales from behind the doors of homes that were the scene of gruesome murders over the last 200 years.'
Daily Mail

'This magnificent volume is a treasure-house of information on the murders and murderers of London.'
Books Monthly

'The chilling details are revealed in a new book identifying London's so-called 'murder houses' – homes which have witnessed terrible crimes and still stand today – and telling their grisly stories. Crime history writer Jan Bondeson – a consultant doctor in his day job – spent 15 years researching and writing his book, *Murder Houses of London.*'
Hampstead and Highgate Gazette

'If you were choosing a city to star as a crime story character, London would be front and centre. Bondeson delves into the many dark corners of the city's history to catalogue the crimes that have occurred everywhere from its narrowest and darkest streets to the stateliest mansions, providing a peek behind its bloodiest closed doors for over two centuries.'
All About History

'Everyone is acquainted with the grisly facts of Jack the Ripper... but there are so many other stories to tell of murder and mystery in London. Jan Bondeson delves into these chilling tales, illustrating that you can never really know what goes on behind closed doors.
Discover Your History

'Every house has a history of some kind but few are as bloodthirsty as these dwellings where behind fresh paint, clean windows and grand entrances lie grisly tales of murder.'
True Detective

'There is more, much more, and although the East End can lay its claim to be a starting point for lurid Victorian murders, Bondeson exhaustively details the grisly history of the rest of London too. So grab the book, grab an A-Z (or actually just tap Googlemaps into your smartphone) and go hunting for London's gruesome past.'
East End Life

'Jan Bondeson is a curious author and I must confess that I approached this book with a mix of apprehension and excitement... there is a fascinating discussion to be had here about murders and 'dark tourism'.'
London Journal

'I once said that Jan Bondeson is incapable of writing a bad book. *Murder Houses of London* once again proves that statement correct... it packs a lot of information into 350 densely printed and liberally illustrated pages. If only walls could talk, what tales they would have to tell. Fortunately we have Jan Bondeson to tell the tales for them. An excellent book, highly readable.'
Ripperologist

'The work contains compelling details not only of famous crimes, but also of homicides ranging from the obscure to the long-forgotten.'
Ripperana

MURDER HOUSES OF GREATER LONDON

Jan Bondeson

Matador
9 Priory Business Park,
Wistow Road, Kibworth Beauchamp,
Leicestershire LE8 0RX
Tel: (+44) 116 279 2299
Email: books@troubador.co.uk
Web: www.troubador.co.uk/matador

ISBN 978 1784623 333

British Library Cataloguing in Publication Data.
A catalogue record for this book is available from the British Library.

Printed by TJ International Ltd, Padstow, Cornwall, UK
Typeset by Troubador Publishing Ltd, Leicester, UK

Matador is an imprint of Troubador Publishing Ltd

CONTENTS

INTRODUCTION

Ah! how unlike the man of times to come!
Of half that live the butcher and the tomb;
Who, foe to nature, hears the general groan,
Murders their species, and betrays his own.
But just disease to luxury succeeds,
And every death its own avenger breeds;
The fury-passions from that blood began,
And turned on man a fiercer savage, man.

> Pope, *Essay on Man.*

This book is the third volume of my comprehensive account of London's topography of capital crime: houses inside which celebrated murders have been committed.[1] Since there is no shortage of London murder houses, this volume will deal with all Eastern suburbs; also Hammersmith and Barnes, the northern part of Camden, Hackney and Stoke Newington, and all Northern and Western suburbs. For a crime to qualify as a 'murder', it has to have been classified as such at some stage of its investigation or prosecution, although it does not matter what the ultimate verdict was, or whether the crime was solved or not. For a house to qualify as a 'murder house', the murder must have been committed inside its walls, not out in the street or in the garden. Moreover, the building in question must survive relatively intact. A Victorian or Edwardian murder house keeps its status after being subdivided into flats, but no 'murder flats' in tower blocks and other ungainly modern developments are included in this book.

Deaths after botched illegal abortions were formerly classed as murders, but they have no business to be in this book. Nor will there be any sad tales of desperate families turning on the taps and gassing themselves. Interesting or unsolved murders have been preferred to simple slayings, and I have not felt it worthwhile to include a profusion of cases of insane women murdering their babies [there are many], or similar-sounding instances of drunken husbands murdering their wives [there are very many]. Only a few modern murders have been included, and I have avoided the activities of the present-day gangsters and mindless hoodlums, to concentrate on older murders that are of interest from a social history point of view. Moreover, I have tended to follow what the distinguished crime historian Jonathan Goodman used to call his forty-year rule: after that period of time, a murder lost its horror and squalidity, and instead gained some degree of historical interest. There are a few notable exceptions, however: for example, a book on London murder houses would have lost much of its credibility if the dwellings of that monstrous serial killer, Dennis Nilsen, had not been included. An unsolved Victorian murder in a location relatively close to central London is quite likely to be covered by this book; a recent case of a young suburban thug killing another in a drunken brawl is not.

There does not appear to be any London murder houses that are relics to crimes perpetrated prior to 1800.[2] But the late Georgian and Victorian builders knew their trade: they were able to produce quality houses that would stand for centuries to come. Even the houses intended for the poor were built to last, as evidenced by many of the humble Victorian terraces surviving to this day, in good order. The historic murder houses of London have faced a trinity of enemies: Decay, the Luftwaffe and the Developer. Clearances of low-quality slum tenements have deprived London of a fair few murder houses. Mr Hitler's concerted effort to rearrange London's architecture meant that his Luftwaffe destroyed many a murder house, not only in the East End, but all over the Metropolis. The Developer has accounted for even more of them, with hideous modern blocks of flats replacing much of the traditional fabric of old London.

Armed with this book and a good London map, you will be able to do some murder house detection work of your own. Read about the 'Hampstead Triangle', home to a surprising number of celebrated murders, and another unexplained triangle of violent death in Kensal Rise. Sometimes, quiet suburban terraced houses hide terrible secrets from the past, as evidenced by the tales of the Kensal Rise Bluebeard, the Demon Barber of Earlsmead Road, the Walthamstow Tragedy and the Acton Atrocity.

CHAPTER 1

CAMDEN

And when, at last, the closing hour of life
Arrives (for Pigs must die as well as Man),
When in your throat you feel the long sharp knife,
And the blood trickles to the pudding-pan;
And when, at last, the death wound yawning wide,
Fainter and fainter grows the expiring cry,
Is there no grateful joy, no loyal pride,
To think that for your master's good you die?

Robert Southey, *Ode to a Pig*.

The central part of the huge monstrosity that is today's London Borough of Camden have been covered in the first part of this book, leaving Regent's Park, Hampstead, Holloway and the other northern regions for the present volume.

Many of the celebrated Camden murder houses still stand, but a good few have been lost, notably the house of horrors at No. 13 Pratt Terrace, a row of slum dwellings on the eastern side of Great College Street, not far from Pratt Street, where the wicked crone Esther Hibner tortured one of her pauper apprentices to death back in 1829. Pratt Terrace still stood in 1863, but nothing remains of it today. One of Kentish Town's most notorious murder houses, the milk-shop at No. 92 Bartholomew Road, site of the mysterious unsolved murder of Mrs Louisa Samuel in

1.1 The milk shop in Bartholomew Road, where Mrs Samuel was murdered in 1887, from the Illustrated Police News.

1887, stood for many decades, but is gone today. No 58 Arlington Road, where the one-legged street musician Ewen Stitchell, who called himself Eugene de Vere, murdered his girlfriend Polly Walker in 1926, no longer stands; nor does No. 30 Hawley Crescent, where the appropriately named Samuel James Furnace murdered Walter Spatchett in 1933, before setting fire to the premises and faking a suicide letter for it to appear as if he himself had perished in the flames. This cunning stratagem did not work, however, and Furnace later destroyed himself while in police custody, through drinking hydrochloric acid.

It is notable that some of the Hampstead murder houses form a sinister cluster: it does not demand much exertion from the curious to visit No. 94 Fleet Road, the Manor House at No. 9 Downshire Hill, No. 23 Upper Park Road and No. 11 South Hill Park. This brief Hampstead murder tour can end at the Magdala Tavern, for some refreshments to be taken as you make your own mind up about the alleged bullet marks in the wall, said by some to have been the result of Ruth Ellis gunning down her faithless lover back in 1955.

A LONDON 'MURDER FARM', 1814

James Dobbins was a turncock, working for the Hampstead Water Work Company, and living at Millfield Farm, near Kentish Town, with his common-law wife Elizabeth Buchanan. They had lived together for twenty years, and were honest, hard-working people. In addition to tending the small farm, Elizabeth took in washing. On October 4 1814, James Dobbins was working with a man named William Clark. When the latter went to Millfield Farm to get some water, nobody let him in. He went back to fetch his colleague Dobbins, and together, they entered the small farmhouse. They saw Elizabeth lying on the floor, her head streaming with blood and gore. When later asked to describe her condition, Dobbins said that "Her head was cut open entirely; the brain I believe was in the head, but the bones were scattered about the place, and I saw my poker standing up by the side of the copper, bent, and all bloody." Remarkably, the poor woman lived on for about a quarter of an hour, in spite of her terrible injuries, although she never spoke a word.[1]

Three hundred yards away from Millfield Farm was a house belonging to a certain Mr Ryner. Three sturdy labouring men were hard at work on the premises, digging the foundation for a boundary wall. When they saw a shifty-looking cove come walking along the road, carrying a large bundle of laundry, the community-spirited workmen immediately stopped him. Since they did not care much for tramps, they thought he had stolen the clothes from a washing-line. When the man claimed to have purchased the laundry for nine shillings, from a gipsy man with a donkey, one of the workmen commented that this was a poor story to tell. They seized hold of the tramp and frog-marched him to Kentish Town. The closer they got to the house where Mr Bash the local constable lived, the more apprehensive the tramp became. He exclaimed, in a strange quivering voice, "For God Almighty's sake, young man, do not bring me any hurt, or trouble, for I am the eldest of eleven children!" The labourers took no notice of this strange appeal, and Constable Bash took the suspect into custody. He turned out to be the 27-year-old vagabond Thomas Sharp, a native of Layton in Bedfordshire.

When he examined the stolen laundry, Constable Bash was surprised to find one of his own shirts, which he had recently sent off to the washerwoman Elizabeth Buchanan at Millfield Farm. Making inquiries, he found that he had arrested not just a thief, but a murderer. Gathering witnesses, he found that the day of the murder, a man named Abraham Tyler had passed by Millfield Farm, seeing the tramp Sharp standing in the doorway, eating a large piece of bread and butter. His testimony, and that of Dobbins and Clark, enabled Constable Bash to reconstruct the crime: the penniless vagabond Sharp had come skulking past Millfield Farm, where Elizabeth Buchanan had given him some bread and butter. Seeing that she was alone and unprotected, he had repaid her kindness by literally bashing her brains out, and stealing her laundry, but only to be apprehended by the vigilant workmen.

Although the murder had taken place outside central London, there was a good deal of newspaper interest, due to the sordid brutality of the crime. The *Morning Post* exclaimed that "Yesterday afternoon one of the most atrocious murders which have ever stained the annals of human crime, was committed on the body of Elizabeth Dobbins, a poor washerwoman, residing at Millfield-farm, Millfield-lane, Kentish-town."[2] At the coroner's inquest on Elizabeth Buchanan, a verdict of wilful murder against Thomas

Sharp was returned, and he was committed for trial at the Old Bailey. The witness testimony against him was rock solid, and he was found guilty and sentenced to death by Lord Ellenborough. After the Judge had pronounced the words 'and may the Lord have mercy on your soul', Sharp unexpectedly replied 'And may the curse of God attend you day and night, both in this world and the next!' Thomas Sharp was executed at Newgate on October 31, 1814. Lord Ellenborough survived the murderer's curse for only four years, expiring prematurely in 1818, aged 68. According to the reliable murder house detective Martin Fido, the murder farm in Millfield Lane still stands, a rare survivor, although it has since been renamed Millfield Cottage.[3]

THE CAMDEN TOWN SHOOTING CASE, 1885

In March 1885, the widow Maria Hammond kept a small lodging-house at No. 7 Caroline Street, Camden Town. Occupying the kitchen and one room herself, she let the remaining five rooms to various needy characters. One of her favourite lodgers was the 31-year-old coachbuilder Charles Wheaton, who had occupied the back parlour on the ground floor for not less than three years. A quiet, industrious man, he had shown no intention at all to move into more salubrious accommodation, preferring to stay in his little room with a cage of 'fancy birds' as his only companions. Another, more adventurous lodger in the same house was the 35-year-old John Rose, who described himself as an author and a journalist. He had already published one book, and was completing the manuscript of another, he claimed. When Mrs Hammond was incredulous, knowing Rose only as a seaman, he produced the book manuscript with a flourish, saying that the publishers would pay him £400 for it, money he would make use of to go to Australia to seek his fortune.

On the early morning of March 6 1885, Rose left his first floor room and walked downstairs, fully dressed. Without explaining what he was up to, he went into Wheaton's room and very soon after, Mrs Hammond heard four shots and a cry of 'Murder!' Bleeding profusely from the head and chest, Wheaton came bursting out from his room. He ran out into the street "in a state of nudity" and kept running at speed "through Caroline-street, Hamilton-street, Bayham-street, Camden-road and Kentish-town-road, to the North-West London Hospital, the blood streaming from his wounds." Mrs Hammond followed him, screaming 'Murder! Murder!' until she was quite out of breath. Some neighbours also tied to keep up with the wounded man desperately running through the Camden Town streets.

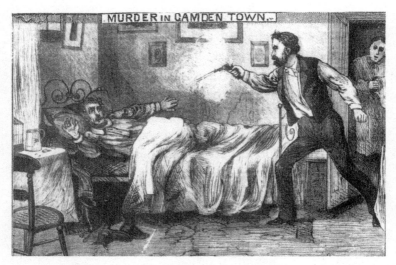

1.2 John Rose shoots Charles Wheaton, from the Illustrated Police News, *March 28 1885.*

Once he safely arrived at the hospital, Charles Wheaton's wounds were bandaged by the house surgeon. Since no bed was available, he was transferred to the North London Temperance Hospital, where three bullets were extracted from his head, chest and belly. In the meantime, the police had gone to No. 7 Caroline Street, to find Rose still there. He seemed quite excited, giving a rambling account of being invited into Wheaton's room to see his birds. When he got into the room, Wheaton had pulled a revolver on him, and Rose had made use of his own weapon to kill him in self-defence. No revolver was found in Wheaton's room, however, and Mrs Hammond denied that her timid lodger had ever possessed any firearm. It also turned out that for many years, Rose had been far from sane. He had more than once been in asylums, but he had escaped from one of them, becoming a sailor and travelling the world. Not less than £39 in gold was found in his room. How he had earned that money remains a mystery, for his yarn about being a journalist was completely untrue according to Mrs Hammond, and no book was published under his name at the relevant time.

For a while, Charles Wheaton seemed to recover, but one of the bullets had perforated the small intestine, and he died painfully from peritonitis. At the inquest, the verdict was wilful murder against John Rose. From his rambling statements, the former sailor seemed quite insane. On trial at the Old Bailey, be was found to be of unsound mind, and was incarcerated at Broadmoor.[4] The 1891 and 1901 Censuses list him as an inmate of Gloucester Second County Lunatic Asylum in Barnwell, and according to Broadmoor records, he was permanently transferred to Long Grove Asylum in January 1920. The murder house at No. 7 Caroline [now Carol] Street is still standing, and it does not appear to have been subdivided into flats.

CHILD MURDER AT CHALCOT CRESCENT, 1891

In 1891, the 40-year-old housewife Mrs Elizabeth Rapley lived at No. 31 Chalcot Crescent, Regent's Park. A gloomy, neurotic woman, she spent much time mourning a child of hers that had died of disease. She also had one living child, 16-month-old Winifred, of whom she was very fond. On November 5 1891, Mr Rapley suddenly shouted to his lodger Marie Woolden, "Oh, Mrs Woolden, come down, she has cut the baby's throat!" When she came down, Mrs Woolden saw that Mrs Rapley had done exactly that. She seemed quite distraught, exclaiming "I did it because he wanted to take the baby from me!" and "Why did I do it? Why did I do it?" A policeman was called, and little Winifred removed to hospital, where she soon expired. Elizabeth Rapley stood trial for her murder at the Old Bailey on November 16 1891. She was found guilty, but not accountable for her actions, and detained during Her Majesty's pleasure.[5]

YOU CRUEL MAUD, KILLING MY BOY! 1901

On January 14 1901, the tram conductor John Harold Shead was travelling on the footboard of a tramcar in Fleet Road, Kentish Town. Suddenly, he heard two reports of a firearm from Mr Griffiths' oil shop at No. 94, and jumped off the vehicle to investigate. Inside the shop, he could see a young man lying in a corner, blood pouring from his head. A well-dressed young woman was also lying on the floor, but she seemed none the worse. Mr George Griffiths came into the shop, explaining that the man who had been shot was his 24-year-old nephew John Bellis, who worked as an assistant in the shop. The woman who had shot him was the 22-year-old Maud Eddington, a former girlfriend of Bellis. Hearing her own name, Maud sat up, and George's wife Mrs Alice Griffiths exclaimed 'You cruel Maud, killing my boy!' 'It is your fault, Mrs Griffiths!' Maud replied defiantly. When a policeman came to take Maud into custody, she willingly walked with him, exclaiming 'I shot him! I only wish I had shot myself!'

John Bellis, who had been shot twice in the head from close range, died seven hour later at the Hampstead Hospital. The murderess had shown considerable determination, shooting her victim in the mouth from close range, knocking out one of his front teeth, and then finishing him off with a second bullet that passed straight through the brain. George and Alice Griffith explained to the police that after John Bellis had jilted Maud, she had become quite deranged, and used to spy on him in the streets. John had tried to ignore her, but this strategy had not worked as planned when she made an unscheduled visit to No. 94 Fleet Road on this cold January day.

1.3 Fleet Road, from an old postcard.

When Maud Eddington was on trial at the Central Criminal Court for the murder of John Bellis, the tram conductor Shead and Mr and Mrs Griffiths gave damning evidence against her. Several witnesses testified that John and Maud had once been 'going out' together, but he had tired of her, and written her an insulting letter. Maud had kept pestering him, however, and one witness said that John had to avoid her in the street. He hardly dared visit the Welsh Tabernacle from fear of Maud waylaying him and making a scene. Once, John had told a friend 'Here is my girl, I do not want to speak to her!' and skulked into an alleyway. Maud was the daughter of a respectable silversmith, and had always seemed perfectly sane. Some letters from her to John were read in court. She blamed Mrs Griffiths for poisoning John's mind against her, and bribing him with £40 to stop seeing her. She would herself receive a dowry of £300, she claimed, but since she intended to remain an old maid, she would never see this considerable sum of money. She then alleged that she was going away as the stewardess on board a ship, but this turned out to be yet another ruse from this artful young woman. Her final letter to John contained her last will and testament, since she had purchased a revolver and intended to kill herself. When she was buried, he was instructed to wear bright-coloured clothes. The revolver should be sold after she had made use of it to destroy herself, and her mother should receive the money. But still, the stony-hearted John did not answer her pathetic letter.

It turned out that indeed, Maud had gone to an ironmonger's shop in King William Street, City, where she had purchased a small revolver and 50 cartridges, without any awkward questions being asked regarding what use she planned to make of this weapon. Giving evidence on her own behalf at the Old Bailey, the young and attractive Maud claimed that in 1899, she had become informally engaged to John. His cruel behaviour had broken her heart, and she had originally intended to shoot herself on London

Bridge. But then she had thought of a better plan: why not destroy herself in front of her callous former fiancé? When she came into the shop, screaming 'I have come here to shoot myself, as I promised!', John acted with his usual indifference to her histrionics. But when she pulled up the revolver, he ran round the shop counter and seized hold of it; in the ensuing struggle, three rounds went off, two of them striking the unfortunate young Welshman in the face and head. She claimed to have carried with her a suicide note and a will, distributing her various possessions among her family, and to have destroyed this note at the police station by throwing it into the fire. But the two police constables in charge of her denied seeing her even go near the fire.

Lord Coleridge, defending Maud, had taken a risk by allowing his client to testify, but it was really his only chance given the amount of damning evidence against her. Described by a newspaper reporter as "a fine, handsome girl with raven hair", Maud turned out a bravura performance in court. The jurymen could not bring themselves to send such a suffering, unhappy flower of British womanhood to the gallows, or even to a prolonged stint in prison. Amazingly, Maud was found not guilty of murder, but guilty of attempting to commit suicide; she was sentenced to just fifteen months in prison.[6] The evening newspapers exulted at this happy outcome of the 'Hampstead Love Tragedy', but some legal authorities were appalled at the extreme leniency shown. A trenchant comment on the case in the *British Journal of Psychiatry* concluded with the words "substantial justice was done, supposing the view of the jury was a true one; but a good deal of doubt is left in the mind of the reader of this report."[7]

Maud Eddington served her time in prison, before returning to her family in London. The 1911 Census has her living with them in Fulham. Remaining faithful to her beloved John, to the end, she died an old maid in Penzance in 1958, having survived her brush with the gallows by not less than 57 years. Her revolver, three bullets inside an envelope, and three hat-pins, reminded visitors to Scotland Yard's Black Museum of her exploits for years to come. The murder shop at No. 94 Fleet Road is today the 'Animal Crackers' pet food and pet equipment store. If, on a cold, dark January afternoon, there are two muffled explosions among the litter-boxes and scratching posts, followed by a squeaky voice exclaiming 'You cruel Maud, killing my boy" in a strong Welsh accent, we now know the reason for it.

MURDER IN ISLEDON ROAD, 1914

In 1912, the 36-year-old newsagent Mr William Charles Lindsay was run over by a carriage in the street. He was quite badly injured, and received £300 in compensation. After his broken leg had healed, he made use of this money to buy the newsagent's shop at No. 56 Isledon Road, Upper Holloway. He would run a prosperous business here, he hoped, and the flat above the shop would come in handy for his growing family. He even invited his father to come and live in this flat, something Lindsay Sr, who still worked as a printer, gratefully accepted.

But it turned out that the shop in Isledon Road had been for sale for a reason, namely that it was not making any money. William Charles Lindsay could do little to stop its decline, except to borrow money to keep his business going. It did not help that his wife Gertrude was a very foolish, thoughtless woman, who spent much money on her various amusements. In May 1914, the situation had become desperate: for three weeks, a moneylender had been calling daily, and the week before, a troop of bailiffs had taken the furniture away. When William Charles Lindsey went to bed on May 22, he got a strong urge to murder his entire family,

1.4 Isledon Road, from an old postcard.

to spare them the disgrace of the workhouse. Early in the morning, he went to get a knife and stabbed his wife hard, exclaiming "We have all got to die!" She screamed and struggled, and old Mr Lindsey came into the bedroom to restrain him. In their bedroom, the three Lindsay daughters wept and cried, when they heard their mother scream. The 14-year-old son William Frank Lindsey had run out into the street to fetch a policeman, and the Isledon Road wife attacker was soon taken into custody. Gertrude Lindsey was taken to hospital, where she made a statement to the police about how her husband had attacked her with the knife, before she expired from her injuries.

At the coroner's inquest on Gertrude Lindey, the pathetic story of the ill-fated newsagent's shop and the couple's domestic discord was considered sufficiently newsworthy to be reported in several papers. The son William Frank Lindsey gave evidence, saying that his mother suffered from 'nerves' and that she often tried to aggravate his father when he was worried. Mrs Laura Prout, mother of Mrs Lindsey, said that her daughter had always been very thoughtless, and not fit to be a wife. She had got involved with bad company and would not take advice, spending money freely when her husband was in dire straits. William Charles Lindsey himself described how he had been worried about his failing business, and the family's near-destitution. The coroner's jury returned a verdict of wilful murder against him, adding that in their opinion, he had not been of sound mind at the time. He was committed for trial at the Old Bailey, where he was found guilty but insane, and committed to Broadmoor.[8]

THE ABOMINABLE CAPTAIN GORGES: MURDER AND MYSTERY AT MOUNT VERNON, 1915

In July 1915, the Hampstead police received a complaint from the local vicar, namely that a shabby-looking, middle-aged man named Gorges had been up to no good, prowling around the neighbourhood and enticing young men to commit homosexual offences. Richard Howard Gorges turned out to be a former army captain, who had been forced to resign his commission because of constant drunkenness. He lodged with a former policeman named Caraher in a small terraced Georgian house at No. 1 Mount Vernon, Holly Hill. Since Captain Gorges was known to carry a loaded revolver, Detective Inspector Arthur Askew and Detective Constable Alfred Young acted with caution. On July 14, they went to the house while Gorges was away drinking, and removed a service revolver and 197 cartridges. When Gorges returned in the evening, having been drinking all day, he was accompanied by a young haberdasher's assistant. Finding that his 'shooter' had been confiscated, he accused Caraher of stealing it. Askew and Young then entered the house, and confronted Gorges. When he heard that he was under arrest, Gorges pulled his *other* revolver from his back pocket, and shot Detective Constable Young dead on the spot. It was only with difficulty that Askew, Caraher, and the other lodgers in the house, were able to overpower the infuriated Captain Gorges, and take him into police custody.

On trial for murdering Alfred Young, a promising young detective with an unblemished record, things were not looking good for Captain Gorges, who did not deny that he had fired the shot that killed the detective. In his defence, he claimed that he had been very drunk, and that he had not known that the men who challenged him were detectives. He had pulled his revolver to defend himself, and it had been fired accidentally in the struggle. There was no doubt that he had gunned the detective down, but the defence argued diminished responsibility. An army character witness pointed out that Gorges had been odd in the head ever suffering sunstroke in the Matabele War. Reduced to the wreck of a man by chronic alcoholism, and trembling like a leaf, Gorges was a pathetic sight in the dock. Still, there was widespread outrage when he was found guilty of manslaughter only, and sentenced to twelve years in prison.[9] The only police killer to make his mark on the Murder Houses of London, Gorges got off lightly, but since his previous life had been colourful indeed, it is well worth reporting some of its most dramatic incidents.

★ ★ ★

Richard Howard Gorges had been born on February 14 1876, in Boyle, Co. Roscommon, into a family of landed gentry who could trace their lineage back to medieval times. In 1890, at the age of just 14, he was 'exported' to the Colonies for some unspecified misdeed. In 1896, he joined the British South Africa Police, serving in the Mashonaland Rebellion, and he later had a stint in

JAN BONDESON

the Cape Police. At the outbreak of the Boer War, Gorges joined
Thorneycroft's Mounted Infantry and initially did well, proving
himself a useful soldier, and being wounded at Spion Kop. But
then there was outrage when Gorges was caught red-handed
committing a 'bestial crime'. Colonel Thorneycroft was so
disgusted that he recommended that Gorges should be shot, but
a staff officer pointed out that this needed a court martial to be
legal. The irate Colonel responded 'Then kick him out of the
Regiment!' and indeed, all the men were lined up, each aiming a
hard kick at Gorges, as he was paraded past them!

After being so shamefully treated, one would expect Richard
Howard Gorges to have stayed away from military life, for good.
But no! He joined Scott's Mounted Infantry instead, and this time
he took his duties more seriously, concentrating on fighting the
enemy, and leaving the drummer-boys alone. A good soldier and a
fearless leader of men, Gorges soon obtained a commission, and at
the end of the Boer War, he found himself a Captain, with several
decorations for bravery. He managed to obtain a commission as an
officer in the regular army, becoming a Captain and regimental
musketry instructor in the Royal Irish Regiment. But after being
posted to Dublin, Gorges returned to his bad old ways. Peacetime
idleness did not agree with him, and he soon drank like the
proverbial fish, and involved himself in various unsavoury intrigues
with accommodating young men. His favourite boyfriend appears
to have been a certain Mr Francis Shackleton, an officer in the Boer
War and the brother of the celebrated explorer of the same name; a
very promiscuous young homosexual, he had already made himself
quite notorious in London.

One of Frank Shackleton's other boyfriends was none less
than the celebrated genealogist Sir Arthur Vicars, the Ulster King
of Arms. Vicars had been born into a respectable upper-middle-
class family in 1864. Unfit for a military career, he concentrated

on the study of genealogy and heraldry. Through a combination of genuine learning in his obtuse field, and effective toadying to those in power, this foppish young dilettante had been appointed the Principal Herald of Ireland in 1893, at the age of just 29. He was also the Registrar of the Order of St Patrick, created by George IV and aimed to reward loyal Anglo-Irishmen who had done sterling work to keep the Irish natives in their proper place. Sir Arthur Vicars, as he soon became, was for many years a loyal servant to the Crown, and a stalwart member of the Viceregal establishment in Dublin. He was allowed to revive various obsolete junior heraldic titles and distribute them among his friends: his nephew Pierce Gun Mahoney was appointed Cork Herald, Frank Shackleton became Dublin Herald, and the wealthy politician Francis Bennett Goldney was made Athlone Pursuivant. Prancing about in their elegant uniforms, the members of Sir Arthur's heraldic court cut quite a dash at various state functions.

Bur Sir Arthur Vicars had been promoted far beyond his capacity. A foolish, credulous man who completely lacked judgment, he associated himself with some very dubious people. He was genuinely fond of Frank Shackleton, although pained by his much younger friend's obvious promiscuity. Sir Arthur banned Captain Gorges from the house he shared with Shackleton at No. 7 St James Terrace, Clonskeagh, since he knew Gorges as a very bad hat, and quite morally corrupt. The Dublin heraldic court had its headquarters at Dublin Castle, and it was here that the regalia of the Order of St Patrick were kept, under the personal guard of Sir Arthur Vicars. The original plan had been to put them inside a state-of-the-art safe inside the strong-room installed at Dublin Castle's Bedford Tower, but since the safe was wider that the door to the strong-room, this could not be achieved. Sir Arthur had the safe put in the library of the

College of Arms instead. He had the key handy at all times, and liked to show off the Irish Crown Jewels, as the regalia were called, to various visitors. The heraldic court was fond of drinking and partying, often inviting various harum-scarum young men along. Shackleton and his jolly young friends were hardened drinkers, but Sir Arthur sometimes passed out after having just a few glasses of sherry. His young friends put him to bed and tucked him in, before continuing their heraldic saturnalia into the wee hours. Lord Haddo, the frolicsome son of the Viceroy of Ireland, Lord Aberdeen, once thought it capital good fun to steal the key to the safe from the comatose Sir Arthur, and to take the Crown Jewels and hide them! Sir Arthur is said to have been completely crestfallen when he was told about this prank the following day, but this regrettable incident did not induce him to improve security at Dublin Castle.

★ ★ ★

On June 11 1907, Sir Arthur Vicars showed the Crown Jewels to a visitor. On July 3, the entrance door to the Office of Arms was found to be unlocked, but with his usual disregard for security matters, Sir Arthur made no effort to investigate this. On the morning of July 6, the door to the strong-room was also found to be open. Later the same day, Sir Arthur ordered the messenger to deposit the collar of a deceased knight in the safe. He found the safe to be open and the unlocked, and the Irish Crown Jewels were nowhere to be seen!

The distraught Sir Arthur Vicars reported the theft of the Irish Crown Jewels to the police. The timing of this heinous crime could not have been worse, since King Edward VII was coming to Dublin just a few days later, and he was unlikely to be particularly pleased that his jewels had just been stolen. In the

1.5 Dublin Castle, home to some distinctly queer goings-on back in 1907; from a postcard stamped and posted in 1916.

police investigation of the theft, the detectives of the Dublin Metropolitan Police received help from one of Scotland Yard's most experienced hands, Detective Chief Inspector John Kane. It was clear to them that the theft had to be an 'inside job': the miscreant must have stolen or copied Sir Arthur's keys to the safe and strong-room, and taken possession of a key to the front door of the Office of Arms as well. They were appalled by Sir Arthur's lax standards of security, and his very lackadaisical approach to guarding the treasure entrusted to him.

The detectives took pains to investigate the various harum-scarum young men surrounding Sir Arthur and his heraldic court. Initially, there were rumours linking Lord Haddo to the theft, perhaps as another prank. A somewhat unbalanced young man, of feeble intellect and vicious habits, Haddo turned out to have an alibi, and anyway there was no clear-cut motive for this wealthy nobleman to risk his future by getting involved in a sordid theft case. Frank Shackleton became the second main

1.6 Newspaper photographs of Sir Arthur Vicars and the collar of the Order of St Patrick. There is no likeness of the abominable Captain Gorges.

suspect when Sir Arthur told the detectives about them being very close friends, and sharing a house together. It would have been easy for Shackleton to steal the keys from the befuddled Ulster King of Arms, to have them copied by some expert in this field, and then to return them before the comatose herald had recovered his senses. But Shackleton turned out to have a cast-iron alibi, having stayed in London for several weeks before the theft. Chief Inspector Kane found it curious that he had signed in at his club every day, and made sure to meet people he knew at various functions, like if he had planned his alibi beforehand. He tried to get his hands on all telegrams sent by Shackleton during the relevant period, but nothing remained to suggest that this slippery character had communicated with his accomplice(s) in Dublin.

Chief Inspector Kane also found some other quite disturbing

matters. Frank Shackleton had been active as a business man, or perhaps rather swindler, for some time. He was also a member of London's homosexual underworld, and the people he regularly consorted with included Lord Ronald Gower, a son of the Duke of Sutherland, known as another promiscuous homosexual. Shackleton's friends ranged from some of the highest in the land to dismal rent-boys and male prostitutes. There were links with the coterie that had once surrounded Oscar Wilde, and with the paedophile ring that had been patrons of the notorious male brothel at No. 19 Cleveland Street back in 1889. Lord Haddo was another of Shackleton's friends, and dark rumours also surrounded the Viceroy himself, the Marquess of Aberdeen, and even the Marquess of Lorne, who had married the Princess Louise, King Edward's own sister. It was clear to the King and his advisors that prosecuting Shackleton would open a can of worms that exposed influential coteries of homosexuals with links ranging from the Royal Family to the rent-boys of the gutter. A vigorous heterosexual himself, King Edward was greatly pained by this state of affairs. There was clearly no possibility to charge Shackleton with the theft, since in cross-examination, he might mention names that would do great damage to the Royal Family and the Anglo-Irish Viceregal establishment.

King Edward instead took out his frustration on the incompetent weakling Sir Arthur Vicars, who was made the scapegoat for the theft. The hapless Ulster King of Arms and his court were all dismissed from their positions, and more reliable men put in charge of running the Irish heraldic establishment. The Irish nationalists were of course gloating that King Edward had lost the Crown Jewels, never more so than in an article in the *Gaelic American* newspaper of 1908. The journalist Bulmer Hodson also pointed out that nightly orgies had been taking place at Dublin Castle, attended by Frank Shackleton and his great

friend 'Captain Gaudeans', a man of absolutely depraved
character, who had once been kicked out of Thorneycroft's Horse
for committing a bestial crime. 'Gaudeans' was clearly Gorges,
and the article implied that he had been Shackleton's accomplice
in stealing the Crown Jewels.

★ ★ ★

The various actors in the Irish Crown Jewels case all came to
abrupt or unsavoury ends. Pierce Gun Mahoney was found shot
dead in 1914, from either suicide, accident or murder. Francis
Bennett Goldney was killed in a motor accident in 1918. Sir
Arthur Vicars was murdered by the IRA in 1921, and his fine
country house burnt down. As for the house at No. 7 St James
Terrace, Clonskeagh [today No. 14 Clonskeagh Road], Sir Arthur
had sold it to the celebrated musician Michele Esposito in 1908,
and it still stands today. The scoundrel Francis Shackleton went
to prison for another swindle in 1913, changed his name and went
to Chichester, where he ran a small antiques business until his
death in 1941.

As for the abominable Captain Gorges, there were interesting
developments in late 1916, when another convict reported that
the captain had been bragging of being involved in the theft of the
Crown Jewels. Sir Basil Thomson, the head of the CID, ordered
two detectives to make careful and thorough inquiries, but either
Gorges clammed up and said nothing, or Sir Basil was informed
by some very high authority that nothing good would come of
pursuing this lead further. Captain Gorges was released from
Parkhurst Prison in 1925, and in 1934, he was living at No. 128
Adelaide Road, Swiss Cottage. In May 1941, he was sentenced to
four months in prison for obtaining goods worth £21 by a
worthless cheque. At some time in the early 1940s, he spoke to a

journalist about his role in the disappearance of the Irish Crown Jewels, alleging that he knew exactly who had stolen them, and also their present whereabouts. In January 1944, the now 69-year-old Richard Gorges, who was registered blind by that time, pitched forward from a crowded platform and landed in front of a tube train at Edgware Road Station, having both legs severed from his body. The coroner's inquest returned an open verdict, without speculation whether he had jumped, fallen or been pushed in front of the train.

Who stole the Irish Crown Jewels? There has been speculation that there was a large-scale conspiracy, either by the Irish republicans or by intelligence agents hoping to undermine the nationalists, but for this there is no solid evidence at all. Nor does the hypothesis that the Jewels were clandestinely returned to London, as the result of an underhand deal, have anything to recommend itself. Sir Arthur Vicars may well have known more than he wanted to admit about the theft, but there is nothing to suggest that he was involved in the crime himself; after all, his entire career was ruined by his failure to guard the Irish Crown Jewels in an appropriate manner.[10] Sir Arthur was adamant that Shackleton was the man masterminding the theft, and here he may well have been right. Captain Gorges is the obvious candidate for having stolen the Jewels, possibly aided and abetted by the mysterious Pierce Gun Mahoney, who later had to be 'silenced' for his part in the affair. There was speculation that the Irish Crown Jewels were delivered to a dealer in Amsterdam, by orders of Frank Shackleton, with instructions that they were not to be broken up, since a 'deal' might still be struck with the authorities. But a more likely version of events is that the Jewels ended up in the hands of Francis Bennett Goldney, before being passed on to an American millionaire for a very considerable sum of money.

THE MURDER OF DOCTOR ZEMENIDES, 1933

On January 2 1933, Scotland Yard was called in to solve a most mysterious murder: Dr Angelos Zemenides, a Professor at King's College and one of the leaders of London's Cypriot community, had been shot dead at his mansion in Upper Park Road, Hampstead. Zemenides was a talented linguist, who had sometimes been employed as an interpreter when his countrymen were in trouble in the law courts. He had taken an interest in Alexander Anastassiou, the Warren Street murderer of 1931, and led a collection of money for his defence. Zemenides was the founder of an organization called the Cypriot Brotherhood, and Archbishop Germanos, of the Greek Church in London, spoke highly of his work in favour of his compatriots. Since Zemenides had been an Anglophile, there were rumours that some ill-disposed Cypriot might have thought he was a spy employed by the British secret service, and 'put out a contract' on the influential Doctor, with the desired result.

The newspapers reported that Zemenides' servant had let in a foreign-looking young man and showed him the way up to the Doctor's first-floor study. The visitor then pulled a gun and shot Zemenides in the chest, before calmly escaping from the premises. But when the police inspected the tall, imposing semi-detached murder house at No. 23 Upper Park Road, they found that it was in fact a boarding-house, kept by an old woman named Jessie Mulligan. She told them that Zemenides had lived in the front room on the first floor. The impoverished former engineer Arthur Deby, who lodged in the ground floor back room, earned some extra money by pretending to be Zemenides' servant, ushering his visitors up to his first floor 'office'. Deby told the police that after he had been alerted by the Doctor's outcry "Mr Deby! Mr Deby! Quick, quick, quick, help me!" he had rushed

CYPRIOT DOCTOR SHOT DEAD AT HAMPSTEAD

1.7 Incidents from the murder of Doctor Zemenides, from the Illustrated Police News, *January 12 1933.*

upstairs to find the Doctor struggling with the stranger in the hallway. Beside himself with terror, the craven Zemenides had tried to cover behind Deby's back, as the old man bravely stood up to the visitor. Deby had seen that the stranger was holding something in his right hand, but he could not understand that it was a firearm. As Deby had tried to go downstairs, with Zemenides hanging on to his back in fear of his life, the stranger had calmly fired a single shot, which penetrated the Doctor's heart. Bizarrely, Zemenides held on to a hat-stand with his last remaining strength, and did not fall down, although he did not say a single word after the bullet struck home. The murderer had then absconded with the greatest coolness, like if gunning people down was something he did every day.

In the hope of finding clues to the identity of Dr Zemenides' visitor, the police made a thorough trawl through London's Cypriot underworld. They also made inquiries about Zemenides' own background, unearthing some very unsavoury facts about the dead man. There was no evidence that Zemenides possessed a doctorate of any description. His only connection with King's College was that back in 1927, he had registered for a B.A., although never attempting to pass any examination. To impress his gullible countrymen, the sneaky Cypriot had his mail directed to King's College, and told lies about being made a professor there. It turned out that Zemenides' only honest work consisted of teaching occasional English classes for foreigners at Poulton School. Otherwise, he was busy as a blackmarket housing and employment agent, finding his countrymen jobs as cooks and waiters at the London restaurants, and accommodation with various slum lords, all for a fee. He was a loan shark and an extortionist, and those who got into his clutches would have years to regret it. This Cypriot Godfather also operated a matrimonial agency. He put advertisements into the country newspapers back home in Cyprus, and built up a 'stable' of village maidens, household servants, and prostitutes, all of whom he put up for sale in London. The procedure for some London Cypriot who wanted to purchase a wife was to pay the 'Doctor' a considerable sum in advance, to finance the young lady's ticket to London, he said. There was strong suspicion that Zemenides was involved in the trafficking of foreign prostitutes into Britain, through nominal marriages with UK citizens.

Not unreasonably, the police linked the murder with the 'Doctor's' wholesale pimping activities. Had he quarrelled with other foreign gangsters who had decided to 'terminate' him, or had he been shot by a dissatisfied 'customer' from his matrimonial agency? It turned out that the 20-year-old Cypriot pastry-cook Theodosius Petrou had once paid Zemenides £15 for a wife, but she had not been to his liking. He had tried to get his money back, but the canny 'Doctor' was not having any of that. One witness stated that the excitable young Petrou had more than once threatened to murder Zemenides, another that the pastry-cook had recently purchased a revolver and ammunition from a countryman. After a search of Petrou's lodgings, this weapon was found hidden behind a bag on top of the coal bin. The experienced gun expert Robert Churchill identified the bullet that ended the 'Doctor's' life as coming from this very revolver.[11]

When he was on trial for the murder of Angelos Zemenides at the Old Bailey, things were not looking good for Theodosius Petrou. It turned out that he had tried to concoct a false alibi, and another witness stated that when he had asked Petrou about Zemenides after the murder, the pastry-cook had replied 'I kill him!' The defence pointed out that Petrou's father was a honest farmer, and that he himself had no prior criminal record. Would it not have been pointless of him to murder Zemenides over such a paltry sum of money? And would Petrou not have had the wits to realize that, having previously threatened the Cypriot Godfather, he himself would become the prime suspect after he was murdered? The defence had their own ballistics experts, who vigorously contested Churchill's identification of the bullet. The key witness Deby could not pick out Petrou in an identification parade, but another witness, who had seen the murderer escape, thought the young pastry-cook resembled the man he had seen, although he was not certain. The Cypriot witnesses against Petrou were shifty-looking characters, and one of them was exposed in court as a convicted brothel-keeper; even the police detectives themselves described them as "an unpresentable-looking crowd". In contrast, to these dodgy foreigners, the handsome Petrou seemed like a guileless and innocent young man. Even the police had to admit that "the fact that he appeared a far better type of man that any of the others may have gone a long way to impress the Jury, *on which there were two women.*"

The outcome of the trial was exactly what these misogynist detectives had feared: Petrou was acquitted. The young Cypriot nearly collapsed in court after the verdict had been announced to him.[12] The police and prosecution were all convinced of his guilt, and they blamed the Cypriot witnesses for their blameworthy untruthfulness, which had allowed a murderer to walk free. Robert Churchill was equally indignant, stoutly maintaining that his identification of the bullet had been the correct one. Speaking out to a representative of the *Daily Express*, Petrou maintained his innocence: he blamed some of his countrymen for perjuring themselves against him, and planting the gun at his lodgings. He would devote the remainder of his life to find the true murderer of Zemenides, he said, and would not rest until the culprit was at the dock and his own name exonerated. But Petrou never found the murderer; in fact, he disappeared from sight altogether and never did anything newsworthy again.[13]

An alternative solution of the murder of Angelos Zemenides would be that the 'Doctor's' wholesale criminal activities had brought him into conflict with an established gang of criminals, with links to the Cypriot community. They hired a hit-man to shoot Zemenides, helped the murderer to get out of the country, and tried their best to 'frame' the young blabbermouth Petrou, who had been talking to many people about his grudge against the dishonest 'Doctor' over the money he had paid for the unsatisfactory 'wife'. It would not have been difficult for the Cypriots to perjure themselves against Petrou, nor to plant the murder weapon at his lodgings. It gives food for thought that Deby, who had definitely seen the murderer, could not pick

Petrou out. And why would Zemenides, who had previously snubbed Petrou with the greatest disdain when the pastry-cook came calling for his money, have become so extremely terrified when he saw who his silent, sinister night-time visitor really was?

The murder house at No. 23 Upper Hill Road still stands. A tall, well looked after Victorian semi-detached mansion, it is today subdivided into flats. The murder victim Angelos Zemenides, exposed in court as a cad, pimp, crook and fraud, and a dodgy foreign doctor if there ever was one, must surely be one of its least distinguished inhabitants ever.

MURDER AND MANHUNT NEAR REGENT'S PARK, 1935

In the mid-1930s, a wealthy London lady named Miss Riley lived in a flat at No. 19 Gloucester Road, Regent's Park. In April 1935, she was invited to go to France for a holiday. Since Miss Riley was the owner of a valuable Siamese cat, she employed a reliable woman named Bertha Louise Gann to look after the animal while she was away.

The 63-year-old Mrs Gann quickly moved into the flat, along with her daughter Maxine. Whereas Maxine worked part time as a shop assistant, Mrs Gann's only occupation was to clean the flat and feed the cat. One day, Maxine brought home a young man who introduced himself as Alan James Grierson. A stoutish, bespectacled, well-dressed cove, he was the son of a respectable Southampton solicitor, and seemed to have received a superior education. He had just lost his job as a salesman, so Mrs Gann put him up as a lodger in the large flat; what Miss Riley did not know would not bother her, the crafty caretaker reasoned, and it was nice to earn some money on the side.

1.8 The deceptively timid-looking Alan James Grierson, executed for the murder of Mrs Gann, from the Illustrated Police News, *November 7 1935.*

Mrs Gann did not at all disapprove of Alan 'going out' with the pretty young Maxine, since he seemed a better sort of bloke than her previous boyfriends. But the well-spoken Alan soon showed another side of his character. He showed no inclination to obtain paid employment, borrowed money from Maxine that he did not repay, and stole some jewelry from Mrs Gann. But Maxine was quite infatuated with her new boyfriend, and Mrs Gann forgave him after he had returned her trinkets.

In late June 1935, Alan told Maxine and Mrs Gann that he had just got a job as a car salesman. He was going to deliver a car to Torquay, and offered to taken them there for a summer holiday. He would pick Maxine up at the Marble Arch, and Mrs Gann from near Regent's Park. His real intention seems to have been to lure the two foolish women away from the flat, so that he could steal every object of value.

But Mrs Gann belatedly developed some sense of duty: surely, she would fail Miss Riley if she deserted the flat and its feline inhabitant, to go cavorting at the Devonian holiday resort. When Alan came calling, she told him she would remain at the flat, although Maxine would go with him to Torquay. Alan did not like this decision, not at all. When Maxine, who had vainly waited for him at the Marble Arch for several hours, returned home, she found her mother unconscious, with serious head injuries. Alan was nowhere to be seen.[14]

The police knew Alan James Grierson as a small-time con artist who preyed on foolish young women and deprived them of their savings. When Mrs Gann died the following day, he became the prime suspect in the murder investigation. His description was widely circulated in the newspapers:

Wanted, for the murder of Mrs Bertha Louise Gann, 19 Gloucester Road, Regent's Park, London, on June 22, 1935.

Alan James Grierson (may use the name of A.J. Forsyth or any other alias), age about 28, native of Southampton. 5ft., 9in., thick build to corpulent, complexion fresh, hair fair (greased to appear dark), eyes blue, clean shaven, Roman nose (almost broken), lobes of ears red and swollen, wears horn and gold rimmed spectacles...[15]

But in spite of this detailed description, and a nationwide search for the fugitive, Alan James Grierson was nowhere to be found. The manhunt escalated, as a breathless *Daily Express* reporter put it:

Hot on Grierson's Tail: All Britain Hue and Cry!
Watch on the Ports!
IN DISGUISE?
Liners and Dance-Halls Searched![16]

But on July 2, two detectives were following up a lead that an out-of-towner was doing odd jobs for a certain Mrs Church, who lived in Oatlands Park, Weybridge. It turned out to be the fugitive Alan James Grierson, the man all Britain had been looking for. He was speedily brought back to London to attend the inquest on Mrs Gann. One would have presumed that Maxine would not particularly have appreciated to be reunited with the scoundrel who stood accused of murdering her mother, but Maxine seems to have been a very naive, foolish young woman. She 'stood by her man' and refused to believe he was guilty, even after Sir Bernard Spilsbury had given the inquest a graphic presentation of how Mrs Gann had been brutally beaten to death with a flat-iron. The case against Alan James Grierson was rock solid, particularly after a jeweller had identified him as the man who had sold an antique silver cruet stolen from Mrs Gann.[17] Convicted of murder at the Old Bailey, he was hanged at Pentonville Prison on October 30, after a last-minute appeal had failed.[18]

The murder of Mrs Gann received a surprising amount of newspaper publicity. The duplicity of the creature Grierson, the dramatic manhunt, and the outpourings from the pathetic Maxine, were the kind of stuff that sold evening newspapers. Even after Grierson had been executed, Maxine clung to the limelight, selling the right to have his love letters to her published in the *Daily Mirror*.[19] This was the end of her brief career as a minor newspaper celebrity, however, and also of public interest in the murder of Mrs Gann, although George Orwell briefly featured it in his *Decline of the English Murder*. But not even Orwell knew what Miss Riley said when she returned home to her murder flat at No. 19 Gloucester Road [today Gloucester Avenue], or what mental trauma the Siamese cat had suffered when this valuable animal was the sole witness to the murder of Bertha Louise Gann. As for poor Maxine, she herself died in late 1937, not from a broken heart, but from tuberculosis according to her death certificate.

MURDER AND SUICIDE IN BRAMSHALL GARDENS, 1935

Mr John Lee-Booker was a wealthy Lancashire barrister and landowner. His son Roland received military training at Sandhurst, before becoming a Cambridge undergraduate, and leaving without a degree in 1912, at the age of 23. Carefree young Roland went for a trip around the world, but at the outbreak of the Great War, he rejoined the army and became a lieutenant in the South Lancashire Regiment. He saw active service in Salonika, where he was severely wounded by a shrapnel impact to the head. Although there was some degree of brain damage, Roland Lee-Booker seemed to recover reasonably well, although it was obvious that his character and personality had changed for the worse.

After being demobilized after the Great War, Roland Lee-Booker remained incapable of any sustained intellectual effort. In particular, he was a bad business man and entirely lacked 'money sense': he spent recklessly, and his family worried what would become of him. After he had married a young woman named Flora McColl in 1927, against the wishes of his family, they wanted nothing further to do with him, although his father kept paying him a small monthly allowance. After a while, this allowance was paid to Flora Lee-Booker instead, to prevent Roland spending it all in a few days. In the early 1930s, Roland and Flora moved into a flat at No. 4 Bramshall Gardens, Dartmouth Park Hill. To make ends meet, he manufactured decorated lampshades, which he sold in the Caledonian Market. But although he considered himself a talented artist, not many people bought his lampshades. Too proud to ask his wealthy family for money, Roland Lee-Booker sank into the mire of poverty. In the end, the former officer and Cambridge man was reduced to collecting rags, bones and other rubbish on a barrow.

In June 1935, Mrs Flora Lee-Booker contacted her father-in-law, to say that her husband's condition was going from bad to worse, and that his odd behaviour had alienated many of the family's friends and business associates. Roland Lee-Booker took a strong interest in politics, particularly the sinister activities of Mr Hitler in Germany, and he lived in fear that there would be another war. He was also becoming increasingly jealous and paranoid about herself, and hardly let her out of the flat. He often questioned her angrily about her movements, and she was becoming seriously frightened what he might be capable of in one of his violent rages. John Lee-Hooker agreed to see his estranged son, probably with some trepidation. But the volatile Roland was in a good mood when they met: he showed his father the large scar on his head from the war wound, and they talked together quite amicably. Mr Lee-Booker agrees to send Flora the monthly allowance in secret, to prevent his son from taking the money and spending it. The wealthy magnate belatedly showed some appreciation for her selfless devotion to his invalid son, and hoped that his timely intervention would enable them to turn their lives around.

But one day in late August 1935, the demented Roland Lee-Booker went on a rampage at No. 4 Bramshall Gardens. He attacked Flora with a chopper, inflicting lethal head injuries. He then ran upstairs and took a headlong leap out of the back second-floor window. A neighbour heard the heavy thud when he landed, and went to investigate, but both the Lee-Bookers soon expired.[20] At the coroner's inquest, held later the same month, Mr Lee-Booker said that he felt deeply shocked to hear that his son had been living in poverty. He spoke out to representatives of the *Daily Mirror* and the *Daily Mail*, blaming the old war wound for the tragedy. The *Mail* added that the Lee-Bookers had owned a large black cat, and that after the murder and suicide, this faithful animal had been keeping vigil in front of No. 4 Bramshall Gardens, waiting for its master and mistress to return. That worthy newspaper promised to keep its readers updated about the further antics of this strange 'Blackfriars Tiddles', but I cannot find anything to suggest that this singular feline, or the tragic Lee-Bookers for that matter, ever made the news again.[21] As George R. Sims eloquently put it, the tragedies pass and are forgotten, and the houses of tragedy are let to new tenants.

MURDER BY A PHONETICIST, 1941

Arthur Lloyd James was Welsh born and bred, born in Pentre in 1884, and a student at Cardiff University before going on to Cambridge. He became an expert in phonetics, and a recognized expert on the pronounciation of the English language. In 1920, he became lecturer at University College London, and in 1933, he was promoted to become professor at the School of Oriental and African Studies. Professor James was the author of several books on phonetics, and the Secretary of the BBC's Advisory Committy on Spoken English. He helped teach the BBC announcers to get their pronounciation right, and regularly appeared in the newspapers with various linguistic advice. One of the earliest 'media academics', he made quite a few radio broadcasts, impressing the listeners with his excellent command of the English language, and his ability to imitate various accents at will. Professor James married the violinist Elsie Owen, a Fellow of the Royal Academy of Music, and they had the son David Owen Lloyd James, who went on to become one of the youngest BBC announcers.

But unfortunately, the outbreak of the Second World War would change Professor James's career forever. His son the BBC announcer joined the RAF, and Arthur Lloyd James himself lived through some tremendous German bombing raids in 1940 and 1941, at his house at No. 43 Hollycroft Avenue, Hampstead. His mind became quite disturbed, and his son made sure he was removed to a nursing home, where a psychiatrist diagnosed him with depressive psychosis. But on January 11 1941, Professor James left the nursing home on his own request, against medical advice, and returned to his house in Hollycroft Avenue, with his wife.

Three days later, the police got a telephone call about a disturbance at No. 43 Hollycroft Avenue. When Detective Constable Walter Whiting knocked on the door, Professor James let him in, saying 'I have murdered my wife. She is in there.' And indeed, the dead body of Mrs James was in another room, with multiple injuries from a fork and a hammer. At the inquest on Elsie James, Flying Officer David Owen Lloyd James formally identified the body. The detective who had arrested Professor James had noticed scratches on his face, and bloodstains on his hands. The unfortunate Professor had that his powers were failing and that he could no longer cope with his work. He had decided that his wife should die rather than face a bleak future. He had wanted to take his own life, but lacked the courage to do so.[22]

On trial at the Old Bailey for the wilful murder of his wife, Professor James was found guilty but insane, and he was removed to a lunatic asylum, where he committed suicide in April 1943.[23] The tragic and sanguinary circumstances of the end of his life had unfortunately meant that a scholar who was once considered one of the greatest living authorities on the English language has become well-nigh forgotten. But in spite of his sad declining years, Arthur Lloyd James was a genuine scholar, sometimes making far-sighted judgments like "A language is never in a state of fixation, but is always changing; we are not looking at a lantern-slide but at a moving picture." In another lecture, he criticized the snobbish BBC announcers of 'being too haw-haw' in their diction; this led to the notorious traitor William Joyce being given the nickname 'Lord Haw-Haw' for his outrageous accent. At a time when many Londoners excelled when facing the German bombings, Professor James collapsed at the immense strain, not due to cowardice, but to the psychiatric disease that later led to him taking his own life as well. The murder house at No. 43 Hollycroft Avenue still stands.

MURDER AT SOUTH HILL PARK, 1954

In 1954, the ground floor flat at No. 11 South Hill Park, Hampstead, was home to the Greek Cypriot waiter Stavros Christofi, his German-born wife Hella, and their three children. Stavros held the well-paid post as wine waiter to the Café de Paris, and the family lived happily at South Hill Park until the day his

1.9 A postcard showing South Hill Park.

37

mother came travelling from Cyprus to join them. An ugly, sinister-looking woman, Mrs Styllou Christofi had a fearsome reputation. As a young woman back in 1925, she had stood accused of murdering her own mother-in-law, by thrusting a flaming torch down her throat, but she had been acquitted. An ignorant peasant woman, she was incapable of learning English, and illiterate even in her own native tongue.

A short-tempered, opinionated woman, Styllou Christofi found much to disapprove of in her son's household. The children were not properly brought up, the food was not right, and Hella did not know her place like a proper wife. Stavros should have married a nice Greek girl instead of this German floozie. Styllou soon became so obnoxious that Hella took the children with her on a holiday to Germany, telling Stavros that when she returned, this harridan of a mother-in-law must be gone. But Stavros was frightened of his mother, and did not have the courage to send her back home. Styllou regarded it as a great insult to have been threatened with expulsion from her son's household, and when Hella eventually returned, her days were numbered: Styllou was not having any sluttish foreign woman tell her where to go.

Styllou behaved less rudely for a while, and even promised to return home eventually, but at the same time, the sinister harridan was busy making plans how to dispose of her rival. On the evening of July 29 1954, when Stavros was at work and the children in bed, she waylaid Hella and knocked her out cold with a blow from the kitchen stove ash-plate. She then strangled her daughter-in-law to death, pulled her out into the garden, doused the body with paraffin, and set it on fire. A neighbour saw the witch-like old woman stoking the fire around what looked like a tailor's dummy. As stupid as she was malevolent, Styllou next ran out into the street, where she stopped a passing motorist, gabbling 'Please come, fire burning, children sleeping!' in her broken English.

But Styllou Christofi's attempt to pass the murder of her daughter-in-law off as an accident did not work, and she ended up on trial for murder at the Old Bailey. As stubborn as ever, she refused to plead insanity, and anyway three doctors certified her as sane. Found guilty of murder and sentenced to death, this mother-in-law from Hell was executed at Wandsworth Prison on December 13 1954.[24] She was buried in an unmarked grave within the prison walls, but her bones were exhumed in 1971, when the prison was rebuilt, and reburied at Brookwood Cemetery. The murder house at No. 11 South Hill Park still stands.

THE TRAGIC CASE OF RUTH ELLIS, 1955

Ruth Neilson was born in Rhyl, the third of six children, although her family soon moved to Basingstoke. Her father was an unsuccessful musician, who became an alcoholic and took his frustrations out on his wife and daughters. Ruth left school at fourteen to work as a waitress. In 1944, the now seventeen-year-old Ruth became pregnant by a Canadian soldier and gave birth to a son, who eventually went to live with Ruth's mother. By that time, she had found out that her faithless swain already had a wife and two children alive back in Canada.

Ruth went on to make a living as a nightclub hostess, although she also did some nude modelling work, and occasionally prostituted herself. In 1950, she married the dentist George Ellis, a much older man who was a customer of the club where she worked. He was quite a nasty piece of work: a violent alcoholic and wife-beater, who suffered from 'brewer's droop'. He was convinced that his wife was having affairs behind his back, and here he might well have been right. Ruth left him several times, after he had beaten her up, but she always returned. They had a

*1.10 A newspaper photograph of Ruth Ellis and David Blakely
in happier days.*

daughter named Georgina, but George Ellis refused to acknowledge paternity and they divorced shortly afterwards.

In 1953, Ruth Ellis became the manager of the Little Club, a raffish nightclub at No. 37 Brompton Road, Knightsbridge [the house still stands]. An attractive 'peroxide blonde', she was lavished with expensive gifts by admirers, and had a number of celebrity friends. She met a young racing driver named David Blakely, a gentlemanly-looking former public school boy, and fell in love with him. Within weeks, he moved into Ruth's flat above the club, despite being engaged to another woman at the time. But Blakely had a vicious side to his nature, particularly when drunk, and beat and kicked her brutally at a minimum of provocation. His snobbish family sneered at Ruth's lack of class and breeding, and made it clear that they would never accept her.

Ruth began seeing a former RAF pilot named Desmond

Cussen, a decent bloke who worked as a director of the family business Cussen & Co., a wholesale and retail tobacconists with outlets in London and South Wales. When Ruth was sacked as manager of the Carroll Club, she moved in with Cussen at No. 20 Goodward Court, Devonshire Street, and became his mistress. If she had married Cussen, and forgotten all about the scoundrel Blakely, much mischief would have been averted. But Ruth was a somewhat flighty young woman, and she kept seeing her younger lover from time to time. Blakely offered to marry her, and she accepted him, but his family would never have accepted a woman of her description as his wife. Ruth became pregnant, but lost the child in January 1955, after a miscarriage induced by a punch to the stomach delivered by the creature Blakely.

On Easter Sunday 1955, Ruth Ellis took a taxi from Cussen's home to No. 29 Tanza Road, the home of Anthony and Carole Findlater, where she suspected Blakely might be. Just as she arrived, Blakely's car drove off, so she paid off the taxi and walked the quarter mile to The Magdala, a large public house situated in South Hill Park, Hampstead. Ruth found her lover's car parked outside. Clutching a .38 calibre revolver, which she had procured from an unidentified source, she lay in wait for him outside the pub. When Blakely and a friend of his emerged, they passed Ruth when she stepped out of a newsagent's shop next to The Magdala. Clearly no close student of what had been written about what women scorned were capable of, he ignored her with his customary caddishness when she said 'Hello, David'.

But this would be the final insult Ruth would take from this boorish and ill-mannered young man. Pulling the revolver, she fired at him from close range. The first shot missed, but the second hit him in the back. Ruth kept firing at her recumbent lover, emptying the revolver when a sixth shot ricocheted off the road and hit a bystander in the thumb. She was arrested by an off-duty policeman, who took the smoking gun from her, and put it in his coat pocket. He heard her say, "I am guilty, I'm a little confused". Ruth Ellis was taken to the Hampstead police station, where she appeared to be calm and not obviously under the influence of drink or drugs. She made a detailed confession to the police and was charged with murder. Psychiatrists found nothing wrong with her, and she was declared fit to stand trial.

On Monday, 20 June 1955, Ruth Ellis appeared at the Old Bailey, before Mr. Justice Havers. She admitted that she had deliberately shot Blakely with intention to kill him, making use of a revolver procured for this purpose, something that guaranteed a guilty verdict. The jury took just fourteen minutes to convict her, and she was sentenced to death. Ruth's only hope was a reprieve from the Home Secretary. In a 2010 television interview, Mr Justice Havers' grandson, the actor Nigel Havers, claimed that his grandfather had written to the Home Secretary recommending a reprieve, as he regarded it as a crime passionnel, but received a curt refusal. The final nail in her coffin is said to have been that an innocent passer-by had been injured, namely the old woman who had been hit in the thumb. In the condemned cell, Ruth revealed more about the motive for the shooting. The gun had been provided by Cussen, she claimed, and he had driven her to Tanza Road. In a final letter to Blakely's parents, she wrote that "I have always loved your son, and I shall die still loving him".

The tragic case of Ruth Ellis caused widespread controversy. Many people found it barbaric to hang a young and attractive woman, who had murdered her worthless lover in a frenzy, after being mistreated by him for months. A petition to the Home Office asking for clemency was signed by 50 000 people, but still the Home Secretary, Major Gwilym Lloyd George, rejected it. The last woman to be hanged in Britain, Ruth Ellis was executed at Holloway Prison on July 13 1955.[25] It has been said that her case did more than any other to strengthen public support for the abolition of the death penalty. It is curious that the murderess Styllou Christofi, who had been executed in December 1954, lived at No. 11 South Hill Park, just a few houses away from The Magdala public house at No. 2A. But whereas the brutal and ugly old Styllou Christofi had walked to the gallows wholly unmourned, the execution of pretty young Ruth Ellis was (not unreasonably) considered distasteful and unnatural.

Ruth Ellis was buried in an unmarked grave within the walls of Holloway Prison. In the early 1970s, she was reburied at St Mary's Church in Amersham, Buckinghamshire. Her disturbed son Andy destroyed her headstone shortly before he committed suicide in 1982. Her daughter Georgina, who had inherited her good looks, and was George Best's favourite girlfriend for a while, later wrote a book of reminiscences of her mother. Ruth's sister Muriel Jakubait also wrote a book, exposing that Ruth had known Stephen Ward, one of the sinister figures involved in the Profumo scandal, and went on to make a very feeble case that Cussen had been the man pulling the trigger, and that the murder was the result of a conspiracy. As for the Magdala public house, it still stands, and looks very much like it had done when Ruth Ellis murdered Blakely just outside it. The bullet holes in its facade are still pointed out to visitors with an interest in criminology, but according to a local 'in the know', they are not the genuine article, but the result of a prank.[26]

THE MURDER OF A HAMPSTEAD MISER, 2004

Allan Chappelow was born in 1919, the son of the wealthy Archibald Cecil Chappelow, whose family originated from Denmark. He was educated at Oudle School near Peterborough,

1.11 A [wrongly labeled] postcard showing Downshire Hill.

and attended Trinity College, Cambridge, between 1946 and 1948. Upon leaving university, he settled down at the family home, the stately Manor House at No. 9 Downshire Hill, Hampstead. Chappelow took an interest in photography, specializing in photos of leading literary and cultural figures, which he sometimes sold to the *Daily Mail* and the *Daily Telegraph*. In 1955, he published *Russian Holiday*, a travel book from Soviet Russia. In 1962 and 1969, he published two critically praised books about George Bernard Shaw.

Allan Chappelow had always been odd and reclusive, but his literary work had kept him occupied and brought him into contact with other people. After the death of his parents in the 1960s, his life gradually went downhill. He shut himself up in the Manor House, only emerging to buy provisions, or to read at the local library. Prominent among his eccentric beliefs was that *a house should look after itself*: he never made any repairs to the roof, windows, guttering or brickwork of the Manor House, apart from sometimes replacing missing roof tiles with planks and plastic bags. The same rule applied to gardens: as a result, both front and rear gardens of the Manor House soon became impenetrable jungles.

Chappelow's neighbours reacted with dismay as the Manor House became the eyesore of Downshire Hill. The wondered whether the old author had lost his reason, but although his house was literally falling to pieces around him, the miser seemed fully lucid. Already in the 1990s, English Heritage approached the local council to take enforcement action to protect the Manor House: after all, it was Grade II listed, as an important piece of Georgian architecture. Reluctantly, the Hampstead councillors remonstrated with Chappelow, but the miser reacted with obstructionism, refusing to allow any person near his house. He claimed that he was too poor [he was in fact still very rich] and too ill [he was fit enough to travel to the United States as late as 2006] to do anything about its obvious decay. Although allowing the wholesale eviction of misbehaving council house tenants, the law was too toothless and vague to allow the authorities to take action against a wealthy miser who let his important listed house decay. Moreover, Chappelow's long-suffering but generous neighbours still tolerated him. They viewed him as a well-spoken old gentleman, and one of life's great eccentrics. He used to wear a double-breasted jacket, an old leather helmet, and small cracked spectacles. He never threw anything away, and every room in the large house was full to capacity.

When the 87-year-old Allan Chappelow returned from the United States in 2006, he was dismayed to find that the front door of the Manor House had been forced. The burglar had rummaged around among the miser's hoard of books, manuscripts and photographs, but nothing appeared to have been stolen. On May 8, Chappelow telephoned the Revenue and Customs to inquire about a tax rebate, which he thought might have been stolen by the burglar. This was the last anybody heard of him. Since the miser emerged from the house so very seldom, nobody noticed anything untoward, except for a postman who found his way through the overgrown front garden blocked by a fallen tree. A stranger came up to him and said that he was related to Chappelow, and that he would make sure the tree was cleared by the next day. This struck the postman as odd, since the stranger was clearly a Chinaman!

In June 2006, the HSBC bank managers noted that large amounts of money had been withdrawn from Chappelow's bank accounts. This was in stark contrast to the miser's usual parsimony, and the bank notified the police: had some miscreant taken Chappelow's bank cards in order to steal the old man's savings? Initially flummoxed by the overgrown garden and the junk-filled house, the police set sniffer dogs to work among the miser's hoard. The sagacious animals promptly sniffed out Chappelow's dead body, buried under three feet of papers and junk in one of the ground floor rooms.

An autopsy showed that Chappelow had been murdered by repeated heavy blows to the head. It was not obvious whether he had been tortured to give out his bank details, or if the murderer had stolen his mail to obtain them. Due to the sighting of the mysterious Chinaman in the garden, and the report that the thief had spoken in what sounded like a Chinese accent when negotiating with the bank, the Oriental tribes received precedence in the police inquiries. A mystery man named Wang Yam, 46 years old and a British citizen born in China, soon became the prime suspect. He had once been a financial trader, but had gone bankrupt in September 2004, owing £1.1 million. He had lived just a few streets from Downshire Hill, but was in arrears with his rent and due to be evicted in June 2006.

Wang Yam was arrested in Switzerland and charged with the murder of Allan Chappelow. It turned out that his past had been colourful indeed: he had been a student leader in the Tiananmen Square protests of 1989, and had fled China for Hong Kong in 1992. Later, it was rumoured, he had become an informant for the British secret services, something he planned to rely on as part of his defence. As a result, part of his trial was held *in camera*, without access by press or public. In March 2008, Wang Yam was found guilty of theft and handling of stolen goods, but the jury failed to reach a verdict on the charges of burglary and murder.[27] A retrial led to Yam's conviction on the charge of murder in January 2009, however, and he was sentenced to life imprisonment, being recommended to serve a minimum of 20 years.[28]

After the death of Allan Chappelow, the crumbling murder house faced further troubled times. As the police investigation was still ongoing, the house was set fire to by a vandal and further damaged. Expert architects were of the opinion that due to the combined effects of damp, dry rot, and general decay, it could no longer be rescued. Still, it was sold for £4.1 million, two distant relations of Chappelow in Denmark receiving an unexpected windfall. The plan was to pull the house down and replace it with a luxury replica. But in October 2010, the neighbours threatened a lawsuit after it had been revealed that the developers were planning to construct two basements underneath the rebuilt Manor House, putting the foundations of their own properties at risk.[29] When I visited Downshire Hill in July 2011, the place looked like a building site, and when I returned two years later, little had changed. The lopsided gatepost of the once-proud Manor House remains a poignant reminder of a strange, wasted life, ending with a brutal and sordid crime.

CHAPTER 2

HACKNEY, STOKE NEWINGTON AND TOTTENHAM

Go, hie thee, hie thee from this slaughter-house,
Lest thou increase the number of the dead!
… A cockatrice hast thou hatch'd to the world,
Whose unavoided eye is murderous.
                        Shakespeare, Richard III

Hackney originated as a village north-east of London. Until the early nineteenth century, it was still a rural area with many gardens, and considered particularly agreeable for a holiday. But frantic house-building in late Georgian and Victorian times changed all of this: brick and mortar took over Hackney's rural acres. Parts of Hackney and Shoreditch soon acquired a dubious reputation. Hoxton was a particular trouble-spot, and noted for the 'Hoxton Horror' of 1872, involving the unsolved murders of Mrs Sarah Squires and her daughter Christiana at No. 46 Hyde Road [the house is long gone].[1] Amhurst Road had two celebrated murder houses: No. 17 where Thomas Morgan shot his wife and son dead in 1893, before committing suicide, and No. 53, where the sinister German nursemaid Emily Newber killed a little baby

2.1 The Hoxton Horror murder shop at No. 46 Hyde Road, from the Penny Illustrated Paper, *July 26 1872.*

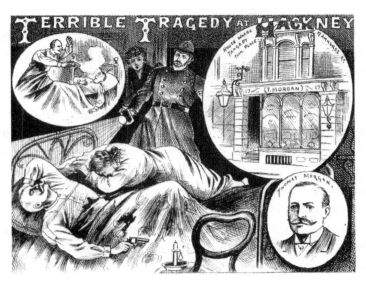

2.2 The shop at No. 17 Amhurst Road, where Thomas Morgan murdered his wife and son, before committing suicide, from the Illustrated Police News, *June 3 1893.*

in 1894; neither of them stands today.[2] The old pawnshop at No. 299 Hackney Road, where the two young hoodlums Samuel Dashwood and George Silverosa beat the 71-year-old pawnbroker Leonard Moules to death in 1942, no longer frowns upon the passer-by.

In 1965, the London Borough of Hackney was formed through the amalgamation of the old Boroughs of Hackney, Shoreditch and Stoke Newington. A large, ethnically diverse, and in parts very rundown part of London, it is home to a number of housing estates built in the 1960s and 1970s, and although some of these blots on the landscape have since been demolished, others remain to this day. Parts of Stoke Newington have always been quite gentrified, with large and attractive houses. Yet it was here, at No. 29 Bethune Road [the house remains] that the French governess Louise Masset lodged back in 1899, with her illegitimate little son Manfred. After another swain had courted her, this sinister woman made the decision that Manfred must be 'disposed of'. In the ladies' lavatory at Dalston Junction Station [the station has been rebuilt, and no original lavatories remain], she bashed him on the head and dumped the body. She was brought to justice, convicted of murder, and hanged, although a deputation of other French governesses in London wrote to Queen Victoria to try to save her.[3]

Although Hackney and Stoke Newington are not home to many celebrated murderers, there is a considerable number of murder houses in its sinister streets. Read about the sinister child-killer of Saratoga Road, and the mysterious murder at the betting shop in Queensbridge Road. And from Tottenham we have the maniac who liked chopping children's heads off, the Italian Gino Ferrari who got away with gunning down his brother-in-law, and the strange burglar 'Silky Bob' Sheppard who murdered his sweetheart.

THE DEVIL MADE HER DO IT, 1888

In 1888, the three-story terraced house at No. 93 Milton Road [today Milton Grove] was home to the 37-year-old Mr Frederick Henry Spickernell and his wife Julia Georgina. They had been married for ten years, and had four children alive. The lodger James Goldring and his wife Mary Ann also lived in the house. On December 29, the normally sane and respectable Julia Spickernell came knocking at Mrs Goldring's door. She waved her arms about in an excited manner and exclaimed 'I have done it!' Fearful that her landlady had gone mad, Mrs Goldring locked her into the back room.

She fetched the neighbour Mrs Lucy Cavalier, who sent a servant for the local doctor. When Mrs Cavalier spoke to Julia Spickernell, she replied "I have done it; the devil made me do it; he has been following me up and down stairs the last five weeks." In her bedroom, the youngest Spickernell child, nine-month-old Mabel Constance, was found thrust head first into a pail of warm water. She was quite dead, as the doctor confirmed when he arrived at No. 93.

On trial at the Old Bailey for murdering her child, Julia Spickernell's barrister described her as a broken woman, enfeebled in both mental and physical health, and practically at death's door. She heard the Devil speak to her, and it was at the Evil One's instigation that she had killed her child. She was found guilty but insane, and was sent to Broadmoor.[4] But Julia Spickernell was discharged into the care of her husband in October 1896.

By the time of the 1911 Census, she was living quietly with him in West Ham. She died in 1944 aged 91, surely not bad going for a woman presumed to have been at death's door back in 1888.

MURDER IN FAIRHOLT ROAD, 1901

William Alfred Adams was a commissions agent, living in a comfortable semi-detached villa at No. 46 Fairholt Road, Stoke Newington. He and his wife Emma were known in the neighbourhood as very respectable people. In 1900, when Mr Adams was 61 years old, he suffered serious financial losses from some imprudent speculations, and became increasingly morose and depressed. He could only afford to keep one servant, and greatly feared poverty in old age.

On April 11 1901, the clerk Mr Henry Gleim, who had been a friend of William Alfred Adams for seven years, received a very strange letter from him. Gleim was asked to take possession of the house at No. 46 Fairholt Road, and to make sure that Mr Adams' three cats were taken care of. When Henry Gleim arrived at the house, Mr Hall and Mr Dodd, two other friends of William Alfred Adams, were already on the premises. They had also received

2.3 A postcard showing old shops in Green Lanes.

letters from him, suggesting that he might have plans to destroy himself, and had entered the house through the open back door. They had found Emma Adams dead in her bed, with her throat cut and her head battered with a blunt instrument. William Alfred Adams was found drowned in the bathtub.[5]

At the coroner's inquest on William Alfred and Emma Adams, it was evident that the husband had stunned his wife with a blow and then murdered her, before drowning himself. A suicide letter indicated that financial difficulties were the reason for this rash act, although it is hard to understand why the gloomy commissions agent preferred such a premature and sanguinary demise for himself and his wife, to eking out his declining years in somewhat straitened circumstances.

MURDER AND MADNESS IN GREEN LANES, 1901

In 1901, the draper's shop at No. 94 Green Lanes, Stoke Newington, was kept by Mr William James Lewis, who employed the dressmaker Caroline Dyer. On July 4 that year, a fire was started in the cellar room underneath the shop. The Fire Brigade was promptly summoned, and did an excellent job saving the shop, although it had become very wet and dirty. A man named Arthur Reed, a member of the London Salvage Corps, took up residence in the shop and Mr Lewis made sure that young Caroline Dyer was found lodgings with his former needlewoman Lizzie Norbury and her widowed mother Ann, in their large flat over Mr Frank Britton's jeweller's shop at No. 52 Green Lanes. Lizzie's brother and two sisters also lived on the premises.

For a while, this arrangement worked quite well, but the nervous young Caroline soon complained to Mr Lewis that she had become fearful that the man Reed had impure designs on her, and that she did not wanted to go near the burnt-out shop at No. 94, where much of the dressmaking equipment was still kept. Nor was she getting on with Lizzie Norbury: the two excitable young women had several angry quarrels about their respective relationships with Reed, and the outcome of these was that Caroline Dyer returned home to her mother's house at No. 223 Lake Road in Portsmouth. Mr Lewis, who had tired of her histrionics, did not think this a great loss. But Caroline Dyer would soon return with a vengeance.

On July 23, Caroline came back to No. 52 Green Lanes, where Mr Britton told her to pack her things and get out, since he did not care for her to stay and make further trouble in the household. Caroline meekly obeyed, but three days later, she returned to the premises, armed with a dagger. With her was her brother, the butcher Ralph Dyer, who was armed with a loaded revolver. Caroline knocked at the door and was admitted. Suddenly, brother and sister dashed upstairs, brandishing their respective weapons. Caroline stabbed Lizzie Norbury hard in the chest, killing her instantly. Ann Norbury was also stabbed twice. Caroline then ran downstairs, but Ralph beat Mrs Norbury cruelly with the butt of his heavy revolver. 'Oh dear! Spare, for God's sake spare, the poor widow!' cried Mr Britton's elderly invalid mother. Two of Mr Britton's shopmen heard her cries for help, but they did not dare to tackle her armed assailant. A sturdy labouring man named Richard Edson, who was at work on a scaffold at No. 50 Green Lanes, came bursting into the house, however. When he saw Mrs Norbury being pummelled by the coward Ralph, he menacingly called out 'What game do you call that?' He seized hold of Ralph with a hearty goodwill, and the dastard did not attempt to shoot him, although his weapon was loaded with six bullets. In the meantime, the demented Caroline ran along Green Lanes, until she reached the fire-damaged shop at No. 94. She knocked at the door, and when Reed opened it, she stabbed him twice in the chest.

Caroline was secured by some passers-by, and both brother and sister were removed to the police station. Caroline seemed quite insane, and had little to say that was coherent. Ralph seemed to glory in his cowardly assault on the harmless old lady. He told the astonished policemen that his sister had told him that Reed had raped her when she was under the influence of a drug that he had covertly administered to her, and that Mrs Norbury and her daughter were accessories to the outrage. It turned out that Ralph had led an adventurous life: he had once been a cowboy in South America, and had then roamed the Australian bush. His butcher's shop in Southsea had a bad reputation for selling diseased meat, and had been at the centre of an unsavoury scandal back in 1894. When Ralph had heard his sister's astonishing story, he had grabbed hold of his 'shooter' and decided on immediate vigilante action.

Since the prison doctors had found Caroline Dyer quite insane, she was unfit to plead. With regard to Ralph, he was considered fit to stand trial, presumably with a narrow margin. When he was on trial at the Old Bailey on September 10, Mr Lewis and Mr Britton described Caroline Dyer's histrionics, and Ann Norbury gave a blow-by-blow account of how her daughter had been murdered and she herself stabbed and beaten up. William Norbury, her son, described how he had met the two Dyers at No. 8 Green Lanes; Caroline had screamed out 'I want to talk to you about Lewis's fire!' and stabbed him in the chest. The medical men who had taken care of the trail of wounded people left behind by the demented Dyers gave evidence about their various injuries: although Lizzie Norbury had expired, on the spot, Ann and William Norbury were both recovering from their wounds, as was Arthur Reed. Another doctor who had examined Caroline Dyer testified that he had found nothing to suggest that she had been raped. A number of witnesses testified as to Ralph Dyer's violent and hostile nature: he had once threatened a schoolmaster, who wanted meat on credit, with a long chisel, and another time, he had gone for a sanitary inspector who had seized diseased meat from his shop, armed with a large cleaver. Mrs Emma Dyer, mother of Ralph and Caroline, testified that apart from these two miscreants, she also had an elder son who was headwaiter at the Grand Hotel in Brighton. She described how Caroline had returned from London, and convinced both Ralph and herself that she had been outraged by Reed and the Norburys. A convinced anti-semite, Mrs Dyer had written to the 'Solicitor-General to the Treasury', saying that "Sir, – My daughter went to London as a fitter they tried to set fire to her she is now inveigled into a Jew's den please see her and see into it the fire was at 94, Green Lanes, London. We are hunted by Jews."

The defendant Ralph Dyer had been sitting smirking in the dock throughout these bizarre proceedings. He stood up and exclaimed "I took up my sister's case to avenge the outrage! I still believe she has been outraged! I plead guilty; that is my answer! I call no witnesses!" The alienist Dr Maudsley and the prison doctor James Scott next gave evidence as to the prisoner's nervous disposition and hasty temper, and his strong antipathy to Jews, which he shared with his mother and sister. It was clear to him that Mrs Emma Dyer was just as crazy as her two children in the dock, and that she had indoctrinated them with her rampant anti-semitism and other eccentric notions. Ironically, neither Reed nor the Norburys had any Jewish blood. Without hearing the counsel for the defence, or the summing-up, the jury returned a verdict of guilty but insane. Just like his sister, Ralph Dyer was incarcerated in Broadmoor.[6] Caroline was transferred to Rampton Asylum in 1913, but she was back in Broadmoor in 1917 and died there in 1939. Ralph's clouded mind improved markedly, however, and he was released from Broadmoor in 1907, travelling to Argentina to start a new life as a cowboy. The murder house at No. 52 Green Lanes still stands, as does Mr Lewis's old shop at No. 94.

THE TOTTENHAM CHILD MURDER, 1904

In 1904, the small end-of-terrace house at No. 10 Bromley Road, Tottenham, belonged to the widowed Mrs Priscilla Holmes. All three of her grown-up children lived in the house: the eldest son Thomas James Holmes, a member of the Tottenham Fire Brigade; the married daughter Mrs Priscilla Copland, with her little son Thomas; and finally the crippled son Albert James Holmes. The 23-year-old Albert was very much at the bottom of the family pecking order. An ugly, awkward youth, he suffered from cerebral paresis, with spastic paralysis in the left side of his body.

The respectable fireman Thomas Holmes did his best to secure his unfortunate brother paid employment, but Albert was not up to much. When employed as a milkman, he scattered the bottles in a random manner along his beat, and he was equally useless as a jobbing gardener. Albert was also very deaf, with a chronically inflamed, aching ear with periodic discharge of pus. When he was employed in Mr Dumbledox' outfitters' shop, his behaviour was very odd. He was constantly swigging from a bottle, and sometimes "his nerves were in a shaking state". Sometimes, when customers came into the shop, he deliberately ignored them, and they had to 'hulloa' at him to make him serve them. Once, when sent out for a bottle of coffee, he returned with a bottle of vinegar instead, and laughed heartily when the mistake was explained to him.

Rather understandably, Mr Dumbledox fired Albert, at the earliest opportunity, and the morose young man returned to the family home, where his angry brother shouted at him for once more losing his job. But Thomas Holmes thought of another stratagem to find his brother employment. He persuaded his friends to donate various unwanted books and magazines, and these were given to Albert, to be sold for a few pennies each. For four months, the luckless lad trudged the endless Tottenham streets, offering this unappetizing reading material for sale, like some bizarre Edwardian 'Big Issue' seller. Rebuffs and ridicule was the street seller's lot in those days, and Albert suffered his fair share of that.

When finally, poor Albert was free of his ordeal, and all but the most tattered books sold, he was determined never to work as a street hawker again. He desperately tried to get a proper job, but without success. In the end, he made use of a quite bizarre stratagem to save himself. Having read a newspaper advertisement, he purchased some pamphlets about hypnotism. Through becoming a master hypnotist, he hoped he could take control of No. 10 Bromley Road, and order the other family members about at will! Mrs Holmes, Mrs Copland and Thomas were all quite unnerved when the weirdo Albert began staring intently at them, and emitting strange magical noises. They thought he must have lost whatever remained of his sanity. But one day, Thomas had 'great news' for his brother: another box of books had been donated, and it was time to walk the streets again! This was more than Albert could take, and he deliberately left all the books outdoors in rainy weather, to make sure that they were all destroyed.

When he saw the ruined books, Thomas Holmes became furious. He shouted at his brother that it was time he was sent to a Cripple's Home, where the keepers would make sure he was kept busy with various chores. 'If I do go you will be glad to get me out of the way!' the gloomy Albert replied. The sanctimonious Thomas replied that the move would be for his own good. Had it not been for his own charity in allowing him to stay at No. 10, Albert would have been a crippled tramp walking the streets, without a roof over his head.

The following morning, the brothers started quarrelling again.

In front of the entire household, Thomas shouted 'You had better be out of the house by the time I come off duty in the morning!' Albert calmly turned to his mother, requesting a clean shirt before he went away. One was given to him, and he went upstairs to change, and to pack his few belongings. On his way downstairs, he went into the nursery, where his little nephew, four-month-old Thomas Copland, lay in his cot. Swinging a poker, he bashed the little boy's head in with repeated heavy blows, before going downstairs and leaving No. 10 Bromley Road, for good.

When Mrs Priscilla Copland, whose husband Joseph was away serving as a petty officer in the Royal Navy, went up to check on her little son, she was distraught to find that he had been brutally assaulted. The skull was broken and the brains protruding. A doctor provided a gloomy prognosis, and blameless little Thomas Copland died just a few hours later. The morose, jealous Albert Holmes was of course the obvious suspect, and the police issued the following communication to the newspapers:

> The cripple's description is given as follows:
> Age twenty-four, height 5ft. 3in., sallow complexion, hair and slight moustache – fair – suffers from paralysis of the left side, left leg shorter than right, left foot withered, cork elevation in boot.

After aimlessly tramping the London streets for two days, Albert Holmes found himself in Kingston-on-Thames. He bought a newspaper with the unflattering headline 'SEEKING A CRIPPLE – Strange Story of the Murdered Baby – Lame Uncle's Jealousy!' Hungry and exhausted, he went into the local police station, went up to the inquiry-window, doffed his cap, and said 'I want to give myself up for killing my brother-in-law's child at Bromley Road, Tottenham, on Sunday.' Albert went on to explain that his brother had turned him out of the house, since he was fearful that he would dominate the household with his hypnotic skills, and he had killed the little boy as revenge.

At the trial of Albert James Holmes, at the Old Bailey, there was no question that he had murdered his little nephew. Dr James Scott, medical officer at Brixton Prison, testified that Albert did not suffer from epilepsy, nor was he obviously insane. Infantile paralysis was sometimes associated with mental impairment, the obtuse doctor went on, and a chronically inflamed ear led to much irritation and pain, as well as deafness. Albert was of mediocre intellect, and his habit of reading various silly pamphlets about hypnotism was unlikely to have done his mental balance any good. The jury found Albert Holmes guilty of murdering Thomas Copland, but due to his various infirmities, he was strongly recommended to mercy. Nevertheless, he was formally sentenced to death, an ordeal unlikely to have edified the poor wretch any further. In the end, the Home Secretary adopted the jury's plea for mercy, and Albert hobbled off into a prison cell, and obscurity.[7] He was transferred to Broadmoor in 1907, and died there in 1923. The murder house at No. 10 Bromley Road, Tottenham, still stands.

CHOPPING CHILDREN'S HEADS OFF, 1906

Arthur Chopping, a morose and backward young man, found it very difficult to obtain paid employment. In August 1906, when Arthur was kicked out of his lodgings, he was taken in by his only friend Charles Yorke, a plumber who lived in a small terraced house at No. 149 Moselle Avenue, Wood Green. Chopping shared the rear bedroom with Yorke's five-year-old son Francis, whereas Yorke, his wife, and two younger children slept in the front bedroom. But although Chopping advertised for work, none was forthcoming. He was financially supported by his father, and willingly performed various household chores, but nevertheless, this needy lodger was becoming a nuisance for the Yorkes, since he was incapable of paying his rent. In better days, he once had £24 saved, but he had spent it all on drink.

On November 16, Charles Yorke told Arthur Chopping that he had to find work within a week, since otherwise he would be taking bread from the children. Yorke was short of work himself, he explained, and had no time for drunken parasites in his household: to make sure Chopping stayed away, he would put a bolt on the door to keep him out. The morose young Chopping listened calmly to this diatribe and merely said 'Good-night!' before retiring to bed.

The next morning, Arthur Chopping went out at nine in the morning and returned at five minutes past seven in the evening. He helped dress the Yorke children and put them to bed. He seemed his usual truculent self, asking Mrs Yorke if Charlie had been home, and if she had done her shopping. Mrs Yorke went out at 7.30 pm, taking her baby son Frederick with her. Chopping wanted her to leave the baby behind, since it was a cold November evening, but she did not follow his advice.

When Mrs Yorke returned home at 8.15 pm, Arthur Chopping was nowhere to be seen. When she went into the rear bedroom to check on Francis, she found her little son lying dead in a pool of blood. His throat had been cut with such force that he had almost been beheaded. In the front bedroom, she found three-year-old Beatrice in a similar condition. Poor Mrs Yorke screamed and ran out into the street.

At about the same time, Arthur Chopping walked into the Wood Green police station. He approached the constable on duty, Frederick Cook, exclaiming 'I have come!' The constable replied

2.4 Arthur Chopping goes on the rampage at No. 149 Moselle Avenue, from the Illustrated Police News, *21 November 1906.*

'Yes, what is the matter, what have you been doing?' Chopping showed his bloody hands, one of which had a deep wound, and yelled out, in a terrible voice, 'I want blood! I want blood!' It took several constables to restrain him, and pull him into the cells.

When Arthur Chopping was committed for trial for the murder of Francis and Beatrice Yorke, at the Wood Green Police Court, Mrs Yorke became hysterical when she saw him: she screamed 'Murderer! Murderer! There sits the man who murdered my innocent babes! Let me get at him! Let me get at him!' As she struggled violently when restrained by some police constables, Chopping seemed to be entirely indifferent.

On trial at the Old Bailey on December 10, Arthur Chopping

remained as inane and half-dazed as before. After the Yorkes and the police constables had given evidence, the defence played the 'insanity card'. Chopping had been drinking excessively, they claimed, and he had several times suffered from delirium tremens. His maternal aunt died in Devizes Asylum, and his two brothers were both very backward mentally. His sister was in Claybury Asylum, suffering from incurable dementia. The medical superintendent of this institution, Dr Robert Jones, testified that he considered Arthur to suffer from exactly the same condition. Indeed, the dull, listless prisoner was hardly able to answer the simplest questions: a sign of congenital weak-mindedness aggravated by intemperance, the doctor pontificated. After the medical officer at Brixton Prison had concurred in this diagnosis, Chopping was found guilty, but insane and not responsible for his actions. He was ordered to be detained during His Majesty's pleasure, and his eventual fate remains obscure, not even the Broadmoor records providing any clue as to his eventual fate.[8]

MURDER IN DURHAM ROAD, 1910

Harry Bright, a young Tottenham lad, caught severe diphteria in 1891 when he was just three years old. In some way or other, the disease resulted in him being paralysed in the right arm and leg. For five months, he was an inpatient in the Hospital for Paralysis, before being discharged as incurable. Harry still had a reasonably normal childhood, attending school until the age of 15, and becoming a useful football player in spite of his deformed leg. In spite of his crippled state, he found full-time employment as a porter, and later as a printer's labourer. He lived his parents at No. 33 Steele Road, Tottenham.

In 1909, when he was 22 years old, Harry felt very proud when he got himself a girlfriend: the 16-year-old Bessie Lester, who lived with her parents at No. 46 Durham Road, Tottenham. They became engaged to marry later the same year. But in late 1910, Harry was becoming a changed man. He was constantly complaining of a cold and a sore throat, and felt very low and depressed. His mother had suffered from periodic insanity for many years, and Harry feared that he would become like her. He was also fearful that Bessie was seeing another swain, and that she looked down on him because of his lowly occupation and crippled arm.

On October 28 1910, Harry and Bessie went out in the evening. They returned to No. 46 Durham Road, seemingly in the best of spirits. But all of a sudden, Mrs Lester heard Bessie give a scream. Her throat had been cut hard with a razor, and she soon bled to death. Harry had absconded from the house, leaving his hat behind.

2.5 Harry Bright and Bessie Lister, from the Illustrated Police News, *November 5 1910.*

Police Constable William Nicholls was on patrol in Mount Pleasant Road, not far from Durham Road, when Harry came running up to him, exclaiming 'I have done my girl in!' He was very agitated, and trembled like a leaf. Harry refused to say where the crime had been committed, instead demanding to be taken to the Tottenham Police Station. Here, he was given pen and paper, and wrote 'H. Bright, 33, Steele Road, Tottenham; Elizabeth Lester, 46, Durham Road'. He pointed at the latter address and said that he had murdered his girl there. And indeed, when a party of police came to the house, they found poor Bessie's lifeless remains, and also the hat and razor Harry had left behind.

When Harry Bright was on trial for murder at the Old Bailey on November 15 1910, before Mr Justice Darling, there was no doubt that he had cut Bessie's throat. No other person had been present in the room, and he had himself admitted the deed to the police. He was unable to explain the motive for this rash act. Dr William Ewin, the local practitioner who had declared Bessie dead, correctly explained the post-mortem findings. He then got into some very murky waters indeed by claiming, when cross-examined, that it was "generally supposed in the medical profession that, where the mother is suffering from insanity at the time she is carrying a child, the insanity may be transmitted to the child"!

Henry Bright, the father of the prisoner, explained that he had been married for 33 years and had 13 children, seven of whom were alive. His wife had thrice been committed to a lunatic asylum. At nearly every pregnancy, or immediately after childbirth, she had become quite insane and violent: "once she nearly succeeded in strangling me; another time she struck me down with a flat-iron; another time she threw a saucepan of boiling water in my face." Still, there was nothing to suggest that Harry himself had been insane at the time of the murder. All his brothers and sisters were fully compos mentis. The jury found him guilty of wilful murder and Mr Justice Darling sentenced him to death. It is recorded that Harry laughed when the sentence was read out to him. But still he was reprieved, his sentence being commuted to life imprisonment.[9] The murder house at No. 46 Durham [now Kitchener] Road still stands, as does the Bright family house at No. 33 Steele Road, Tottenham.

BABIES UNDERNEATH THE FLOORBOARDS, 1913

Frederick Robertson, a young man with a wooden leg, worked as a relief stamper, making embossed picture postcards that were popular at the time, and lodged at No. 12 Saratoga Road, Clapton. His wife Lily and their three children lived with him in their ground floor flat: the two-year-old twins Frederick and Nellie, and the 10-month old baby Beatrice. In 1913, Lily fell ill with what was thought to be tuberculosis, and was taken into Homerton Infirmary. Frederick found it irksome to look after the children, and he was not a good parent. He pinched and beat the poor children when they annoyed him with their squalling. To save himself the trouble of dressing and undressing them, he put them to bed in their day clothes. Mrs Phoebe Smith, who also lodged at No. 12 Saratoga Road, thought him a very cruel and unnatural father. She suggested that he should 'give the children away', as she expressed it, and Frederick thought this a capital idea. He took the children to various children's homes, but either they charged too much money, or would not take in the dirty little wretches.

On June 28 1913, Frederick asked Phoebe Smith to help him put the children to bed. He wanted them to be fully dressed, so that he would not have to exert himself to dress them the following morning. With some relief, he said that the Salvation Army's children's home had accepted all three children, and they would be going soon. And indeed, the next day baby Beatrice was gone. The following morning, Phoebe Smith found Frederick in the kitchen eating a hearty breakfast. He said that earlier that morning, the Salvationists had come to pick up the twins.

In the following week, Phoebe Smith became suspicious. Frederick had always been a very cruel parent, and she suspected he might have lied about the disposal of the three children. The wooden-legged scoundrel was as defective as a husband, seldom visiting his ailing wife, and instead 'carrying on' with a young floozie named Gertrude Flude, who he had met at the postcard

2.6 The dead children are found at No. 12 Saratoga Road from the Illustrated Police News, *July 31 1913.*

factory. Mrs Smith found it strange that after the children had gone, Frederick always kept the curtains drawn in the front room, and that he did not allow any person to enter it. Phoebe Smith went to the Clapton police station, where the constables did not pooh-pooh her concerns, particularly since the family lodging upstairs at No. 12 had already been complaining to the landlord about a nauseating smell. Instead they resolutely searched the house. In the ground floor flat, there was a noxious smell in the two front rooms. When the floorboards were lifted, the putrefying corpses of all three children were found underneath them, a dreadful sight that horrified even the experienced police constables.

Frederick Robertson was speedily arrested at the postcard factory, and questioned about the find. He denied ever experiencing any noxious smell in his flat, and thought some tramp might have hidden the dead children there as a joke. He admitted once having had three children himself, but claimed to have abandoned them in the street and never seen them again. The police of course did not believe him. At the coroner's inquest on the dead children, the sordid truth about Frederick Robertson's sinister activities at No. 12 Saratoga Road was relentlessly exposed. His wife Nellie could remember that before she had gone into hospital, Frederick had given her a yellowish fluid to drink, and also some white pills supposed to be good for her health. These pills had made her very ill, she said, and she had vomited profusely after drinking some tea made by her husband. She had since been discharged from hospital, and the doctors had told her she did not have tuberculosis, a diagnosis originally suggested by her husband.

On trial at the Old Bailey, Frederick Robertson was found guilty of murder and sentenced to death. There was nothing to suggest that he was insane, just cruel and egotistic; he was hanged at Pentonville Prison on November 27 1913.[10] The landlord at

2.7 Robertson is taken out of court, from the Illustrated Police News, *July 31 1913.*

No. 12 Saratoga Road must have found it difficult to let the ground floor flat for some time, but today the triple murder is all but forgotten. This once-notorious murder house looks like a very ordinary terraced house, and hopefully it is not haunted by the crying of spectral children.

THE TOTTENHAM SHOOTING CASE, 1913

Gino Ferrari, an Italian immigrant, managed a small café in Blackfriars Road. A steady, diligent man, he saved money and opened two confectioners' shops in Old Street and Aldersgate. He married an Englishwoman named Florence West and they had a son named Falda. In one of his shops, Gino employed his brother-in-law Serafino Fazzani, who had married his sister Jesuina, but they soon quarrelled and Serafino opened a confectioners' shop of his own at No. 53 West Green Road, Tottenham.

Gino and Serafino were both proud, stubborn men, and their feud went on for years. They kept spreading malicious gossip about each other, and writing poison-pen letters. It particularly angered Gino that his sister Jesuina took the part of her husband. In July 1913, Serafino Fazzani, his wife Jesuina and her sister Aida went to the Old Street Police Court to take out a summons against Gino Ferrari for libel, after Gino had written a letter suggesting that after having tired of Jesuina, Serafino was 'carrying on' with young Aida instead.

The mean-spirited Gino Ferrari, who had a healthy fear of police courts, thought it great effrontery of Serafino and his sisters to take out a summons against him. On July 21 1913, he went to Serafino's shop at No. 53 West Green Road, asking for his brother-in-law. When told that Serafino was not at home, he showed Jesuina a loaded revolver and said "You'll be a widow and you will lose your brother! It is not safe for Serafino to walk about. I will shoot him in the street!" When she replied "You won't do that; you have a wife and child of your own!" the angry Italian snapped back "I don't care for anybody!"

Late in the evening the same day, Gino Ferrari returned to No. 53 West Green Road. Amazingly, considering his dire threats earlier in the day, Jesuina let him in and showed him into the kitchen, where Serafino was sitting. They began negotiating, and Serafino offered to withdraw the summons if Gino paid certain expenses for his children. All of a sudden, Gino screamed out "You won't have any more expenses for your children!" and Serafino shouted back "Yes I shall!" Then three revolver shots rang out. Jesuina ran into the kitchen and saw her husband lying lifeless on the floor. The shop assistant Celeste Ostrachini tried to stop

2.8 A postcard showing West Green Road, Tottenham; the shop at No. 53, where the short-tempered Italian Gino Ferrari made use of his shooter back in 1913, is on the right side in the distance, before the railway bridge.

Gino from escaping, but received a bullet in the shoulder for his trouble. Another assistant named Casali was shot through the cheek by the trigger-happy gunman. Gino ran out into the yard, leapt a fence, and disappeared.

'Aliens' Feud Tragedy!' exclaimed the headline of the *Daily Mail*, and a number of other newspapers followed suit with xenophobic comments about the undesirability of importing various excitable, trigger-happy foreigners into England's green and pleasant land. The coroner's inquest on Serafino Fazzani returned a verdict of wilful murder against Gino Ferrari.[11] The problem was that the murderous Italian was nowhere to be found: with the swiftness of a four-wheeled Ferrari, he had absconded to the continent, leaving the London detectives in a cloud of dust. From France, he wrote some angry and mean-spirited letters to his wife, threatening to return to London and kidnap young Falda if the lad was not sent to Italy to be brought up by Gino's parents.

The Scotland Yard detectives corresponded with their Paris colleagues, but Ferrari had made haste to reach his native land, where he once more went to ground.

In the Great War, Gino Ferrari decided to join the Italian army. In 1917, he was arrested for some minor offence, and completely by accident, it was discovered that he was a wanted man. 'Murder Will Out!' and 'Long Arm of the Law!' exclaimed the London newspapers, hoping that Gino Ferrari would be returned to the Metropolis, to stand trial for his past misdeeds in the Tottenham Shooting Case. But the Italian authorities did not extradite Gino to London, where he would have been likely to have faced the death penalty for murder. They debated whether he should stand trial in his native land, but since a number of the original witnesses had died or disappeared, and others could not be communicated with, this was not considered practical.[12] The Italians instead allowed Gino Ferrari to remain in the army, obviously hoping that the West Green Road murderer would make use of his lethal shooting skills against the German and Austrian soldiers. What happened to him in the end will be a challenge for some clever Italian genealogist, but what is certain is that he never stood trial for his crimes in London.

MURDER BY AN ARMY SERGEANT, 1919

Arthur Pank, a young Tottenham lad, joined the army in 1900, serving in India for nine years. Throughout the Great War, he served in Turkey, and advanced to become a sergeant in the military police. In 1919, having suffered from malaria and depression, the now 38-year-old Pank was stationed at Aldershot, awaiting transfer to an army unit in Russia.

Arthur Pank had a brother, the labourer George William

Pank, who had married a woman named Beatrice Downes; for some reason or other, he had taken her name. When he was in leave, Arthur liked going to London, and he always stayed with his brother and sister-in-law, in their first-floor flat at No. 15 Suffield Road, Tottenham. Beatrice did not approve of his drunken and quarrelsome behaviour, however. Arthur was a hardened toper, who kept swigging hard at the whisky bottle; he did not get particularly drunk, only morose and unhappy. George and Beatrice objected to the drunken Arthur staying with them, but the tough military policeman kept coming to their flat, and they did not possess the courage to have a quarrel with him.

In the evening of April 22 1919, a police constable on patrol at Seven Sisters Corner saw the drunken, dishevelled Arthur Pank come reeling along the pavement. Seeing the policeman, he exclaimed that he had just shot a woman. And indeed, Beatrice Downes was found dead in the flat at No. 15 Suffield Road, with several bullet wounds. Arthur explained that he had brought a loaded revolver back from Constantinople, and that he had made use of this weapon to murder his sister-in-law. He did not provide a motive for his actions.

Dr W.D. Higson put Arthur Pank under special observation at HMP Brixton. He could soon report that Arthur had broken off his engagement to a local girl in 1918, after suffering from malaria. He had been drinking excessively, and needed treatment to stave off the DTs. There was a strong history of melancholia in his mother's family, and there were "strong grounds for suspicion that the act which he has committed is the first prominent symptom of a disease of the mind that will develop further in the course of time." At the coroner's inquest on Beatrice Downes, Captain Hunt of the military police testified that Arthur Pank had nineteen years of meritorious army service, with several good conduct medals. Still, the evidence against him was rock solid, and a verdict of wilful murder was returned.

When Arthur Pank was on trial for murder at the Old Bailey, before Mr Justice Darling, the helpful Dr Higson gave evidence in his favour. Arthur had told the doctor that the day of the murder, he had lunched with his brother and sister-in-law. After George William Downes had returned to work, his wife had insisted that Arthur should come home to No. 15 Suffield Road with her. Once home, she had shown him some pornographic pictures, and suggested that he should go to bed with her. When the virtuous Arthur had objected that he would not make a cuckold of his brother, adding "If you were my wife I would do for you!" Beatrice laughed at him and replied "No man would frighten me like that!" Without any further discussion, Arthur had pulled his revolver and shot her dead. In his hostile summing-up, Mr Justice Darling made it clear that he did not believe in this story, and he also effectively undermined the 'insanity defence' that Pank's counsel had put forth. The jury found Arthur Pank guilty of murder, and Mr Justice Darling sentenced him to death. "Defending Honour of his Brother! – Story of Confession by a Soldier! – Sentence of Death!" exclaimed the breathless headline of the *Daily Mirror*.[13]

As he was languishing in Brixton Prison awaiting execution, Arthur Pank received a letter from the army, informing him that after being found guilty of murder, he had been stripped of his sergeant's stripes and reduced to the ranks. But elsewhere, more benevolent forces were trying their best to save him from the gallows. Aided by Dr Higson, Pank's legal counsel made an appeal to the Home Secretary. By some stratagem or other, they had found evidence that Beatrice Downes had been a 'nymphomaniac' for some time, possibly from the after effects of an operation, and that Arthur Pank's story might well be true after all. Even Mr

Justice Darling admitted that if he had known about this evidence, he would have been less harsh in his summing-up. Accordingly, Arthur Panks was respited and sentenced to life imprisonment. The former sergeant was released on ticket-of-leave as early as May 1927, having served eight years behind bars. It is recorded that he went to visit his brother, who was now living in South London with his new wife, without causing any further bloodshed. But the end of the story is a tragic one: in early September 1927, Arthur Pank was found drowned near Bournemouth. "Death of Reprieved Murderer – Identification of Man 'Found Drowned'" the *Times* laconically put it.[14] The murder house at No. 15 Suffield Road is the only reminder of yet another of London's many forgotten tragedies.

MURDER BY 'SILKY BOB', 1923

The rather sinisterly named Gallowstree Common is a hamlet in South Oxfordshire, about 4.5 miles north of Reading. Back in March 1922, the Crown and Anchor pub outside Gallowstree Common was run by the widow Sarah Blake. She was a very shy and reclusive woman, and had just one close friend, Ellen Payne, who lived next door. On March 4, Sarah had to make a business trip to Reading and asked Ellen if she would mind the pub until she returned. But when Ellen went to the pub to get some last minute instructions, she found the front door locked. After getting no response to knocking, she forced the door open and was faced with a bloodbath. Sarah's body was lying on the kitchen floor in a pool of blood and more was splattered across the walls. A post mortem showed she had suffered more than 60 wounds to her head, hands, face, neck and arms. Her skull was fractured and one ear almost severed. In the woods the police found a bag, similar to the one in which Sarah kept the pub's takings, as well as a blood-stained knife with hairs attached that were similar in colour to the victim's. Suspicion fell on the 24-year-old professional burglar Robert Alfred Sheppard, also known as 'Silky Bob'. Soon after the murder, he was arrested on a burglary charge. At Reading Police Station, Bob freely admitted murdering Mrs Blake. He was in a very agitated state, and shuddered when the blood-stained knife was shown to him. The police knew that Bob had a habit of being far from truthful, and found it strange that his clothes were not blood-stained. Still, he was charged with the murder, and many people thought him guilty.

But when Silky Bob was brought before the Caversham magistrates, there had been sensational developments elsewhere. The 15-year-old lad Jack Hewitt had been observed peering into the hedge where the knife was found, like if he wanted to find out if it was still there. He had called at the pub on the night in question for a glass of 'raspberry champagne' and a ginger stout. A workmate confirmed that the knife was Hewitt's. On this flimsy evidence Jack, who was not very bright, was arrested by the police. After a grilling that lasted for hours, he made a confession which he later retracted, saying that the police had terrified him. Asked by his interrogators why he had killed the landlady, he was alleged to have said, "Blame it on the pictures." That was a history-making remark, because this was the first time in Britain anyone had claimed that violence on the screen could lead to violence in real life by way of imitation. On June 2 1922, Jack Hewitt was found guilty of murder at Oxford Assizes, Because of his youth, he was sentenced to be detained during His Majesty's pleasure. At the same Assizes, Robert Alfred Sheppard was sentenced to six months in prison for burglary.[15] A note addressed to a householder by this mocking burglar, and left on a kitchen table with some empty plates on it, was read out in court:

Dear Sir – Many thanks for your breakfast and rest. I didn't like your sherry, but I can recommend your whisky. Sorry I cannot stop to make your acquaintance. Yours sincerely, Silky Bob.

In the summer of 1923, we find Silky Bob lodging at No. 41 Drayton Road, Tottenham, together with his common-law wife Florence Jones. They did not get on very well, and had many angry quarrels. On the morning of July 7, Bob came running out into the kitchen in a most agitated state. Poor Florence was lying lifeless on the front-room couch, and he feared that she was dead! A doctor arrived to confirm that this was indeed the case, and that the cause of death was carbon monoxide poisoning. The belt of a coat was wound round her neck, like if somebody had tried to strangle her as well. Since Bob looked like a nasty piece of work, the police arrested him. They soon found out all about his formidable reputation as a burglar, and also that a few months earlier, he had given himself up for trying to strangle Florence, but she had not wanted to prosecute him.

At the Tottenham police court, Bob was charged with murdering Florence Jones, through causing her to inhale coal gas. On trial at the Central Criminal Court on September 20 1923, Robert Alfred Sheppard's defence team had an amazing story to tell. Both Bob and Florence had been very depressed, and they had made a 'suicide pact' to gas themselves. Florence went through with her part, but Bob regretted this rash act and pulled the gas pipe out of her mouth, but too late to save her. There was no independent evidence that either the rogue Bob or the floozie Florence had seemed particularly depressed, however. Mr Justice Swift pointed out to the jury that even if the accepted the 'suicide pact' theory, the prisoner was still guilty of murder. After deliberating for forty minutes, the jury returned a guilty verdict, with a strong recommendation to mercy. When asked if he had anything to say, Silky Bob smiled and replied 'I have had a fair trial, and I am rather glad of the verdict!' It is not known if he was equally jolly when Mr Justice Swift donned the black cap and sentenced him to death.

Robert Alfred Sheppard did not want to appeal against the sentence. In a letter to his sister, he made a full confession, saying that Florence had wanted to die, but that she had not possessed the courage to kill herself. He had willingly obliged when she asked him to gas and strangle her. In the end, his sentence was commuted to life imprisonment.[16] It is not known how closely the Reading police were following this remarkable trial for murder, or whether they still had niggling concerns about the safety of the harsh verdict against young Jack Hewitt the previous year. After all, Silky Bob, who had once confessed to the Gallowstree Common murder, had now shown that he was perfectly capable of murdering a woman in cold blood.

MURDER IN TERRACE ROAD, 1939

In 1939, the small newsagent's shop at No. 7 Terrace Road, Hackney, was kept by the 40-year-old Arthur Haberfield. He lived in the first floor flat above the shop, with his wife and children, and sub-let a ground floor kitchen and living-room, and two second-floor bedrooms, to the 41-year-old painter Sidney Charles Pitcher and his family. As war broke out, Mrs Haberfield and her children were evacuated, as were the two Pitcher children.

Sid Pitcher had lodged with the Haberfields for many years, and the families were good friends. But the war changed all of this. Sid Pitcher knew that Haberfield was very friendly with his female customers, touching their arms and shoulders, and paying them various compliments. After Mrs Pitcher had started helping out in the shop, the jealous Sid was becoming fearful that the amorous shopkeeper would be paying her attention as well. And sure enough, Haberfield and Mrs Pitcher were becoming very good friends. Sid resented that he took all his meals with the family, and that he occupied the second-floor bedroom vacated by the Pitcher children.

Sid Pitcher once threatened Haberfield that he should leave his wife along, or else, but the shopkeeper pooh-poohed his concerns, saying that they were just friends. Another time, when Sid saw that his wife had brought Haberfield a cup of tea, he grabbed her by the throat and shook her angrily. On December 18 1939, Haberfield had enjoyed a hearty meal with the Pitchers. He sat contentedly in an armchair, puffing at his pipe. Sid Pitcher very much resented his intrusive behaviour, and feared that his marriage might not last much longer. All of a sudden, he seized a knife and stabbed Haberfield hard in the chest, pursuing him into the corridor leading to the shop.

Mrs Pitcher called the police, and when they arrived, Sid Pitcher gave himself up for murdering his landlord. When he was on trial at the Old Bailey, his wife said that he had always been very jealous, although she had never given him cause. A former army soldier in the Great War, Sid Pitcher had an excellent character, and his wife testified that he had always been an excellent husband and father. He was found guilty but insane and was committed to Broadmoor.[17] There is reason to believe that he eventually emerged from its walls, however, and a Sidney Charles Pitcher died in Hackney in 1979, aged 81. The ground floor of No. 7 Terrace Road is still home to a newsagent's shop.

MURDER AT THE ANIMAL CLINIC, 1942

Mr Christopher James was a respectable, middle-aged engineer, who lived at No. 8 Coningsby Road, Finsbury Park [the house stands], with his wife Lilian. They had been married for twelve years, but had no children. They were both fond of animals, and kept a pedigree Chow Chow, and also an old cat. In September 1939, the dog fell ill, and it was taken to the Green Lanes Animal Clinic at No. 626 Green Lanes, Harringay. A young vet named William James Dulieu managed to save the valuable animal's life, and he afterwards visited the James family home, at regular intervals, to check on the Chow's health. During one of these house-calls, the lecherous veterinarian seduced Mrs James, or perhaps vice versa, and their affair continued until 1941. Dulieu kept extracting money from Mrs James, to the tune of more than £1000. In the end, she confessed all to her husband, who seems to have been much more concerned about the money than about his wife's infidelity. He easily forgave his errant wife, but instructed a solicitor to draw up an agreement for Dulieu to pay all the money back, something the proprietor of the Green Lanes Animal Clinic reluctantly agreed to do.

It is sad but true that Mrs Lilian James continued her sinful life of histrionics and unfaithfulness. She kept seeing Dulieu when her husband was at work. In November 1941, she confronted her lover at the Animal Clinic, to tell him that she was pregnant and he the man responsible. When she demanded that he should confront her husband, and marry her after her divorce, he bluntly answered 'Bollocks'! In a furious temper, Mrs James started smashing bottles in the surgery, until forcibly restrained and ejected from the premises. Dulieu demanded compensation for the damage, but Mr James ignored him. Mrs James later claimed to have suffered a miscarriage, perhaps as a result of Dulieu hitting her in the stomach during the scuffle at the Animal Clinic, hut her husband felt certain that she was lying, and that she had never been pregnant in the first place. Instead, there were other developments, namely that William James Dulieu, who had been 'carrying on' with married women all over North London, had finally acquired a permanent girlfriend, the 24-year-old Miss Patricia St John Smythe. She had moved into the flat above the Animal Clinic, with her aunt, and it had not taken long for the lecherous veterinarian to win her heart. Furious at being cast aside by her lover, Mrs James exchanged some very unpleasant letters with her rival. Young 'Pat' gave as well as she got, pointing out that the handsome young Dulieu no longer had any need for the 'old bag' he had merely been 'working' for money to clear his debts.

These cruel and unkind letters from her younger rival drove the already unbalanced and frustrated Lilian James over the edge. She brought a knife with her to the Animal Clinic, and made use of it to stab Pat hard in the chest, killing her. An old woman, who was at the premises to obtain veterinary treatment for her dog, tried to restrain the murderess, but Mrs James broke free and ran out into Green Lanes. She confessed the murder to a police constable on patrol, and was promptly taken into custody. The investigation of the murder revealed some spicy secrets: the lecherous tendencies of the creature Dulieu, the forgiveness of Mr James, and the violent passions of his deranged wife. Not the least remarkable disclosure was that Dulieu entirely lacked veterinary credentials: for all those years, the Green Lanes Animal Clinic had been run by a quack! The Chow had been very lucky to survive its visit to this ill-fated establishment; the James family's old cat, which had also been one of Dulieu's patients, had not been equally fortunate.

When Mrs James was remanded in custody for the murder of Patricia Smythe, Mr James gave an evasive question as to whether he had sufficient means to have his wife represented, and she was granted legal aid. Miss Julie Smythe, aunt of the murdered young woman, said that she had been perfectly happy with Dulieu, and that they would have married in a month's time. The pathetic aunt had already started to prepare for the wedding, ordering a cake and other paraphernalia. On trial for murder at the Central Criminal Court on April 27 1942, before Mr Justice Oliver, Mrs James was found guilty but insane, and was ordered to be detained during his Majesty's pleasure.[18] As for her former paramour William James Dulieu, he appears to have married another girl and lived happily ever after. Hopefully, for the sake of London's four-legged inhabitants, he refrained from any further pseudo-veterinarianism, and supported himself through hard graft and honest toil. The murder house at No. 626 Green Lanes still stands today, and has not changed much since 1942. By a curious coincidence, there is a veterinary surgery at No. 638 Green Lanes just a few doors away, operating with more conventional methods than Dulieu's former clinic at No. 626.

CARNAGE IN STIRLING ROAD, 1954

Thomas William Shadrach, a native of Wales, was born in June 1920. He joined the R.A.F. in 1937, and remained in this service for many years to come, although he was not considered fit for flying duties. He married a woman named Margaret Cleverly in 1942 and had three children with her. In 1947, he returned to Britain from an air base in Italy, with the rank of temporary Flight Sergeant. But due to a fondness for gambling, he soon got into financial difficulties, which he tried to resolve by stealing money from the R.A.F. sergeants' mess, and forging withdrawal forms from a 'doctored' P.O. saving book. In 1948, he was caught for this exhibition of dishonesty, dismissed from the R.A.F., and sentenced to six months in Swansea Prison.

In 1949, Thomas William Shadrach was living in his father's

house in Wales, with his wife Margaret and the children. But he soon got fed up with her snide remarks about his imprisonment and military disgrace. In 1950, he deserted his family and went to London, where he lived off various odd jobs. In 1952, he bigamously married a woman named Irene Mansell, who already had two children from a previous marriage to the concert artist Frank Mansell: the sixteen-year-old Thalia and the ten-year-old Katrina. Shadrach got a job as a clerk and moved into a Wood Green flat with his new family. In August 1953, there was another mouth to feed, namely baby Thelma, although the family was already very poor. They had to take in a lodger, a man named Albert Gurney, who was soon 'carrying on' with the eighteen-year-old Thalia, although he was already married, and the father of twelve children! Mr and Mrs Shadrach, who had little claim to moral high ground themselves, found this miserable state of affairs hard to bear. After she had found Thalia sitting on Gurney's bed, wearing only her dressing-gown, she asked her daughter to choose between her family and her lover. Young Thalia quickly packed her bags and left the family home at No. 14 Stirling Road, Wood Green, for good, with her much older 'boyfriend'!

Poor Irene Mansell, or Mrs Shadrach if we are to be charitable, took the loss of her teenage daughter, under such dismal circumstances, very badly indeed. She wept and cried that Thalia did not love her, and that she had preferred going off with a howling cad who was already married, with a large family. Thomas William Shadrach was also badly affected by this family disgrace, and he became increasingly depressed. In the end, he thought it would be best to put his poor 'wife' out of her misery, and to murder the two remaining children as well. On November 16 1954, he strangled his wife and his stepdaughter to death, before smothering baby Thelma with a cushion. He tried to slash his wrists with a razor, but not with much conviction. Instead, Shadrach wrote a letter to the Chief Constable of the Metropolitan Police, admitting his crimes, and adding that he was now going out to commit suicide by jumping in front of a lorry. But instead of attempting to destroy himself, he meekly gave himself up to a police constable he knew, with the words 'Taff, I have got to tell you. I have been meaning to give myself up. I've done them in!' A prison doctor found a scratch mark to his face, resulting from Irene Mansell's final struggle with her demented husband. Although profoundly depressed, he was found sane and fit to plead.

When the triple murder case was heard at the Tottenham police court, the magistrates saw fit to reproach that disreputable pair, Albert Gurney and Thalia Mansell, for their immorality and unseeming light-heartedness in court. As for Thomas William Shadrach, he was committed for trial at the Central Criminal Court, where he was found guilty but insane, and committed to Broadmoor.[19] There is reason to believe that he did not remain within its walls for very long, however, since a Thomas W. Shadrach of the relevant age is recorded to have married in 1963, and died in Fulham in 1973.

MURDER AND MYSTERY IN
TOTTENHAM, 1960

On April 1 1960, the 22-year-old Mrs Pamela Masterson was found shot to death in her flat at No. 30 Clifton Gardens, Tottenham. The tabloid newspapers first believed she had been shot through the head after surprising a burglar, perhaps with a gun fitted with a silencer. They described her as very pretty, and a model young mother; her 18-month-old son Michael was found crying in his cot next to his mother's bed. One of the detectives speculated that the Clifton Gardens burglar turned murderer had forced open the flat's window, and stepped on the sleeping woman, whose bed was just by the window. He had then panicked and shot her dead, before making his escape. Mr Patrick Masterson, who worked as a scaffolder in St Neots and only spent the weekends at his home, told the police that their three-year marriage had been very happy, and that as far as he knew, his wife had no enemies. The manager of the nearby chemist's shop where Pamela Masterson worked as an assistant agreed, adding that she had been very popular with the customers.

The newspaper articles on the mysterious murder of Pamela Masterson soon acquired a new spin, however. Nobody had broken into the flat, and there were signs that the murdered woman had smoked cigarettes with a visitor before she had been killed. It also turned out that Pamela Masterson had a background as a Soho nightclub hostess. It was speculated that she might have met one of her old friends from the vice business, and the police were keen to track down the driver of a green car seen in Clifton Gardens early in the morning after the shooting. On April 4, they had their man: the unemployed 26-year-old van driver Joseph Edward Martin, who was charged with murder the following day. He had been showing people a loaded Luger pistol he was carrying around, and had visited the murder house in Clifton Gardens before.

When Joseph Edward Martin stood trial at the Central Criminal Court for the murder of Pamela Masterson, the medical evidence spoke in favour of Mrs Masterson having been shot in the head with the muzzle only seven inches away from her face. Martin admitted that he had been to No. 30 Clifton Gardens several times before, to visit a girlfriend of his named Mrs Freda

Dunne. The night of the murder, the unemployed, gun-toting hoodlum came prowling around as usual, after having drunk a good deal at a club. When he wanted to enter Freda's room through the window, he woke up Pamela Masterson, who told him that Freda was not at home. She invited him into her flat, where they smoked some cigarettes before going to bed and having intercourse. She wanted him out of the flat by 6 am, but Martin could not resist taking out his pistol and showing it to her. As he demonstrated its mechanism, a shot went off hitting her in the face. Blood was gushing from her nose and mouth, and she leant against the wall. Making no attempt to help her, Martin grabbed his overcoat and made a rapid getaway, stopping on the way home to throw the gun over a park wall into a small lake.

The prosecution alleged that the shooting had been deliberate, although they were not in a position to prove a motive. Martin seemed like a nasty piece of work, a work-shy drunkard who admitted that he had no license for his firearm, but he did not have a history of committing serious crime. With must have been a quite narrow margin, the jury found him Not Guilty of capital murder, but Guilty of manslaughter. He was sentenced to six years in prison.[20] In June the following year, his name again hit the newspapers when he escaped from a Wormwood Scrubs working party at Ashford. Together with the robber Colin O'Neill, the sturdy, dark-haired Martin was still on the run two days later. In a newspaper interview, Martin's wife said that she thought her husband had escaped because she and their two children were being evicted from the flat they lived in. His mother Mrs Ellen Martin said that her son was a silly boy, and that if she saw him, she would turn him in. It would appear as if the Clifton Gardens killer was eventually recaptured, and that he served his sentence and disappeared into obscurity.[21]

MURDER IN WOOD GREEN, 1960

Hubert Roy Lane was born in Gloucester in 1906, and worked as a dining car attendant on the railways for many years. He married but eventually left his wife. In the 1950s, he met Mrs Beatrice Monica Wiles, who was also married but lived apart from her husband. He moved into her flat at No. 457 High Road, Wood Green, but the relationship did not end well. In early 1960, Mrs Wiles applied for a court order forbidding Lane to visit the house.

On August 29 1960, the 40-year-old Beatrice Monica Wiles clocked into the factory where she worked, at 8.15 in the morning. At shortly after 1 pm, her 14-year-old daughter Irene returned to No. 457 High Road, having done some shopping. She saw her mother slumped in a chair, and Hubert Lane stood in the room wiping blood from his hands. Terrified, the girl ran off and called the police. They found Mrs Wiles with severe stab wounds to the neck, and she died half an hour later. When Hubert Lane was arrested and charged with the crime at the Tottenham Magistrate's Court, the court was cleared when the dead woman's daughter gave evidence, due to its distressing nature. On trial for murder at the Central Criminal Court on October 19 1960, Hubert Lane was found Not Guilty of murder but Guilty of manslaughter on the ground of diminished responsibility, a not uncommon verdict at the time, and he was sentenced to life imprisonment.[22]

A FORGOTTEN HACKNEY MURDER, 1971

In 1971, the betting shop at No. 242 Queensbridge Road, Hackney, was owned by the 55-year-old Mr Frederick Campbell. On Thursday July 1, two young black men forced themselves into the shop and demanded money. The manager went to press the alarm button, and the men ran away. But the very next day, when Mr Campbell and his assistant were counting their takings, two youths again came bursting into the betting shop, with a third acting as lookout. When they demanded money, Mr Campbell moved to press the alarm button, but one of the robbers blasted him with a shotgun. When the assistant came to his aid, he was shot as well.[23]

The two youths made a dive for the till, before escaping in a Ford Cortina. A Trinidadian chef named Augustine Marks, who saw the robbers escape, followed them in his own car for a few blocks, and later claimed to have seen the face of one of them quite clearly. Mr Campbell died from his injuries, but the assistant recovered. The police made a trawl of the Hackney criminal underworld, and found Walter Fitzgerald Fraser, who had been born in British Guyana in 1946, and lived in London since 1962. He was a nasty piece of work, with two convictions for larceny and one for robbery. A loaded revolver was found in Fraser's flat, and the witness Marks identified him as one of the two men in the Ford Cortina. The police were confident that the Queensbridge Road murderer had been found.

When Fraser was on trial for murder and attempted murder in January 1972, the basis of his defence was mistaken identity. And in spite of Marks giving evidence identifying Fraser as the man he had seen in the car, he was acquitted due to lack of evidence. No theory emerged as to the identity of the second robber. The book *Black Community on Trial* by Rudy Narayan points out the prosecution of Fraser as an example of institutional racism from the police, but the police file on the Queensbridge Road murder makes it equally clear that several experienced detectives thought Fraser the guilty man.[24] At any rate, the robbers turned murderers were never caught, and a both dastardly and pointless crime went unavenged. The murder shop at No. 242 Queensbridge Road is today the Queensbridge Supermarket.

CHAPTER 3

KENSAL RISE, WILLESDEN, BRONDESBURY, KILBURN AND CRICKLEWOOD

Mysterious was my cause of Death,
In the Prime of Life I fell;
For days I Lived yet ne'er had breath
The secret of my fate to tell.
Farewell, my child and husband dear
By cruel hands I leave you,
Now that I'm dead, and sleeping here,
My Murderer may deceive you.

Though I am dead, yet I shall live,
I must my Murderer meet,
And then in Evidence, shall give
My cause of death complete.
Forgive my child and husband dear,
That cruel Man of Blood;
He soon for murder must appear
Before the Son of God.

From an inscription on a memorial stone
in Beverley Cathedral, dated 1853.

This chapter will cover a large chunk of northwest London, from Harlesden, Willesden, Kensal Rise and Kilburn in the south, extending north to include Brondesbury and Cricklewood. Although many murder houses in these parts of London survive in good order, there are some notable exceptions. No. 76 Mayo Road, once home to the baby farmer Polly Palmer and her husband Arthur, no longer stands, but the house of Polly's infamous mother Amelia Dyer, the doyenne of Victorian baby farming, survives to this day at No. 45 Kensington Road, Reading.[1]

No. 60 Milton Avenue, Harlesden, where the villainous chemist Arthur Devereux murdered his wife Beatrice and their twin sons in 1905, no longer stands. Nearly all the northern terrace of houses in Milton Avenue has been replaced with modern housing, although the southern terrace still remains, containing houses that match a contemporary drawing of the murder house. Devereux put the bodies of his three victims in a large trunk, which he stored in a warehouse at No. 2 Buller Road, off Kilburn Lane [it no longer stands]. But the bodies were discovered, and Arthur Devereux arrested, tried and convicted of murder, and later hanged at Pentonville prison. To support the murderer's surviving son Stanley, whose entire family had been wiped out, all Devereux' effects were sold at auction, including the trunk in which the bodies had been stored.[2]

No. 11 Victoria Villas, once situated off Victoria Road, Kilburn, where Leonard George Hucker murdered his girlfriend's mother Mary Alice Moncrieff in 1939, has been lost to a large development of modern blocks of flats.[3] The murder shop at No. 18 Hillside, Willesden, where the robber Donald Brown murdered the tobacconist Herbert Blades in 1955, has also been lost to modern developments. Brown was sentenced to death for murdering the harmless old man, but he received a late reprieve and was sent to Broadmoor, where he hanged himself in 1964.[4]

But northwest London still has a wealth of historic murder houses, some of them infamous dwellings, others obscure and little-known. Kensal Rise has what can only be called a sinister cluster of murder houses, with No. 43 Wrentham Avenue [formerly Ladysmith Road], once home to George Albert Crossman, the Kensal Rise Bluebeard, at its centre. Both the houses connected with that prolific serial killer, Dennis Nilsen, also still stand today. Both No. 195 Melrose Avenue, Cricklewood, and No. 23 Cranley Gardens, off Muswell Hill Road, appear to be subdivided into flats. Expensive and well looked after houses, they are both in good repair today, although their period of rehabilitation is not yet complete: many people living nearby know all about their horrible secret.

TERRIBLE CRIME OF A DRUNKEN MOTHER, 1897

In the 1890s, the engine-fitter James Symmonds, who was employed at the Neasden Works of the Metropolitan Railway, lodged in the first floor front room over a shop at No. 239 High Road, Willesden Green, with his wife Emma and their four children. Emma also worked, as a laundress, in spite of having young children. The Symmonds family lived happily until Emma started drinking more gin and beer than was good for her. Her husband persuaded her to take the pledge at a temperance society, but she soon broke it. Although a kind and even-tempered woman when sober, she became a perfect virago when drunk.

On Wednesday July 14 1897, Emma Symmonds started drinking already in the afternoon. Her husband was dismayed to see the state of her when he returned home from work as 6.20. He sent his six-year-old son James Jr to fetch a fellow lodger

High Road, Willesden Green, showing Library.　　　Reeves' Series.

3.1 A postcard showing Willesden Green High Road.

named Bill Bruce. The dismal James Symmonds warned his friend that his drunken wife was on the rampage again, and that she was likely to make a racket, since he knew that she had a bottle of gin hidden away. He asked Bruce to pawn his watch and lend him some money, so that he could spend the night to another lodging-house. Bruce turned out to be a true friend, and returned with the money and without his 'ticker'. Exclaiming 'I am going to clear out of it, Bill, since there is going to be a row!', Symmonds rapidly made himself scarce. None of the two men seems to have thought twice about the four children they left alone with their drunken and angry mother.

Perhaps feeling some belated concern for his children, James Symmonds sneaked back to No. 239 High Road at one in the morning. Entering the room, he was horrified to see that the walls were liberally sprinkled with gore, and that his daughter Minnie was lying in a large pool of blood on the floor with her throat cut. Symmonds screamed and ran upstairs to fetch his friend Bill

Bruce. When they dared to re-enter the flat, they saw that the frenzied Emma Symmonds had cut the throats of all her children, and her own as well. Minnie and baby Eva were both dead, but Emma Symmonds and her sons Charles and James were taken to the Willesden Cottage Hospital in a very precarious condition.

At the coroner's inquest on Minnie and Eva Symmonds, their father testified that Emma Symmonds had been drinking hard for a fortnight, and that when drunk, she had often threatened to murder her children. There was insanity in her family, and her brother had hanged himself in Leeds. The murderess and her two surviving children were all on the mend at the cottage hospital. She had not provided any explanation for her frenzied assault, apart from saying 'They made me do it! They were walking up and down!' Although the coroner's inquest returned a verdict of wilful murder against Emma Symmonds, she would never face trial at the Old Bailey, since she had already been sent to Broadmoor Asylum, by order of the Home Secretary, as a lunatic.[5] The murder house at No. 239 Willesden Green High Road still stands, and the first floor front room, over what is today a small pizza shop, does not appear to have changed a lot since the time it was the subject of a detailed drawing, showing the position of the murder victims, which is today kept in the police file on the case in the National Archives.

THE KENSAL RISE BLUEBEARD, 1903

In early 1903, a dapper-looking cove named George Albert Crossman took the lease of No. 43 Ladysmith Road, Kensal Rise. He sub-let the ground floor of this recently built end-of-terrace house called 'Sunnyside' to a family named Dell. The Dells found Crossman more than a little odd: he did no work at all, and had a great many flashily dressed female acquaintances visiting the premises, and sometimes making angry scenes. In addition to these volatile floozies, Crossman had a little son named Bertie, of whom he appeared to be quite fond; when not busy dealing with the women in his life, he strolled round the neighbourhood leading the little boy by the hand, and puffing contentedly at a large cigar.

George Albert Crossman said he was in the furniture business, and indeed, some dodgy-looking workmen sometimes came to deliver large cabinets, tables and armchairs to the premises, but Crossman used them to furnish the house and made no attempt to sell them. He could sit smoking in his armchair for hours on end, looking out at the sleepy suburban street. But there was something else worrying the Dells, namely a very foul smell emanating from the cupboard underneath the stairs. When they complained, Crossman blamed the drains, but these were found to be in good working order. Instead, Mr Dell tracked down the smell to a large tin trunk in the cupboard, and demanded that Crossman should remove it.

Habitually disinclined to do any work himself, Crossman went to a carrier named Ryden, hiring this individual to remove the trunk and some other pieces of furniture. But the noxious and powerful smell emanating from the trunk was such that Mr Dell became very uneasy, and called in the police. When Ryden's van came to 'Sunnyside', two constables were hiding at the premises; two more were dodging behind a hedge opposite. As Crossman stood arguing with Ryden, who was unwilling to have anything to do with this foul-smelling trunk, he suddenly saw the policemen spying on him across the road. He ran off into Dundonald Road, then into Okehampton Road, and finally into Hanover Road, with the four constables in hot pursuit. The chain-smoking Crossman gasped for breath as the police were steadily

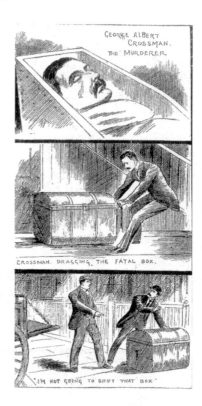

3.2 Scenes from the career of
George Albert Crossman, the
Kensal Rise Bluebeard; like the
three following, it is from the
Illustrated Police News,
April 2 1904.

gaining on him. Suddenly, he pulled out a large razor and cut his
throat with great force, giving a terrible, spluttering yell as the
blood gushed up in great cascades. When the constables came up
to him, they found that his head was nearly severed from the body.

When the police looked into Crossman's past, they found that
this dishonest, work-shy fellow had several convictions for
thieving. Eschewing the convention of monogamy, he had not
fewer than nine wives; the first of them, the mother of little
Bertie, had died from what was alleged to be natural cases. The
next seven wives were all alive and well; one of them had in fact
taken Crossman to court for bigamy, and caused him to be
sentenced to five years penal servitude in December 1898. All

3.3 *The murder house at No. 43 Ladysmith Road.*

3.4 *Crossman cuts his throat.*

3.5 The discovery of the sinister trunk.

these wives had been recruited through advertisements inserted by Crossman into various matrimonial magazines, which appear to have served various crooks and perverts nearly as well as the Internet does today. Under different aliases, Crossman had relieved each wife in turn of her paltry savings, easily finding novel victims through his advertisements.

Wife number nine, the nurse Ellen Sampson, was the lifeless inhabitant of that sinister trunk; unfortunately for Crossman, he had not put down enough cement in the bottom of the trunk to prevent various body fluids from seeping out. The Kensal Rise Bluebeard had murdered her the day after their marriage, in January 1903, after one of his other wives had been making

He fell, bleeding profusely.

3.6 Crossman commits suicide, from Famous Crimes Past & Present.

threatening comments about taking him to court for bigamy. That would have meant prison, and Crossman had had enough of that; as a result, Nurse Sampson had to be disposed of.[6] Since the remains of the unfortunate nurse had been in the trunk more than fourteen months, there is no wonder the cupboard became a bit smelly.

There was outrage in respectable Kensal Rise after this ghastly trunk murder had been detected. It was suggested that the name of Ladysmith Road ought to be changed, to blot out the memory of this heinous act. Eschewing the suggestion of Trunkville Road, brought forward by some joker, the local worthies decided on Wrentham Avenue.[7] I can find nothing to suggest that the houses were renumbered, and the present-day No. 43 looks very much like an original sketch of the murder house. I wonder if there might still be a faint, malodorous smell in the understairs cupboard?

MURDER IN DUNDONALD ROAD, 1906

No. 11 Dundonald Road, Kensal Rise, is just a few doors away from No. 43 Ladysmith Road, home to the trunk murderer George Albert Crossman, the man of many wives. In 1906, No. 11 Dundonald Road was home to the upholsterer Alfred Robert Rogers, his wife, brother, and four children. He had lived there for several years, and was well liked locally as a honest, hard-working family man. Alfred's upholstery business in Kilburn was not a success, however. Although his brother Albert returned from New Zealand to help him, the upholsterer's shop failed miserably in June 1906, something that made Alfred very depressed and worried about the future. Albert tried to cheer him up, but they failed to find another suitable shop. On September 6, Alfred had been out all day looking for a shop in Finchley, but without finding one. All the inhabitants of No. 11 Dundonald Road went to bed between nine and ten: Alfred Rogers, his wife Jessie and their three-year-old daughter Ethel in the front bedroom, the two daughters Dorothy and Florence Mabel, aged 14 and 9 respectively, in the room behind that. The 11-year-old William Rogers had a room of his own, as did Albert the brother.

In the early morning of September 7, Albert Rogers heard a frenzied shouting from his brother's bedroom. When he opened the door, he could see Alfred attacking his wife and youngest daughter with a large razor. Both of them were bleeding profusely. Albert dashed into the room and seized hold of his brother. Both were strong men, and a violent struggle ensued. Albert managed to seize hold of the razor and throw it out of the window, but Alfred got hold of another one, cutting hard at his brother's throat with it. Albert knocked his brother downstairs with a well-aimed blow, and threw him into the kitchen, but Alfred got hold of a large carving-knife instead. He cut his brother several times, but

3.7 The desperate struggle at No. 11 Dundonald Road, from the
Illustrated Police News, *September 15 1906.*

the sturdy Albert managed to seize him in a powerful wrestling hold. The demented Alfred seemed to calm down, and the brothers went into the bathroom to change their blood-soaked clothing. But Alfred gave a yell and ran out again. He threw a large flower-pot at his brother, but it missed its target and went through a window. It was not until the neighbours Mr Ralph and Mr Elliott had entered the house through the broken window that the frenzied Alfred Rogers could be pacified. When asked where all his children were, the maniac screamed 'I have killed the lot!' And in the side bedroom, the two girls Dorothy and Florence were found with their heads nearly severed from their bodies by their father's razor. Mrs Rogers, the heroic Albert, and young Ethel were all seriously injured.

Arriving at No. 11 Dundonald Road, the police were amazed to see how the house had been turned into a blood-spattered battleground. Alfred Rogers was taken into custody, and the three wounded people were sent to St Mary's Hospital, where they all made a good recovery. When charged with murdering his daughters at the Willesden Police Court, Alfred Rogers seemed extremely depressed. He stood with his head bowed, and had to be supported by two warders. At HM Prison Brixton, Alfred Rogers was kept under close observation by Dr James Scott. There was no family history of insanity, nor had Rogers himself ever been in an asylum, but he had been subject to frequent attacks of headache and mental depression. Dr Scott concluded that at the time of the murders, Rogers had been in a state of insane melancholia, but at the present time, he was fit to plead and stand trial for his crimes.

When Alfred Rogers was on trial for murder at the Old Bailey, Albert Rogers testified that his brother had been very worried about the failure of his business, although the family was reasonably well off. The brothers had an income of £100 each per annum from some property, and were certainly in no danger of poverty. The neighbours testified that Alfred Rogers had always been a steady, industrious man, and very fond of his family. He was found guilty of murder, but it was considered that he had been insane at the time, and he was detained at Broadmoor, where he died in 1920.[8]

THE DEMON BARBER OF EARLSMEAD ROAD, 1910

Oliver Smith was born in Chesterfield in 1877. At the age of just 15, he was apprenticed to a local barber, but instead he joined the army in 1901, serving in India in 1903. In 1908, Oliver deserted his regiment, although he would have served his full time the following year. He went to London, where he lay low for a while, doing various menial jobs.

In April 1910, Oliver Smith secured steady employment in Mr Henry Lampard's barber shop in Harrow Road. This success allowed him to rent the downstairs flat at No. 67 Earlsmead Road, Kensal Rise, together with his common-law wife Harriet Lucy Gasson. She was four years older than him, and already had a two-year-old child, born out of wedlock. This child had been 'put out to nurse' with a woman in Ongar, at the cost of five shillings per week.

On October 7 1910, the man occupying the upstairs flat at No. 67 Earlsmead Road heard a woman moaning downstairs. Shortly after, Oliver Smith left his own flat, humming merrily to himself. Three days later, when the neighbour looked through the curtains of a downstairs window, he saw the body of a woman lying in a pool of blood. After he had called in the police, Inspector Arthur Macer and his colleagues examined the murder flat.

Harriet Gasson's throat had been cut with a razor, which was lying on the dresser. A pair of blood-stained trousers lay on the floor, indicating that the murderer had changed his trousers before leaving the flat.

On October 11, Oliver Smith walked into Grays police station in Essex, to give himself up at the murderer of Harriet Gasson. They had been very poor, he explained, and he had resented losing the five shillings that Harriet needed for the care of her child. Nor did he like the fact that she was obviously pregnant with another child conceived before she had moved in with him. After an angry quarrel, Harriet had retired to the kitchen, threatening to cut her throat. She had returned with a small gash on her throat, begging Oliver to finish the job, something that he had done with enthusiasm. After changing his trousers and collar, he had hurriedly left the flat. Pondering whether to destroy himself, he had purchased some hydrochloric acid at a pharmacy, but he had lacked the courage to swallow it. When Oliver's pockets were emptied, they contained only the bottle of acid and a farthing.

When Oliver Smith was on trial for murder at the Old Bailey on November 15 1910, his defence council presented a number of witnesses whose testimony suggested that he had been a very disturbed man since an early age. His half-sister said that as a youth, Oliver had been notable for his abnormally large head. He had been quite simple-minded, and given to violent temper tantrums. His cousin, and his mother's uncle, had both been in lunatic asylums. The hairdresser to whom Oliver had been apprenticed as a young man thought him a very sullen and morose young lad, who would go into a violent rage and temper at the slightest provocation. Several witnesses referred to Oliver's motiveless desertion from the army as further proof of his insanity. But the medical officer of Brixton Prison, who had spoken to the prisoner at length, explained that there had indeed been a reason for him to desert. Oliver had been married, but he had left his wife and was badly in arrears with his payments to her. In his view, Oliver Smith was definitely not clinically insane. Although the murder may not have been premeditated, Oliver had shown concern for his own fate, as judged by his change of collar and trousers after the murder.

The jury found Oliver Smith guilty of murder, and Mr Justice Darling sentenced him to death.[9] But a surprising number of people did their best to save the Demon Barber of Earlsmead Road from the gallows. His family had a good reputation, and they managed to get Mr John O'Connor MP interested in the case. Mr O'Connor petitioned Winston Churchill, pointing out Oliver's indifferent health and abnormally large head, and also the lack of motive for the murder, and the fact that he had speedily given himself up. Had Mr Justice Darling misdirected the jury?

This appeal was dismissed, but still, Oliver Smith's sentence was eventually commuted to life imprisonment. In 1919, when Oliver was in Maidstone Prison, one of the guards was attacked by a dangerous prison bully named Patrick Russell. The unfortunate guard would have received a brutal thrashing, had Oliver not confronted the bully and rescued the guard. There was another petition for his release, but again it was turned down. Interestingly, it is recorded that Oliver's wife, who he had once so basely deserted, showed an interest in securing his release, along with the remainder of his family. The Demon Barber of Earlsmead Road remained behind bars until November 1923. He got a job as a printer upon release, but died from pneumonia in April 1925.[10] The razor used by the Demon Barber to cut poor Harriet's throat was deposited in Scotland Yard's Black Museum, and may well be there still.

MURDER IN CHEVENING ROAD, 1935

Philip Quarry, a 22-year-old joiner, shared the basement flat at No. 32 Chevening Road, Kensal Rise, with his one year older wife Angela. The dark, damp, insalubrious flat had a kitchen, a bed-sittingroom, a bath and a scullery. Philip and Angela had got along quite well in the early stages of their marriage, but as time went by, their relation went from bad to worse, and they were often at loggerheads. Philip was very fussy about his food, which he wanted served as soon as he came home from work. He resented that his wife got pregnant, and could be very cruel to her. Angela moved in with her brother for a while, but Philip soon managed to persuade her to return to the gloomy little flat in Chevening Road.

On June 9 1935, Philip and Angela had another furious quarrel, which she ended by seizing up a stair banister and hitting him hard in the eye with it. She then took refuge in the upstairs

3.8 An old postcard showing Chevening Road.

flat. After a while, Philip came staggering upstairs with a black eye, saying that his wife had hit him with a banister, and that he wanted it back. The upstairs neighbour, Mr Stanley Evans, politely handed him the banister. After a while, Angela also appeared, and Philip offered her a cup of tea and a cigarette if she returned to the basement flat with him. But after they had gone downstairs, Mr Evans heard them quarrelling angrily, before Angela gave a loud scream. He went down to the front window of the basement flat and asked Philip if his wife was all right. His neighbour just grunted in reply, and Mr Evans saw that he had a knife in his hand. When Mr Evans had returned to his own flat, he could see Philip running away. After the police had been called in, to break down the door to the basement flat, they found Angela stabbed to death.

Later the same day, Philip Quarry went into the Kilburn Police Station, doffed his cap to the constable in charge, and said 'Excuse me, Sir, I have murdered my wife at No. 32 Chevening Road, and I wish to give myself up!' On trial for murder at the Central Criminal Court, things were not looking good for him. There was no doubt that he had stabbed his wife to death, and a mental specialist had declared him fully sane and fit to plead. The defence called a number of witnesses who testified that Philip Quarry had suffered from epileptic fits, and medical experts who tentatively suggested that he might have committed the crime in a state of unconsciousness.

But the Lord Chief Justice, Lord Hewart, delivered a hostile summing-up, pointing out that the attempt to set up an 'insanity defence' was based on some very flimsy evidence. He was surprised that 'apparently qualified doctors' would take part in such shenanigans in court. If they succeeded, they would be responsible for a perfectly sane man being incarcerated in an asylum for criminal lunatics. Philip Quarry's defence team had eloquently entreated the jury to show their client mercy, but the prerogative of mercy was not for the jury, or for himself. And could the jurymen imagine something less merciful than to stigmatize a sane man as a criminal lunatic? After an absence of nearly an hour, the jury returned a verdict of Guilty, adding a strong recommendation to mercy. Lord Hewart then sentenced the prisoner to death for what he called "a brutal and ferocious murder".

There was a brief newspaper debate about the validity of the insanity defence in the Quarry case. Not unsurprisingly, a writer in the *British Journal of Psychiatry* criticized Lord Hewart for his uncompromising language and disrespect for the psychiatric profession. In the end, Philip Quarry's death sentence was commuted to penal servitude for life.[11] The basement flat at No. 32 Chevening Road still remains.

MURDER AND MYSTERY IN BRONDESBURY VILLAS, 1940

In 1919, Sergeant Major John Howell Jones had belonged to the British forces occupying parts of Germany. He was friendly enough with the local population to marry one of them, Frau Karolin Getta Muller, who had already been married twice. They lived together in Cologne for a while, before returning to London. Mrs Karolin Jones took time to adapt to her new country, and she was a poor linguist, but the marriage seems to have been reasonably happy. They had no children of their own, but they adopted the boy Friedrich Joseph, a son of Karolin Jones' first marriage, and he changed his name to Frederick Jones.

When the Sergeant Major died in 1930, Karolin Jones became a prostitute. She later opened a small brothel at No. 52 Marchmont Street, and was convicted and fined for this offence. In 1938, she moved into a small first-floor flat at No. 21 Brondesbury Villas,

Kilburn. It did not take long for her to become very unpopular locally. An ugly woman with a fierce temper, she often quarrelled with her neighbours, and sometimes started screaming at complete strangers in the streets for no apparent reason. Although she was comfortably off, she was an inveterate shoplifter, sometimes making use of simple tactics like exchanging her own old hat for a new one on a department store hat stand. By 1940, she had four convictions for theft and shoplifting, and one for hitting a woman with an umbrella. Understandably for a Jewess in the 1930s, this fierce woman was very much against the Nazis; indeed, she used to attend the meetings of Mosley's Blackshirts, to heckle the speakers. She falsely represented herself as a refugee from Nazi Germany, in order to gain sympathy, but the neighbours knew the truth about her sordid background.

In early 1940, the neighbours in Brondesbury Villas remarked that they had not seen the bugbear Mrs Jones for quite a while, but this did not induce them into inquiring what had happened to her, or even to ring her doorbell. But on April 10, when the rent-collector Alfred Scott came around, there was no answer when he rang the bell at Mrs Jones's door. The neighbours said that they had not seen her for a month. Scott, a former police constable, suspected that she had absconded, in order to avoid paying her rent. He got hold of a duplicate set of keys from his firm, and opened the front door to the flat, which turned out to be very dirty and poorly furnished. He found Karolin Jones bound, gagged and quite dead in the back room. She had been brutally hit about the head and then strangled to death. It was considered peculiar that she was wearing her overcoat.

It was estimated that Karolin Jones had been murdered about two weeks earlier. The other inhabitants of Brondesbury Villas made evasive noises when the detectives berated their lack of neighbourly concern. One woman said that she had heard noises from Mrs Jones's flat around April 5, and notified the rent collector, but the police suspected that she was lying. Since Karolin Jones's flat had been ransacked by the murderer, the detectives of course thought robbery the motive. It was well known locally that Mrs Jones was well off, and perhaps some local burglar had decided to rob her. The flat had not been broken into, suggesting that she had either invited her attacker in, or that she had been on her way out, wearing her overcoat, when she was surprised by the robber.[12]

It turned out that Karolin Jones was good for not less than £2 928, a small fortune in those days. Wisely, she had put her assets in the bank instead of keeping them back home. The sole beneficiary in her will was her son Frederick, but he was never a suspect for the murder, since he was serving abroad with the British Expeditionary Force at the time. At the inquest, it was commented that Mrs Jones was a very secretive, mysterious woman. Often, she went out alone late at night. The police found it surprising that she had been able to save nearly £3000 in spite of not having paid employment. There was speculation that the former brothel madam had been involved in blackmail, and that one of her victims had 'silenced' her, but it was never explained how she could have found information sensitive enough to blackmail somebody with. The robbery theory has more to recommend it, since although Mrs Jones kept her money and valuables in the bank, the intruder would not have known that. There had been much gossip locally about her wealth, and her foreign origins, and the neighbours had disliked her intensely. No close students of the Nazi persecution of the Jews, they tarred all people with a German accent with the same brush. It is ironic that Karolin Jones, who was notable for her fierce anti-Nazi views, might well have lost her life due to the anti-German sentiments fuelled by the Second World War.

POINTLESS MURDER IN HANOVER ROAD, 1940

Jack Cuthbert Fennell, a 41-year-old unemployed catalogue folder, lived with his mother, wife and two brothers at No. 6 Hanover Road, Brondesbury Park. In 1940, he applied for war work, but was turned down because of his poor physique and lack of adequate training. This annoyed him, and he took it out on his wife Naomi, a waitress at the Harrods Store Restaurant. After he had got drunk and beaten her up a number of times, she filed for divorce, but eventually moved back into No. 6 Hanover Road. On June 18 1940, Jack and Naomi had a furious quarrel that ended in blows. Jack pulled a small-calibre revolver and shot his wife dead. He was found guilty of manslaughter and sentenced to ten years in prison.[13]

MURDER BY 'GUARDSMAN MICK', 1958

On December 19 1958, the naked body of Veronica Murray, a 35-year-old prostitute, was found in the front bedsit she rented at No. 58 Charteris Road, Kilburn. She had been brutally murdered, and her body had been mutilated after death. In younger days, Veronica Murray had been an attractive and successful prostitute, but as she got older, she had to consort with all kinds of dangerous riff-raff. The former convent school girl from Londonderry had been well known in many of Soho's shady clubs.

Murders of prostitutes are notoriously dangerous to solve, due to the absence of a previous relation between murderer and victim, and the scarcity of reliable witnesses. Fortunately, the man who had murdered Veronica Murray had not been wearing gloves, and he had left some good fingerprints behind. Since he did not have a criminal record, the prints did not identify him, but the brutality of the murder made the detectives involved in the murder investigation certain that he would he heard from again.

And these detectives were not mistaken. In early 1959, the very same prints were found at the scene of a burglary at the Westbury Hotel, Westbury Avenue. In October the same year, Mrs Mabel Hill, living at No. 5 Ismailia Road, Fulham [it has since been demolished], brought a young man home to her flat, presumably for some 'fun'. But once he was inside the flat, the visitor turned nasty, trying to rape and strangle her. Mrs Hill was found in a senseless condition, well-nigh strangled by a pair of her own nylon stockings. She was able to give a rough description of her attacker, a short young man with cropped hair, who had seemed quite harmless until he had attacked her in a furious temper. His fingerprints matched those of the murderer of Veronica Murray.

The Charteris Road murderer next made himself known by breaking into a number of Chelsea and Pimlico flats and hotel rooms. Constitutionally averse to the traditional burglar's habit of wearing gloves, he left nice fingerprints behind each time. In one of these burglaries, he had amused himself by cracking a sleeping old woman over the head with a poker, nearly killing her. He then burgled the hotel suite of the actor George Sanders, stealing a number of objects, including a pair of the actor's shoes. Instead, he left his own footwear behind: a pair of dirty shoes marked 'W.G.' Were these his own initials, the police pondered, or did these letters have any other significance?

Soon after, the gloveless killer again left some useful fingerprints behind at yet another Chelsea burglary. One of the objects stolen was a very distinctive cigarette lighter. When the police issued a description of it, a soldier in the Welsh Guards came forward to say that he had purchased this very item, for five shillings, from another soldier, the 19-year-old drummer Michael

Dowdall, also known as 'Guardsman Mick'. This individual was promptly arrested, and his fingerprints were an exact match with those of the murderer of Veronica Murray.

A native of Llanhilleth, not far from Abertillery, Michael Dowdall had joined the Welsh Guards at the age of 15, as a drummer boy. He had not taken his military career very seriously, and had been incapable of learning to play the flute, or of becoming a proper military musician. The other soldiers said that 'Guardsman Mick' often went for drunken 'benders' in London when on leave, and that he sometimes was very well supplied with money when he returned, enough to pay them for washing his shirt and cleaning his boots. When questioned by the police, Dowdall said that he could recall that back in December 1958, when he had been very drunk, he had been taken home by a street prostitute. When they quarrelled, she called him 'a filthy little Welsh bastard' and this sent him over the edge. After a fierce fight, he had knocked her down, and quite possibly killed her.

On trial at the Old Bailey for the murder of Veronica Murray, all Dowdall's legal team could do was to try playing the insanity card. Remembering the case of Derek Lees-Smith, the Bryanston Court killer of 1942, they made sure their client had an electroencephalogram, which turned out to be abnormal. They claimed that when sober, Dowdall was a capable soldier and a decent human being, but when going on a drinking binge, he turned into a veritable Mr Hyde, capable of both theft and murder, since his brain reacted abnormally to the alcohol. But in his summing-up, Mr Justice Donovan pointed out that the section in the Homicide Act that dealt with diminished responsibility was not intended as a charter for drunkards. Dowdall had chosen to go drinking on his own volition. The jury took the hint and 'Guardsman Mick' was found guilty of wilful murder. He was sentenced to imprisonment for life, and the Judge pointed out that due to the savagery of his crimes, it was clearly unsafe to impose any minimum sentence. Dowdall would remain in prison until the authorities were satisfied that he could safely mingle with his fellow creatures.[14] It is not known how long he spent behind bars, but he is unlikely to have been included among the individuals who today have an official or unofficial 'whole life tariff', meaning that he has probably been released from prison. The murder house at No. 58 Charteris Road still stands.

MURDER IN BRENTHURST ROAD, 1968

Vincent Bonitto was born in April 1935, a native of St Anne's, Jamaica. From an early age, he showed strong criminal tendencies, with many convictions for theft, burglary, assault, and robbery with violence. Borstal, prison with hard labour, and beatings with a cat o' nine tails had no effect on this hardened villain. Having just spent two years in prison for assault, Bonitto moved to London with his wife in April 1958. He kept to the straight and narrow for a while, and settled down in a small terraced house at No. 3 Brenthurst Road, Harlesden. Bonitto and his family lived in the three upstairs rooms, and they sub-let the three rooms downstairs to other impecunious West Indians. One of them was the former Barbadoes police constable Henderson Kinch.

In July 1964, Vincent Bonitto was sentenced to four years in prison for robbery, burglary and assault. He was released in March 1967 and returned to the house in Brenthurst Road. He blamed his wife for giving information to the police, and tried to discipline her using his fists, but the tall and strong Henderson Kinch protected her. Bonitto could behave like a complete madman when he had smoked too many 'reefer cigarettes', and his constant violence caused his wife to move out of the house.

Henderson Kinch, who was becoming fearful that his demented landlord's threats to murder him in his sleep were not as empty as he had previously presumed, decided upon a pre-emptive strike. In the early hours of July 15 1968, he crept into Bonitto's bedroom, murdered him with a dagger, and proceeded to dismember the body. He boiled some of the body parts in a pressure cooker, cleaned up the crime scene and the bath where the butchery had been performed, rented a Vauxhall Victor car and loaded the mangled remains of his former landlord into the boot. He brought with him a spade and other garden tools, planning to bury what remained of Vincent Bonitto in the countryside.

But unfortunately for Henderson Kinch, who had made such impressive progress in committing the perfect murder, he was quite a bad driver. Having only got to Windsor, he drove the Vauxhall into a fence, damaging it severely. The suave West Indian, who was himself uninjured, at first managed to distract the police constables who attended the accident from the contents of the boot. When they turned their backs, he kicked Bonitto's severed head, which he had kept in a box inside the car, into a hedge. But the constables became suspicious, removed the car's rear seat, retrieved the body parts, and arrested Henderson Kinch.

On trial for murder at the Old Bailey, Henderson Kinch pleaded guilty and was sentenced to imprisonment for life. The *Sunday Telegraph* started a scare that cannibalism had been involved, and that Kinch had eaten the boiled remains of Bonitto. "The blood-chilling report of a case of suspected cannibalism in a house in North London occupied by coloured immigrants can hardly fail to exacerbate racial tensions!" exclaimed that worthy newspaper. Since there was in fact no solid evidence that cannibalism had taken place at all, the *Sunday Telegraph* journalist was harshly spoken to by the Director of Public Prosecutions, since the article might well constitute contempt of court. In the end, the newspaper was not prosecuted for its racist exhortations, however.[15]

MASS MURDER IN OLIVE ROAD, 1971

In 1971, the little terraced house at No. 17 Olive Road, Cricklewood, was inhabited by the West Indian immigrant Winston McKenzie, his wife Edna, son Michael and daughter Candy. On July 29, for reasons unknown, Michael McKenzie decided to exterminate his entire family. Drugs may well have been involved. Going on a rampage through the house, he stabbed both his parents to death, seriously injured his sister, and killed her boyfriend, the American sailor Richard Simms. The murder house was surrounded by armed police, but Michael McKenzie had entrenched himself in one of the bedrooms. Since the frenzied killer had shown what he was capable of, a police sergeant obtained permission to use CS gas to incapacitate him. McKenzie was captured unharmed, and later found guilty of manslaughter.[16]

DENNIS NILSEN'S MURDER HOUSES, 1978-1981

Dennis Nilsen, one of the most prolific serial killers in modern history, was born in Strichen, Aberdeenshire, in 1945. His father, a drunken Norwegian soldier, soon absconded, and Dennis was brought up by his grandparents for a while, before his mother remarried and took him back. His childhood does not appear to have been particularly unhappy, and his mother and grandparents took good care of their little boy. Still, he took the first opportunity to leave the drab Scottish outback, through joining the army in

1961. He became an army cook and served abroad for lengthy periods of time. Although a homosexual, he kept his urges under tight control, fearful of being kicked out of the army, in disgrace, if caught 'in the act'.

After leaving the army in 1972, Dennis Nilsen briefly served as a police constable, before becoming a civil servant at a jobcentre. He was reasonably competent at his job, albeit surly and sarcastic to his superiors. A firm trade union activist, he looked like the archetypical 1970s 'leftie': long-haired, bespectacled, scruffily dressed and lacking a tie. He admonished his colleagues for reading the tabloids, instead recommending the *Guardian* newspaper as the proper reading material for a true left-wing intellectual.

Although he had worked full time all his adult life, Dennis Nilsen never had much money. He drank a good deal, but was never an alcoholic. An ever-active homosexual, he liked 'cruising' round central London's many gay pubs, picking up various dodgy coves and taking them back to his lodgings. The years in the army had made him unfastidious with regard to living accommodation, but in late 1975, he and his younger boyfriend moved into the ground floor rear bedsit at No. 195 Melrose Avenue, Cricklewood. They spent much time clearing the long garden, to which they had sole access, and planting fruit trees there. They got hold of a gloomy-looking mongrel dog, which they renamed Bleep, and also a cat and a budgerigar. The relationship lasted only for a year and a half, however, since Nilsen considered his boyfriend to be his intellectual inferior, and often shouted at him for his stupidity. Both of them were notoriously unfaithful, bringing home various undesirable types to No. 195 Melrose Avenue, until the boyfriend [wisely, as we will see!] decided that he had seen enough of the sinister Nilsen, and moved out in the summer of 1977.

Alone in the Melrose Avenue flat, a gloomy Dennis Nilsen pondered his future. He kept on picking up various young homosexuals, quite a few of them alcoholics, drug addicts or rent boys, getting them drunk and then having sex with them in his tiny flat. In 1978, something seems to have snapped in his head, and he began murdering his evening visitors, one after one. After plying them with drink until they were well-nigh comatose, he strangled his defenceless victims, or drowned them in the bath. Nilsen was himself a very hard drinker, and still clear-headed even after imbibing quite a quantity of lager and whisky; his needy victims, many of whom had been living in the street, had the unexpected dose of strong spirits go straight to their heads, with disastrous results for them. The vile Nilsen then took the corpses to bed with him, fondled them, and had sex with them. When he tired of his repulsive 'sex toys', he made use of his army butchering skills to cut his victims up, and hid the body parts underneath the floorboards. It is not known whether the dog Bleep was given a few bones and meaty chunks to cheer her up, after she had been the sole witness to these perverted practices. When the bodies underneath the floorboards were becoming too 'high', the resourceful Dennis Nilsen lit a bonfire in the garden and burnt them to a cinder. In all, twelve young men were murdered at No. 195 Melrose Avenue, nearly all of them homeless drifters who Nilsen had picked up in central London and brought home to his flat. Most of the victims had severed all family ties, and nobody missed these feckless young tramps, drug addicts and rent boys. One intended victim managed to fight off the frenzied attacker, but although he immediately called the police, they took no particular notice of what they thought were two silly 'poofters' having a domestic disagreement.

In 1981, the owner of the house at No. 195 Melrose Avenue wanted to 'develop' it into two nice flats. To get rid of the various

3.9 Across the road from Dennis Nilsen: an old postcard showing the house at No. 38 Cranley Gardens.

undesirables occupying its shabby bedsits, they were offered a neat lump sum in cash. After having made sure that the remains of all his victims were safely buried in the garden, Nilsen moved into a tiny second-floor flat at No. 23 Cranley Gardens, Muswell Hill. Again it is unclear why he chose such dismal living accommodation; after all, alcohol was cheap and so were his rent boys. Nor was a second-floor flat ideal for a serial killer, who needed to dispose of his victims. Nilsen kept on working at the jobcentre, appearing as strange and respectable as before, and taking a vigorous interest in trade union activities. But the urge to kill and kill again was too strong for him to fight. In November 1981, he thought he had 'finished off' one of his victims, a Camden drag queen, by drowning him in the bath. But the dog Bleep licked the intended victim's face, and when the half-drowned drag queen came to, he lashed out at Nilsen and managed to escape. Three more victims were not as lucky: they were all murdered, 'used' and butchered by the demented murderer.

From his new second-floor flat, Nilsen had no access to a garden, nor could he store large quantities of human flesh beneath the floorboards. Instead, the ever-resourceful killer stored various body parts in his wardrobe, and in his bath. He had a large pot that he used for making curry: in this container, he boiled the remains of his victims before flushing them down the toilet. But the drains were soon blocked by the lumps of flesh, and when a company was called in to unblock them. When the police came calling in February 1983, Nilsen feigned surprise and innocence, exclaiming 'Good grief, how awful!' when he was informed the drains were full of human flesh. But one of the detectives smelt rotting flesh inside the flat, and roughly asked him 'Don't mess about, where's the rest of the body?' Nilsen calmly indicated two very smelly plastic bags in his wardrobe. When he was asked how many people he had killed, he replied 'Fifteen or sixteen!'

Dennis Nilsen was taken into custody and charged with multiple murder. The poor old dog Bleep, who had seen the grossest scenes enacted in front of her innocent canine eyes, was taken to the Battersea Dogs' Home. Although she was far from an attractive dog, and blind on one eye after being mauled by a cat, many people offered to give the traumatized animal a new home. This never happened, however, since Nilsen had neglected to have her properly vaccinated; poor Bleep died from a parvovirus infection, the sixteenth (or perhaps seventeenth) victim of the demented serial killer.

In the newspapers, there was sensation that the outwardly respectable civil servant could have committed such gruesome murders. Both murder houses were named and shamed, being pictured in all the tabloids. The *Daily Mirror* even managed to take some snapshots inside the sparsely furnished, shabby Cranley Gardens flat, still full of empty beer cans from Nilsen's final drinking binge. As the police were digging away in the garden of No. 195 Melrose Avenue, finding one body after another, a huge crowd of journalists gathered outside. One of them managed to get an interview with the builders who had just put the finishing touches on the two nice new flats. There were buyers for both of them, the builders said, nervously hoping that contracts had already been exchanged.

Dennis Nilsen was convicted of six murders and two attempted murders and sentenced to life imprisonment.[17] Initially, his minimum term was 25 years, but he is now believed to have received a whole life tariff, meaning that he will never be released. His existence behind bars has been far from untroubled. In December 1983, he was slashed hard across the face with a razor at Wormwood Scrubs. A barrack-room lawyer just like in his trade union days, he vigorously fought the decision not to allow him access to gay pornography. In 1998, he tried to publish his autobiography, but without success, since the authorities placed an injunction on it. In 2005, a number of his letters to an outside friend were published, alleging that he regularly got drunk on potent prison 'hooch'.[18] He still regarded himself as intellectually superior, disapproving of inane TV shows like *Big Brother* and *Coronation Street*, and claiming to read several books each month; whether he was still poring over his old favourite, the *Guardian* newspaper, was unfortunately not revealed. At any rate, Dennis Nilsen is still with us, at Full Sutton high security prison, aged 70 in 2015. His leather jacket is kept at the curious Crime Through

Time museum in Littledean, where I have seen it; it is unlikely that the two will ever be reunited.

The two murder houses also faced further troubled times. The two flats at No. 195 Melrose Avenue appear to have sold in 1982, just as planned by the developer of the house, but it is unlikely that the purchaser of the downstairs flat was particularly happy about what had been kept stored underneath the floorboards by the previous tenant. In 1984, after Nilsen had been jailed, the ramshackle house at No. 23 Cranley Gardens was also tidied up and developed into four flats. The estate agents selling them did not have an easy job, however, since many people found it eerie to move into a house where such horrible and depraved crimes had been taking place. In 1994, the owner of the lower ground floor flat at No. 23 expressed her relief that the flat had finally been sold after two years on the market.[19] The new owner had never heard of Dennis Nilsen. Today, both Dennis Nilsen's murder houses are still standing, and in good condition, although many people living nearby know about their sinister past.

CHAPTER 4

HAMMERSMITH AND BARNES

On the lone bleak moor,
At the midnight hour,
Beneath the Gallows Tree,
Hand in hand
The Murderers stand
By one, by two, by three!
　　　　Richard Harris Barham, The Nurse's Story
　　　　　　　(from the Ingoldsby Legends*).*

The murder houses of Fulham have been described in the first volume of this work, but this chapter will deal with those in Hammersmith, Barnes and Shepherd's Bush. Many of the murder houses of these parts survive today, although not No. 187 Sterndale Road, Shepherd's Bush, where Charles Everard Fox murdered his son in 1908, or No. 32 Davisville Road, where Bernard Cooper murdered his wife in 1949. The murder house at No. 7 Roseford Gardens, where Mrs Ada Fortescue was murdered by her lodgers in 1936, no longer frowns upon the passer-by; in fact, the entire street has been 'developed'.

　　Barnes is home to one of London's most mysterious murder houses: No. 3 Grove Villas, Grove Road, home to the baby-farmer and murderess Ada Chard Williams. Grove Villas was a row of three houses built in August 1899; No. 1 was called 'Grove House' and No. 3 was 'Durban House'. In the years following the trial and execution of Ada Chard Williams in 1901, the remainder of Grove Road was constructed and the houses renumbered. Attempts to elucidate the position of Grove Villas using the Post Office directories were unsuccessful, and a visit to Grove Road failed to show up a 'row' of three distinctive-looking houses. Parts of Grove Road have been 'developed', and blocks of flats constructed, but many old houses remain; if the mystery house once known as No. 3 Grove Villas is one of them, it has managed to keep its secret.

Hammersmith and Barnes have a fair few murder houses standing. Read about the French aristocrat who was gunned down in his fine Thames-side residence, marvel at the immorality of the extraordinary Barnes killer Horace Robinson, ponder the mysterious murder of John O'Shea, and have a look at one of London's most remarkable modern murder houses in Dewhurst Road, Brook Green.

THE FINEST MURDER HOUSE IN BARNES, 1812

The present-day No. 27 Barnes Terrace was constructed around 1760 as a two-story Georgian cottage, enjoying an attractive position just by the Thames. Its most notable occupant was the Comte d'Antraigues, a French nobleman from a distinguished family. A cunning politician, he had initially supported the French Revolution, but during the tyranny of Robespierre, he became fearful for his life and escaped to Germany. Employed by the Russians, he began plotting against the French revolutionaries. Napoleon Bonaparte did not at all appreciate the Comte

JAN BONDESON

4.1 The Comte d'Antraigues.

d'Antraigues, since the nobleman was ceaselessly travelling around
Europe, spying and stirring up trouble for the French. In 1797,
Comte d'Antraigues was arrested in Venice at Napoleon's orders,
but the slippery nobleman managed to escape to Milan. He was
later employed at the Russian diplomatic mission to the court of
Dresden. In 1806, he came to London, with credentials from the
Emperor of Russia. The Comte d'Antraigues found many friends
in London government circles, where his knowledge of European
politics was much appreciated. The wealthy nobleman had a town
residence at No. 7 Queen Street West, and also the attractive
Thames-side house that is today No. 27 Barnes Terrace.

In July 1812, the now 56-year-old Comte d'Antraigues was
staying at his country residence. The Comtesse, who had once
been a celebrated opera singer and actress, was with him; their
only son was away studying law at Manchester University. They
had a staff consisting of a coachman, a footman and two

124

4.2 Barnes Terrace, an old print.

maidservants, and also a 'servant out of livery' named Laurence Stelli. On the morning of July 22, the Comte and Comtesse wanted to drive to London. But when she was standing in the doorway, and he was coming downstairs, there was the sudden and unexpected loud report from a pistol, and a cloud of smoke in the hallway. One of the housemaids screamed 'Murder! Murder!' As the smoke subsided, the servant Stelli was seen to run upstairs. He soon returned, brandishing a large pistol on one hand, and a dirk in the other. With the latter implement, he stabbed the Comte d'Antraigues hard in the shoulder, before plunging the dirk into the chest of the Comtesse. She screamed 'It is Laurence! It is Laurence!' and fell to the ground. When Stelli ran back upstairs, the Comte pursued him, although bleeding badly from his wound. For a minute, the horror-struck domestics stood staring at each other. Then, there was another loud report from a pistol shot.

Not unreasonably, the frightened servants did not dare to go upstairs, fearful that the demented Laurence Stelli would be waiting up there, intent in finishing off the remainder of the household. One of them fetched a doctor, another went for the police, and the coachman managed to flag down a sturdy passer-by, who armed himself with a poker and resolutely went upstairs. He found the Comte d'Antraigues lying on the bed, in a dying condition. Stelli was lying on the floor, having blown his brains out with a shot from the large pistol. Medical attention could do nothing for either Comte or Comtesse: they both expired within an hour, without speaking a word. At the coroner's inquest, the verdict was that Laurence Stelli had wilfully murdered the Comte d'Antraigues and his wife, afterwards committing suicide. No motive for this outrage could be discerned. Stelli might have disliked his employers, or he might just have gone mad.

Considering the background of the Comte d'Antraigues, there have also been some conspiracy theories. The pistols and the dirk had been kept in the Comte's room, for reasons of self-protection. The nobleman had been well aware that Napoleon had 'put out a contract' on him, and that an assassin might be calling on him at his Thames-side retreat. Another conspiracy theory, favoured by French 'alternative historians', is that the British secret service had murdered the Comte d'Antraigues, to steal his papers. Neither of these theories explains why Stelli committed suicide after committing the double murder, however; after all, he could quite easily have subdued the other domestics with the pistol, and then taken off in style in the Comte's carriage. Laurence Stelli was buried in a shallow grave at the crossroads of Barnes Common. The locals thought it would be fun to open the grave and have a look at the corpse, however, and when the hearses containing the coffins of the Comte and Comtesse came travelling across the common, the undertakers stopped to take a peek at the murderer themselves.[1]

In the 1870s, two more stories and some nice wrought-iron balconies were added to the murder house at No. 27 Barnes Terrace.

4.3 Houses in Barnes Terrace, from a postcard stamped and posted in 1906.

'd'Antraigues', as it has been renamed, is today one of the most handsome Thames-side residences of Barnes Terrace. When the house was sold around ten years ago, for a very considerable sum, by Savills estate agents, its history was summarised in the particulars, although it was left out that the nobleman after whom it had been renamed had actually been murdered on the premises, along with his wife, and that the murderer had committed suicide there.

SHOCKING MURDER IN WEST LONDON, 1896

The life of Mrs Annie Florence Chambers certainly had its ups and downs. The daughter of a poor, drunken labourer, she became a barmaid already in her teens. Since she "possessed considerable personal attractions" and was not averse to having some fun with the chaps, she soon had many admirers. One of

4.4 The murder of Annie Florence Chambers, from the Illustrated Police News, *February 1 1896.*

them, the theatrical designer Joseph Chambers, became so besotted that he actually married her in 1870. He was a friend of Sir Henry Irving, and advanced to become treasurer of the Lyceum Theatre. For a number of years, the Chambers' led a happy family life, and had not less than nine children alive. But Annie Florence's fierce and angry temper, and her husband's infidelity and lack of professional success, meant that eventually, the marriage broke down. Annie Florence Chambers settled down in a house at No. 12 Greenside Road, Shepherd's Bush, with her numerous brood of children. Her husband supported her as well as he could, which did not amount to very much, but the kind Sir Henry Irving sent her a pound a week after he heard of her domestic difficulties.

In spite of the support from the generous thespian, Annie Florence Chambers soon had to take in lodgers. Her house was not a particularly clean or attractive one, and the lodgers were of a corresponding quality. A one-legged, drunken sailor, a drunken old bookseller, and some ladies of very dubious virtue all came and went. Angry quarrels were the order of the day: the lodgers complained of the dirty rooms, the noisy children, and the badly cooked food, and Annie Florence, who had seen better days, was equally annoyed by their drunken and immoral habits. A nurse named Mrs Holland was a slightly more desirable lodger: although she kept complaining of the food, at least she paid her rent on time, and even contributed to the cleaning and dishwashing when she felt like it. There were problems when Nurse Holland's son Joseph joined the household in late 1895, however. Not only was he a very idle, drunken young fellow, but Annie Florence found out that although he was just 26 years old, he had just spent five years in Dartmoor Prison for house-breaking. The reason he settled down at No. 12 Greenside Road was not that he liked the dirty, crowded house, but that as a convict released on license, he had nowhere else to go but the house where his mother was lodging.

Joseph was soon the major troublemaker in the household. He more than once declared that the food compared unfavourably to the prison 'grub' to which he had become accustomed. After he had dashed a pint of stale beer into the face of one of Annie Florence's children, and thrown a boiled potato at another, Nurse Holland and her son were threatened with eviction from the premises. But after the nurse had apologized for Joseph's behaviour, and promised to try to find alternative accommodation for her malcontent son, they were allowed to remain at No. 12. Since Annie Florence was seriously fearful that Joseph would injure one of her children in one of his fits of rage, she purchased a large mongrel dog, to set upon the miscreant if he tried any further potato-throwing antics.

On January 20 1896, Annie Florence Chambers took Joseph's

luncheon up to his room. Sounds of an angry quarrel were soon heard, and Annie Florence gave a piercing scream and came running downstairs. Mary Chambers, one of her daughters, ran out into the street, where she politely told Police Constable Dickinson that she thought her mother was being murdered at No. 12. Entering the premises, Dickinson saw a large dog sleeping peacefully by the fire. He found the lifeless body of Annie Florence Chambers in the basement passage. She had been stabbed hard, and struck a number of blows with a blunt instrument. The policeman went up to Nurse Holland's room, where he found the dismal Joseph skulking in a corner. Two blood-stained knives and a blood-stained hammer, were found in the room, and the miscreant's clothes were also heavily stained with blood. A broken plate of very unappetizing 'grub' was found on the floor. Clearly, the demented ex-convict had had enough of his landlady's dismal cooking, and taken drastic action to make sure he would never taste her food again. At the coroner's inquest, the jury returned a verdict of wilful murder against Joseph Holland.

At Joseph Holland's trial for murdering Annie Florence Chambers, at the Old Bailey, two doctors testified that Holland was insane and unfit to plead. He was detained in Broadmoor during her Majesty's pleasure, ending his days there in February 1927.[2] His knives and hammer were deposited in Scotland Yard's Black Museum, and may well still be there today. What happened to Annie Florence Chambers' numerous brood of children after her untimely death is not known. The murder house is still standing, and appears to be well looked after. A large and valuable house in a relatively quiet Hammersmith street, it is far from the dismal lodging-house where poor Annie Florence Chambers had to pay such a heavy price for her indifferent cooking.

THE GOLDHAWK ROAD FISHMONGER MURDER, 1902

In 1902, the shop at No. 62 Goldhawk Road, Hammersmith, belonged to Mr W.S. Evans, a successful fishmonger who owned a string of shops all over West London. One of his employees at the Goldhawk Road fishmongers shop was the 23-year-old Frederick Charles Meaker, who had been working for Mr Evans not less than ten years. In spite of his feeble intellect and great fondness for drinking beer, Fred was a reliable enough workman, and good at cutting up fish. He could also be trusted with a daily delivery round in the neighbourhood.

But in late 1902, Fred Meaker's habits went from bad to worse. His girlfriend left him after he had knocked her about in a drunken rage. Miss Ethel Beatrice Evans, who worked as book-

4.5 A postcard showing old shops in Goldhawk Road, stamped and posted in 1906.

keeper to her father, and supervised the staff at No. 62 Goldhawk Road, more than once had to admonish young Fred for lurching through his delivery round in an alcoholic daze, scattering fish among the Hammersmith households in a random manner. In particular, Fred was at loggerheads with another fishmonger's assistant named Edward Girling, who objected to his drunkenness and general incompetence.

On December 17 1902, Fred Meaker and Edward Girling started a fight inside the fishmonger's shop at No. 62 Goldhawk Road. Fred waved his arms about, but was too drunk to score any hits. Girling gave Fred a couple of hard knocks, sending him sprawling. A witness saw him kneeling on top of Fred, to prevent him from getting up. "Let me go, you bastard, I will settle and murder you!" the furious Fred screamed, as his opponent held him down.

A police constable came to break up the fight, and Miss Evans went up to him, saying that she did not want to charge anybody with assault. The constable suggested that the drunken Fred should be sent home to 'sleep it off'. Miss Evans invited Fred up to the rooms above the shop, and made him a large cup of strong coffee to sober him up. She saw that he looked angrily at Girling, and picked up a knife from the fish slab. "Put that knife down at once, Fred!" she ordered him, and the fishmonger's assistant meekly obeyed. He started to cry, saying that he was sorry for getting drunk and misbehaving himself. After emptying the cup of coffee, he staggered off home.

The next morning, a morose-looking Fred came to work half an hour late. The stern Mr Evans himself came into the shop at No. 62 Goldhawk Road, and he was of course not at all pleased with Fred's recent shenanigans. He went up to the till, asked for sixpence, gave this coin to Fred in lieu of two weeks wages, and said "You had better go!" Fred meekly returned his apron to Miss Evans and walked off.

But on December 23, Fred returned with a vengeance. Blind drunk and foaming at the mouth, he burst into the shop, seized a large knife, and stabbed his enemy Edward Girling to death with it. The startled fishmonger only had time to say "Don't, Fred!" before the knife struck home. The other shop assistants seized hold of Fred and held him down on a large block of ice. When a police constable took him into custody, he said "He has done me a lot of harm. I am sorry I did it, I was in drink!"

When Frederick Charles Meaker was on trial for murder at the Old Bailey, there was no question that he had murdered his old enemy Edward Girling. But many witnesses testified as to his feeble intellect, and also some strange 'fits' he had been suffering, grinding his teeth and clenching his fists. Since an early age, he had been a very heavy drinker, and the month of the murder, his consumption of beer and gin had been truly prodigious. Dr James Scott, medical officer at H.M. Prison Holloway, testified that Fred was definitely sane, and that during the seven weeks he had been in prison, he had suffered no epileptic fits. The jury found him guilty of murder, but added a strong recommendation to mercy on account of his youth and weak-mindedness. His death sentence was later commuted to imprisonment for life.[3]

In 1914, Fred Meaker was released from prison. Twelve years without access to alcoholic beverages had made him a saner and healthier man, and he served as a private soldier throughout the Great War, before marrying and settling down to an ordinary life back home in London. The murder shop at No. 62 Goldhawk Road is today the Vanni Patisserie. The remainder of Goldhawk Road would remain murder free until 1949, when Fred Hukin murdered his mother Clara Adelaide at No. 279 [it still stands], before committing suicide.

MURDER AND IMMORALITY IN BARNES, 1921

Mr Horace Robinson, a tall, barrel-chested cove who owned a ramshackle art and antiques business, also did some bookmaking on the side. Indolent and work-shy, the 45-year-old Robinson still kept poverty from the door by some stratagem or other, and could afford to live in a small villa at No. 2 Clavering Avenue, Barnes, with his much younger mistress Ivy Perry. Horace and Ivy had two children, both of whom had been 'farmed out' to Ivy's mother. They led a riotous life, with much drinking and partying. In April 1921, the 23-year-old Ivy wanted to move in with another bloke she had met, a professional skater named Ernest McManus. He was a much better man than her present lover, she declared, and on this point she may well have been right. When Ivy told Horace about her plans, he was not best pleased. Weeping piteously, he pleaded with her to consider their children, but she knew what a howling cad he was, and did not budge.

On April 12 1921, Ivy Perry had threatened to invite her new boyfriend to No. 2 Clavering Avenue. Fearful of being beaten up, Horace hid in the garden. And indeed, McManus and another man named Thomas soon came calling at the house. When these two humourists saw Robinson skulking in the garden, they called out 'Hullo, Robbie, are you a night watchman?' With as much dignity he could muster, Horace said 'What are you doing here?' 'Why, we are going in to see Ivy! We've come for a drink! Aren't you coming in?' All the indignant householder could come up with was 'This is a funny business, is it not!' The two men only answered him with a loud guffaw of laughter, before being invited in by the jolly young Ivy, who was wearing a fur coat over her nightgown.

As all four started drinking beer thirstily, Horace pleaded with McManus not to wreck his happy home, but the forthright skater said 'Ivy loves me more than she does you, and why should I not

4.6 *Dramatic scenes from the murder of Ivy Perry, and a drawing of the murder house, from the* Illustrated Police News, *April 21 1921.*

have her?' Poor Horace wept miserably. The 'funny' Mr Thomas said 'It is a fine jump from Hammersmith Bridge into the water for a miserable man on a night like this!' and McManus and Ivy both joined in his guffaws of laughter. Eighteen large bottles of beer had been emptied before Ivy decided that she had had enough. When she returned to her bedroom, the maudlin Horace followed her there, pleading that she should think of the children and not ruin his happy home, but she refused to listen. He then pulled out a small pen-knife and stabbed her in the neck. Ivy screamed and ran downstairs, where she threw herself into the arms of McManus. 'You'd better grease!' the angry skater told Robinson, and the shaken householder made himself scarce.

A doctor arrived at No. 2 Clavering Avenue, but it turned out that the knife had hit Ivy Perry in a major artery, and she rapidly bled to death. Horace Robinson gave himself up to a police inspector in Hammersmith Broadway and was charged with her murder. At the coroner's inquest, a story of remarkable depravity was revealed. Horace Robinson had once married Bessie Perry, Ivy's elder sister, and had five children with her. But after young Ivy had moved in with them, the lustful Horace had seduced her, and their first child had been born when she was just twelve years old. He had then kicked Bessie and her children out of No. 2 Clavering Avenue and installed his young sister-in-law as the new 'Mrs Robinson', a role this immoral young wench was quite willing to play. She had only been fourteen years old when their second child was born.

The inquest returned a verdict of wilful murder against Horace Robinson, but when on trial at the Old Bailey, he was very ably defended by the eloquent Sir Ellis Hume-Williams. It was pointed out that in spite of all Robinson's blameworthy caddishness, Ivy had not been behaving much better, stealing her own sister's husband, before deserting her lover and two children to go off with some dodgy bloke. It was accepted that Horace had stabbed Ivy in a sudden rage, that there had been considerable provocation from the heartless jokes and comments made by McManus and his companion, and that it was clearly not a case of deliberate murder, due to the diminutive size of the pen-knife, which is still kept in the police file on the case. In the end, Horace Robinson got off with five years in prison for manslaughter.[4]

But this sordid story does not end here. It is sad but true that the real Mrs Robinson, born Bessie Perry, sued for a decree nisi at the Divorce Court in December 1922. She described Horace Robinson as the devil incarnate: he had beaten and mistreated her, and forced her out onto the street as a prostitute, before misconducting himself with young Ivy, and evicting Bessie and her children from No. 2 Clavering Avenue. The decree nisi was promptly awarded.[5] But in 1924, the King's Proctor, the solicitor representing the crown in cases of probate and divorce, referred the case to the High Court of Justice, since Bessie Robinson had clearly lied in court. She had in fact been living with another man, with whom she had at least one child, from 1916 until 1921. Although Sir Ellis Hume-Williams, whose services were again requested, did his best for his unworthy client, the decree nisi was rescinded and Mrs Robinson had to pay all the costs.[6] When the dismal outcome of the High Court of Justice case was duly reported in the *Times* and other newspapers, hollow laughter must surely have emanated from one of the cells in Wandsworth Prison, where Horace Robinson was still languishing.

MASS MURDER IN BARNES, 1927

Alexander Bell Filson was born in Portaferry, Co. Down, in 1877. His father, the local doctor, died when he was a young boy. After an unhappy childhood, he enlisted in the army and went to India as a private soldier, but in some unspecified sub-continental calamity, he lost a leg. Invalided back home, he became clerk to the accountant Maurice Chater. In secure if unspectacular employment, he could afford to marry a barmaid, and they soon had three children. In his crippled state, Filson was not fit for service in the Great War, and during the war years, his business career began to prosper. In 1920, he was made a partner in the firm of Chater & Filson, earning a very respectable salary. His son John was sent to Westminster School, and his daughters Margaret and Mary also received very decent educations. In 1924, the Filson family moved into a large ground floor flat at No. 19 Riverside Gardens, Castlenau.

In the mid-1920s, Alexander Bell Filson's life began going seriously wrong, however. He lost his wife to throat cancer in 1925, after a long and distressing illness, leaving him a single parent with a 17-year-old public schoolboy son, and two daughters of twelve and seven. Worried about continuing to be able to educate his children in the station of life to which he felt they must belong, Filson started embezzling money at the accountant's firm. Mr Chater caught him red-handed and he was dismissed from the partnership. He tried setting up business on his own, but it turned out that Chater had spread the word about his activities, and nobody wanted to employ an accountant with a proven track record of dishonesty. Filson was soon back home at Riverview Gardens, unemployed and unemployable.

Although the family was still comfortably off, with money in the bank, Filson became increasingly depressed and worried about the future of his family. He began drinking to excess, more than two bottles of whisky a week. He was jolly when drunk, but very miserable when sober. He could still afford to keep a housekeeper named Ruth Parrish, but she thought her employer an odd cove, who got annoyed by the slightest trifles, like one of his daughters

FATHER AND THREE CHILDREN FOUND SHOT DEAD AT BARNES

4.7 Alexander Bell Filson and his murdered children, from the
Illustrated Police News, *January 20 1927.*

being untidy. In January 1927, Filson seemed to perk up when his
only brother James, a senior police officer in India, came to visit
London. The two arranged to meet for Sunday lunch on January
16. On Thursday January 13, after his brother had called him,
Filson even seemed quite jolly, although Miss Parrish got the
impression that he was worrying about his son John, who was just
going off to join the R.A.F.

The very same night, Ruth Parrish, who had a room of her
own in the spacious flat, had difficulties sleeping, since her
employer had left the hallway lights on. In the middle of the night,
she heard some odd noises, but she did not go out of bed to
investigate. The following morning, it seemed as if Mr Filson and
his children were all having a lie-in. She was worried to see that a

letter marked 'Cemetery. East Sheen' was lying on Mr Filson's desk, and that a box of pistol bullets had been put on a table. At 9.30 am, one of John's friends called to see him, but when Miss Parrish knocked at his door, there was no response. Entering the room, she saw him lying dead on the floor. The two girls, and Alexander Bell Filson himself, were also dead and still. The demented father had risen in the middle of the night, shot all three children, and then killed himself. The weapon used had been a small .25 calibre browning automatic pistol.

At the inquest on Alexander Bell Filson, the sad story of his wife's death and his professional ruin was retold. It was thought that the visit of his successful brother, and the departure of his beloved son, might have temporarily unhinged his mind. Filson left a suicide note saying that it had broken his heart to see his wife's home going to rack and ruin. The story was front page fare for the Press. "THREE MURDERS BY A FATHER: NOISES HOUSEKEEPER HEARD IN THE NIGHT… Edgar Allan Poe conceived few stories as strange as that which a woman related to the Mortlake Coroner's Court today… " exclaimed the *Evening News*. The police concluded that financial worries might well have been at the bottom of things, and they may well have been right, but still, Filson left in excess of £1000, money that went to his brother. The inquest found that he had committed the murders while of unsound mind.[7]

THE LAW OF 'RED ANGER', 1942

In the 1930s, London had a not inconsiderable Cypriot community. One of them was Savas Constantine Haji Savva, a married man with two children, who lived in a flat at No. 59 Parfrey Street, Hammersmith. He was called up for military service in 1940, and Mrs Iris Savva and the two children were evacuated to Norfolk. But there were soon worrying signs that Mrs Savva was 'carrying on' with an army corporal, and with a man named Macready as well. Private Savva, as he had become, offered to forgive her, but as a 'modern woman', she demanded a divorce.

In December 1941, Savas Constantine Savva went home on leave. Reaching the Parfrey Street flat, he found it empty, but there were some men's clothes in the bedroom. The angry, cuckolded Cypriot had brought with him an army rifle, and some ammunition, and when his wife returned with her lover Macready, he shot her dead, on the spot.

Promptly arrested and charged with murder, Savas Constantine Savva stood trial at the Old Bailey in late January 1942. On the advice of his legal team, he pleaded not guilty, claiming that he had only fired his rifle to frighten the guilty pair when they returned to the flat. In court, Mrs Savva's misconduct with various men was exposed for everyone to see, and her husband's magnanimity was made much of. He had used to write her long and eloquent love letters, with phrases like 'I want to believe my love for you is in extinguishable. Light of my eyes, light of my whole soul and body.'

Mr Christmas Humphreys, prosecuting, told the jury that "If a man finds his wife with a lover and in his fury and red anger kills one of them, the crime may be reduced to manslaughter." And indeed, the jury returned a verdict of guilty to manslaughter, and Savva was sentenced to fifteen months in prison.[8] He was one of several World War soldiers 'saved by their uniforms' when standing trial for gunning down their rivals or errant spouses. Lieutenant Douglas Malcolm and Count Ludomir Cienski both walked free from the Old Bailey after shooting dead interlopers in their respective marriages, and then we have Ronald Light, of

Leicester notoriety, and the wife-killing Private Chandler of Ballard's Lane. Savas Constantine Savva served his time, rejoined the army, survived the war, and remarried in 1950. He died in 2006, aged 93, having survived his dice with death at the Old Bailey for more than 64 years.

BLOODBATH IN EDITH ROAD, 1949

Elizabeth Klassen, a young native of Munster in Germany, got a job as an interpreter for the British Control Commission. In 1948, the now 23-year-old Elizabeth emigrated to London, since she wanted to improve her English, and since she feared becoming unpopular in Munster after the occupation had ceased, for having aided the English *Schweinhünde*.

Elizabeth Klassen first worked as a maid at the Three Tuns Hotel in Windsor, and then became housekeeper to a certain Commander List, of No. 14 Pitt Street, Kensington. She took lodgings at No. 6 Edith Road, Hammersmith. At Windsor, Elizabeth had befriended a Polish ex-army railway worker named Stefan Mizgalski, who fell very much in love with her. He told his friends that he wanted to marry this beautiful German girl. But Elizabeth, who had been brought up as a member of the *Herrenvolk*, and indoctrinated with the Nazi race theory of Polish *Untermenschen*, soon tired of her lover. Once, she told a friend that she had only seen him to get the opportunity to speak her own language, and the friend agreed that she could do much better than to marry a wretched Pole.

But the amorous Pole remained hell bent on marrying his faithless Elizabeth. On July 26 1949, he stood waiting for her at No. 6 Edith Road when she returned from work. They went up to her second-floor room. At midnight, the inhabitant of the first-floor room noticed blood dripping through his ceiling, and rapidly informed the police. The jilted Pole had cut Elizabeth's throat with a razor blade, before cutting his own brachial artery; the resulting bloodbath was repulsive even to the experienced police constables. On August 4 1949, the Hammersmith Coroner's Court returned a verdict of wilful murder against Stefan Mizgalski, who had then committed suicide whilst the balance of his mind was disturbed.[9]

MURDER IN GODOLPHIN ROAD, 1954

The twenty-year-old Patricia Wood, a canteen assistant at the BBC studios in Lime Grove, shared a flat at No. 91 Godolphin Road, Shepherd's Bush, with her widowed mother. She had a boyfriend, the 23-year-old salesman Christopher George Owden, who also lived in Godolphin Road. But Owden was quite a strange fellow,

4.8 A postcard showing Godolphin Road.

143

and sometimes behaved in a very immature and unbalanced manner. Patricia Wood decided to break off their engagement on November 30 1954. This came as a fearsome blow to the weirdo Owden, and would have terrible consequences for both of them.

On December 1, the day after the engagement had been broken up, Owden telephoned the BBC, presenting himself as a police officer, and asked for Patricia Wood. Disguising his voice, he told her that her former boyfriend Christopher George Owden had just committed suicide by leaping into Thames. At 10 am, the distraught Patricia Wood arrived home at No. 91 Godolphin Road. Showing considerable cunning, Owden was waiting for her there. He burst into the hallway, knocked her down with a large milk bottle, and stabbed her 25 times.

After murdering his former girlfriend, the demented Christopher George Owden went on the run. But the police found out about the bogus telephone call to lure Patricia Wood back to her flat, and made the correct deductions; Owden was soon the prime murder suspect, and a wanted man. After a report that a young man was hiding in Richmond Old Deer Park, these premises were searched with police dogs, and the fugitive was hounded out of his lair.

Once he was in police custody, the Godolphin Road murderer freely admitted his guilt. He told all about his cowardly trick to lure Patricia back to her flat, and described how he had deliberately murdered her. Once the engagement had been broken off, he had gone out to purchase a large knife, and made plans how to dispose of his faithless Patricia. Owden had a history of psychiatric disease, although obviously not severe enough to convince people that he needed help, or that he might prove dangerous to other people. Once, he had attacked his mother without provocation, and when briefly serving in the R.A.F., he had attempted suicide. On trial for murder at the Central

Criminal Court in January 1955, Owden was found guilty but insane, and incarcerated in Broadmoor.[10] Nothing is known about his later activities, except that a Christopher G. Owden died in Richmond in late 1967. The murder house at No. 91 Godolphin Road still stands.

THE MURDER OF JOHN O'SHEA, 1956

John O'Shea was a thrifty, hard-working Irishman. Although an unskilled labourer, he did plenty of overtime and made it a habit to live as cheaply as possible. An occasional pint of Guinness and a small flutter on the dogs at the White City track were his only pleasures in life. He did not trust banks, and made a habit of carrying a large sum of money in his wallet, sometimes several hundred pounds.

In 1956, the 43-year-old John O'Shea was living in a small room at an insalubrious lodging house at No. 22 Cambridge Grove, Hammersmith. Mrs Margaret Twyford, the landlady of the house, cannot by any means be called a security-conscious woman. The front door was kept unlocked at all hours, to allow the lodgers to come and go like they pleased. She does not appear to have performed any checks on the lodgers, or even obtained proof of their identity, as long as they were able to pay for their rooms. As a result of this slack policy, the lodgers were a rowdy and colourful lot, many of them hailing from the Emerald Isle.

On April 27 1956, the lodger James O'Brien was returning to No. 22 Cambridge Grove in a jolly frame of mind. When the tipsy Irishman went to give some winnings from the dog-track to another lodger, he saw that the door of John O'Shea's room was open, and shouted 'Hello, Kerry!' since he knew that O'Shea came from those parts. But since there was no response, O'Brien had a look inside the room. He found John O'Shea in bed, stiff and cold. He had been murdered with two powerful blows to the head from a blunt instrument, probably administered from behind. His room had been ransacked and his money stolen.

The police investigation of the murder of John O'Shea made a thorough trawl of Hammersmith's seedy underworld. It was of course considered important to investigate the antecedents of the past and present lodgers at No. 22 Cambridge Grove, also those who found it convenient to go under an alias. The problem was that the landlady's slack record-keeping, and the secretive manner of some of the lodgers, made it impossible to track them down. Mrs Twyford described John O'Shea as a very quiet, industrious man, a teetotaller with no interest in women. He had a widowed mother and two married sisters alive, and they added the information that the reason he had been so very thrifty was that after twenty years as a builder's labourer in Hammersmith, he dreamt of buying a farm back in Kerry, and looking after his mother in her old age.

The police concluded that John O'Shea had been murdered for profit, probably by some person who knew the house at No. 22 Cambridge Grove well. O'Shea had been a strong, fit labouring man, and the killer must have been lucky to be able to knock him unconscious without a fight. Or had the killer perhaps been a man who John O'Shea had known and trusted? The coroner's inquest returned a verdict of murder against some person or persons unknown.[11]

Several years went by without any worthwhile clues emerging in the O'Shea murder investigation. But in August 1959, the unemployed and homeless Irishman Richard Hodson went to Mr Gerald Byrne, the chief crime reporter on the *Empire News*, to confess that more than three years earlier, he had murdered John O'Shea. He claimed to have met O'Shea in a pub, and noted the large wad of cash in his wallet. He had followed John O'Shea home, made a note of his address, and returned another day armed with a hammer, to bash the thrifty labourer's head in and steal his hoard of banknotes. Byrne called the police and Hodson was removed to the Hammersmith police station. When sternly told "You have been brought here in connexion with the murder of John O'Shea", he replied "Yes, I did it!"

The police were encouraged to find that most of Richard Hodson's statements were consistent with the known facts about the murder of John O'Shea. But once Hodson had been deprived of alcohol, marijuana cigarettes, and various other drugs he had been abusing, the Irishman began to change his tone. He had been 'high' on some particularly strong 'reefer' cigarettes when he had confessed to the murder, and in real life, he had never even met John O'Shea. Indeed, he had been in Dublin in late April 1956. On trial at the Central Criminal Court, Hodson pleaded not guilty. He explained that he had been very depressed in August 1959, and that he had gone to Gerald Byrne to confess to a famous unsolved murder, so that he could be hanged and put out of his misery. He had lived in Shepherd's Bush for a while, and heard of the hunt for John O'Shea's murderer from other Irishmen in the pubs. Two men gave Hodson a solid alibi, claiming that they had seen him in Dublin every day in the last week of April 1956.

The case rested entirely on Richard Hodson's confession. The police had not been able to unearth any corroborating evidence against the Irishman, who made a much better impression in court after the alcoholic fumes had cleared from his brain. In his summing up, Mr Justice Cassels reminded Hodson that he only had himself to blame for the position he was now in. He asked the jury to consider whether Hodson was a guilty man plagued by his conscience, or just a drunken waster of police time. The jury went for the latter alternative, and Hodson was a free man.

The murder of John O'Shea remains unsolved, and the relevent police file in the National Archives is still closed.[12] The murder house at No. 22 Cambridge Grove still stands, although it looks rather bedraggled, situated on a busy road, close to the tube line to Hammersmith.

WIFE MURDER IN CASTLENAU, 1963

Mohammed Hussain Arbaney received a very good education in his native land of Pakistan, graduating as a B.A. in Karachi in 1949. He married his wife Zubeyda and they had two sons. Mohammed Arbaney's wealthy parents supported him when he went to England in 1952 to start a career as a business man. Initially, he had good success, but in the early 1960s, things were no longer looking good, although a foreign exchange business he had set up for his countrymen remained profitable. Arbaney started to drink to excess, and he suffered bouts of depression. In February 1963, he took an overdose of sleeping tablets, and three months later, he was taken into Putney Hospital in a comatose condition after a prolonged drinking bout.

The doctors at the Putney Hospital were unable to make Arbaney see reason, however, and he returned to the ground floor flat at No. 38 Castlenau, Barnes, where he lived with his family. He drank harder than ever, drove dangerously, and kept a loaded shotgun ready for use. On July 4, he ended an argument with his wife by shooting her dead with this weapon. Remarkably, his nine-year-old son Fiesal, who had been an eyewitness to his mother's murder, grabbed the shotgun from his father, and himself fired off a shot through the window to attract attention.

When the 47-year-old business man Mohammed Arbaney was charged with murder at the Mortlake police court, the prosecuting

4.9 Castlenau looking north; the future murder house at No. 36 can be seen on the right side of the road.

counsel praised young Fiesal for his calmness and bravery. Arbaney was sent for trial at the Central Criminal Court for murdering his wife. Dr Brisby, the Brixton prison doctor, certified that Arbaney suffered from endogenous depression, and that this, in combination with his excessive intake of alcohol, substantially impaired his mental responsibility. Arbaney was found guilty of manslaughter under diminished responsibility, and imprisoned for life.[13] His later activities remain obscure, although he is likely to have left prison alive, perhaps to return to his native land?

MURDER IN DEWHURST ROAD, 2011

Over the years, the West London mystery man William John Saunderson-Smith built up a formidable property empire, in London and elsewhere. He owned flats and houses in London, rental homes in Dorset, and various properties abroad. His London tenants more than one complained about his high-handed attitude and reluctance to maintain the properties, but when they took him to court, he represented himself with good success. The jewel in the crown in Saunderson-Smith's property empire was a large terraced house at No. 20 Dewhurst Road, Brook Green, which he had owned since 1981, and kept as student lets. All of a sudden, in 2011, Saunderson-Smith evicted all the students and himself moved into house. The neighbours were relieved when an eerie silence replaced the raucous music that used to emanate from No. 20. Instead, Saunderson-Smith filled the tiny front garden with a stockpile of building material, causing the neighbours to suspect that he was renovating the building, and perhaps converting it back to a family house.

In October 2011, the 58-year-old Saunderson-Smith was still building away at No. 20 Dewhurst Road. The neighbours, although pleased to be rid of the students, found him very strange indeed. He came and went at odd hours, and was very reluctant to discuss what plans he had for the house. Nobody ever visited this strange, lonely man, apart from some builders who helped him renovate the house. On October 21, one of these workmen found Saunderson-Smith murdered inside the house, his head battered by a series of savage blows.

The detectives found that a ground-floor window to the house was unlocked, but it was still possible that Saunderson-Smith had let his killer into the house. As forensic officers searched the murder house, which was full of building material, debris and junk, the detectives began finding out more about the victim's background. They soon established that Saunderson-Smith had been a homosexual, and a frequent visitor to various gay clubs in the Brompton Road and Kennington districts. They also found out that the murdered tycoon had used different identities to conceal the size of his property empire. They were unable to find any relatives, business partners or friends of the murdered man, only a handful of acquaintances. In spite of this, there was little trace of the murdered man in official databases and records. Although Saunderson-Smith's ugly, bloated face was staring at the readers of newspapers all over the country, no valuable leads about the mystery man's strange life were forthcoming.

But in the meantime, there had been noteworthy developments elsewhere. A total of £350 000 in £50 and £20 notes were found packed into plastic bags at No. 20 Dewhurst Road and another property in nearby Sedlescombe Road. The police were unable to fathom what the property tycoon had been planning to do with this mountain of banknotes, except that it was unlikely to be something legal.

There were various hypotheses how the murder of Saunderson-Smith could have happened. Firstly, it was possible that some homophobic thugs had killed him, or that a planned meeting with another homosexual had gone wrong. Secondly, Saunderson-Smith might have disturbed burglars out to steal his hoard of cash. Thirdly, old enemies of the Brook Green mystery man might have entered the house to settle the score with him.[14]

When Tates Estate Agents put the murder house on the market, the West London Today had the headline "'Fantastic' Brook Green murder home for sale at £1.8M" This newspaper did not thing that even a grisly murder would put off potential buyers in this very convenient part of London, and they were proved right, since the murder house was quickly under offer.

The police soon had a vital lead. Three Polish builders named Dawid Rymar, Slawomir Bugajewski and Ireneusz Mydlarz, had been working for Saunderson-Smith. They had left London after the murder under suspicious circumstances, and had spent money freely. It turned out that the three villains had heard rumours that Saunderson-Smith kept a large stash of money in his house. They had carefully planned the murder, particularly how to avoid CCTV cameras. But they had been spotted by a camera mounted on a West Kensington hotel. It is remarkable that although the murderers had planned their crime, and had plenty of time to search the murder house, they had failed to spot £250 000 in cash stored in the attic, as well as £100 000 in cash kept at another of Saunderson-Smith's houses.

All three Poles were taken into custody. One of them felt so confident that he had cheated justice that he agreed to fly back from Poland for questioning without an extradition warrant. It turned out that Saunderson-Smith's DNA had been found in a Land Rover belonging to Bugajewski, and along with the CCTV evidence, and records of the three men's lavish spending after the murder, this was enough to convict them. It was considered particularly damning that they had clearly intended to 'beat it out of' Saunderson-Smith where he had hidden his hoard.

After a three-week trial at the Old Bailey, all three Poles were sentenced to life imprisonment, with a minimum of 30 years before parole. Had they been more clever and ruthless, they could have committed the perfect murder and got £350 000 or so in cash to share.[15] As things were, they merely managed to serve as a dire warning to other foreign criminals that in modern London, murderers are nearly always caught and convicted, and that the courts have no sympathy for those who commit a brutal murder for gain.

P1-1 No. 7 Caroline [today Carol] Street, Camden Town, where John
Rose murdered Charles Wheaton in 1885.

*P1-2 No. 94 Fleet Road, Kentish Town, where young
Maud Eddington gunned down her boyfriend John Bellis in 1901.*

*P1-3 No. 23 Upper Park Road, Hampstead, where the bogus
Dr Zemenides was shot dead by an unknown assailant in 1933.*

P1-4 No. 19 Gloucester Road [today Gloucester Avenue], Regent's Park, where Bertha Gann was murdered by Alan James Grierson in 1935.

P1-5 No. 4 Bramshill Gardens, where Roland Lee-Booker murdered his wife Flora in 1935, before committing suicide

P1-6 No. 43 Hollycroft Avenue, Hampstead, where Professor Arthur Lloyd James murdered his wife Elsie in 1941.

P1-7 No. 11 South Hill Park, Hampstead, where Styllou Christofi murdered her daughter-in-law Hella in 1954.

P1-8 The Magdala Tavern, just outside which Ruth Ellis gunned down her boyfriend David Blakeley in 1955.

P1-9 The purported bullet marks on the wall of the Magdala Tavern.

P1-10 *The derelict Manor House at No. 9 Downshire Hill, where the Chinaman Wang Yam murdered the author Allan Chappelow in 2006.*

P1-11 *Two years later, in late 2013, the Manor House is in the same sorry state.*

P2-1 The old shop at No. 52 Green Lanes, Stoke Newington, where Ralph and Caroline Dyer went on a rampage in 1901, murdering Lizzie Norbury and severely injuring several other people.

P2-2 No. 46 Durham [today Kitchener] Road, Tottenham, where Harry
Bright murdered his girlfriend Bessie Lester in 1910.

P2-3 No. 12 Saratoga Road, Clapton, where Frederick Robertson murdered his three children in 1913.

P2-4 No. 15 Suffield Road, Tottenham, where Arthur Pank murdered his sister-in-law Beatrice Downes in 1919.

P2-5 No. 41 Drayton Road, Tottenham, where the burglar 'Silky Bob' Sheppard murdered his girlfriend Florence Jones in 1923.

P2-6 No. 7 Terrace Road, Hackney, where Sidney Charles Pitcher murdered Arthur Haberfield in 1939.

P 2-7 The former Animal Clinic at No. 626 Green Lanes, Finsbury Park, where Lilian James stabbed Patricia Smythe to death in 1942.

P2-8 No. 14 Stirling Road, Wood Green, where Thomas William Shadrach murdered Irene Mansell in 1954.

P2-9 The former betting shop at No. 242 Queensbridge Road, site of the unsolved murder of the manager Frederick Campbell in 1971.

P3-1 No. 43 Ladysmith Road [today Wrentham Avenue], Kensal Rise, where George Albert Crossman murdered Ellen Sampson in 1903.

P3-2 No. 67 Earlsmead Road, Kensal Rise, where Oliver Smith murdered his common-law wife Harriet Gasson in 1910.

P3-3 No. 32 Chevening Road, Kensal Rise, where Philip Quarry murdered his wife Angela in 1935.

P3-4 No. 21 Brondesbury Villas, site of the unsolved murder of Karolin Jones in 1940.

P3-5 No. 58 Charteris Road, Kilburn, where Michael Dowdall murdered
Veronica Murray in 1958.

P3-6 No. 195 Melrose Avenue, Cricklewood, where Dennis Nilsen murdered twelve young men between 1978 and 1981.

P3-7 No. 23 Cranley Gardens, Muswell Hill, where Dennis Nilsen dispatched three more victims before he was caught in February 1983.

P4-1 The present-day No. 27 Barnes Terrace, where Laurence Stelli murdered the Comte and Comtesse d'Antraigues in 1812, before committing suicide.

P4-2 No. 12 Greenside Road, Hammersmith, where James Holland murdered Annie Florence Chambers in 1896.

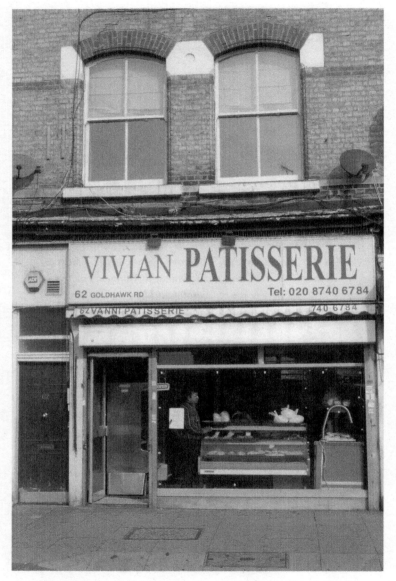

P4-3 The former fishmonger's shop at No. 62 Goldhawk Road, Hammersmith, where Frederick Meaker murdered Edward Girling in 1902.

P4-4 No. 2 Clavering Avenue, Barnes, where Horace Robinson killed his mistress Ivy Perry in 1921.

*P4-5 No. 91 Godolphin Road, Shepherd's Bush, where Christopher
Owden murdered Patricia Wood in 1954.*

P4-6 No. 22 Cambridge Grove, Hammersmith, site of the unsolved murder of John O'Shea in 1956.

P5-1 No. 3 Herbert Villas [today No. 6 Cowper Road], Acton, where George Pavey murdered the girl Ada Shepherd in 1880.

P5-2 No. 1 Florence Terrace [today No. 39 The Mall], Ealing, where George Henry Perry murdered Annie Covell in 1910.

P5-3 No. 5 Kingsley Avenue, Ealing, where Arthur James Benbow murdered Sophia Baker in 1912.

P5-4 *No. 16 Winscombe Crescent, Ealing, where Linford Derrick killed Arthur Wheeler in 1936.*

P6.1 *The former wine-shop at No. 62 Colindale Avenue, Hendon, where Arthur John Biggin killed John Thomas Gregory in 1919.*

P6.2 The murder maisonette flat at No. 620 Finchley Road, where Donald Hume murdered Stanley Setty in 1949.

P6.3 No. 8 Ashcombe Gardens, Edgware, where Daniel Raven murdered his parents-in-law in 1949.

P6.4 The former surgery at No. 98 Sheaveshill Avenue, Hendon, where Elias Georgiou murdered Dr Johannes Pulfer in 1957.

P6.5 No. 768 North Circular Road, where the serial poisoner Graham Frederick Young claimed his first victim, his stepmother Molly Young, in 1962.

P7-1 *No. 126 Portway, West Ham, site of the unsolved murder of Amelia Jeffs in 1890.*

P7-2 The sinister-looking house at No. 7 Moyers Road, Leyton, where Walter Harry Sudul murdered his mistress Henrietta Howard in 1906, before committing suicide.

P7-3 No. 9 Bethell Avenue, Forest Gate, where George Cutler Nadin murdered three of his children in 1908.

P7-4 The Coopers Arms murder pub, Chadwell Heath, where Tom West killed his wife Bertha in 1912.

P7-5 No. 24 Stork Road, Forest Gate, where Walter James Limpus murdered his wife and son in 1912.

P7-6 No. 13 Stukeley Road, Forest Gate, where Henry Perry, alias Beckett,
murdered the entire Cornish family in 1919.

P7-7 *No. 12 Bartle Avenue, East Ham, where George William Barton murdered his sister-in-law Mary Palfrey in 1923.*

CHAPTER 5

WEST LONDON

There's a black gibbet frowns upon Tappington Moor,
Where a former black gibbet has frown'd before:
It is as black as black may be,
And murderers there
Are dangling in air,
By one!— by two!— by three!
　　　　Richard Harris Barham, The Nurse's Story
　　　　　　　　(from the Ingoldsby Legends*)*.

This chapter will deal with the murder houses of Ealing, Acton and all western suburbs. Ealing's most famous murder house is at No. 22 Montpelier Road, where Ronald Merrett, alias Chesney, murdered his wife and mother-in-law in 1954. Remarkably, Merrett had once stood trial in Edinburgh for murdering his own mother at No. 31 Buckingham Terrace [the house stands] after she had caught him passing cheques in her name. The Scottish verdict had been 'Not Proven', and as cool as a cucumber, Merrett cashed in his £50 000 legacy, changed his name to Chesney, and set out to spend the money quickly. He became a smuggler and forger, and led an adventurous life; his experience with boats led to him being commissioned into the RNVR in 1939, and advancing to become a Lieutenant-Commander. After the war,

5.1 A contemporary photograph of the murder house at No. 22 Montpelier Road.

Chesney continued his career of crime, before murdering his estranged wife Veronica and her annoying old mother at the old people's home they ran in Montpelier Road.[1] Finding the murder house at what was once No. 22 was hard work, since many old houses have been pulled down for the construction of modern blocks of flats. Nor can it be excluded that a renumbering of the houses had been performed at some stage, when the road was 'developed'. But comparing a bona fide photograph of the murder house to the existing older houses in Montpelier Road led me to conclude that it no longer stands.

But although Ealing's most famous murder house is long gone, West London had much to offer with regard to murder houses. Read the sad tale of the Acton Atrocity, and visit the murder house in Cowper Road; ponder the tragedy of Florence Terrace, and make up your mind about the mysterious Winscombe Crescent murder of 1936.

THE ACTON ATROCITY, 1880

Mr John Shepherd was a successful builder and house decorator, who employed several workmen. He lived at No. 3 Herbert Villas, Cowper Road, Acton, with his second wife, his young son, and his four daughters. The oldest daughter, ten-year-old Ada, was reliable enough to take care of her younger sisters. On Friday October 22 1880, Mr Shepherd and his wife went to visit Mrs Shepherd's mother, who lived at Norwood Junction. He brought with him a large cheque for a house he had just sold, which he cashed in a bank on the way. Mrs Shepherd took the baby with her, but Ada was instructed to take the other three children to Mrs Perry's private school at No. 2 Churchfield Villas, where they were pupils, and to give them their luncheon. George Pavey, a workman who had been in Mr Shepherd's employ for six months, was left in charge of the house, which doubled as Mr Shepherd's office. Pavey was a 'cripple' affected with partial spastic paralysis in one arm and leg, and he was supposed to be very grateful to Mr Shepherd, who had shown him much kindness in the past.

Just before two o'clock, the three children came home to No. 3 Herbert Villas, where Ada made sure they were fed, before she escorted them back to school. But when some customers of Mr Shepherd came knocking at around three and four, nobody answered the door. When the little children arrived home from school a little later, they were equally surprised that Ada was not there to let them in, and they went off for a stroll. Mr and Mrs Shepherd returned to the deserted house at half past six in the evening, wondering where Pavey and the children had gone. In the back kitchen, Mr Shepherd stumbled over a large object lying on the floor. He gave a cry of horror when he realized that it was the dead body of his daughter Ada, lying in a large pool of blood. Her face was covered with a handkerchief.

5.2 The discovery of the murder of Ada Shepherd, with a view of the murder house, from the Illustrated Police News, *November 6 1880.*

At first, the distraught Shepherds thought that their entire brood of children had been murdered, but the other three eventually turned up, none the worse for their late-afternoon stroll. Police Constable Walter Millar, who had been on patrol nearby when he heard an excited local shouting 'All of Mr Shepherd's children have been murdered!' as he ran along the pavement, went to Herbert Villas to investigate. He expressed relief when he saw the remaining children alive and well, and then horror as he was confronted with Ada's mangled corpse. The surgeon Mr Clement Murrell also arrived and examined the blood-soaked corpse, declaring that Ada had been brutally 'outraged' [raped] and then deliberately murdered with a deep stab wound to the throat. A blood-stained kitchen knife was found nearby. Ada's face was bruised and livid, like if her attacker had struck her, and held her in a stranglehold. She had been dead about three hours and a half.

The question on everybody's lips was of course what had

5.3 Ada Shepherd, and the apprehension of George Pavey, from the
Illustrated Police News, *November 6 1880.*

happened to the man Pavey, who was supposed to have been
looking after the house. When Inspector Frederick Savage, an
experienced officer from the Metropolitan Police, arrived at
Herbert Villas to take charge of the murder investigation, it was
clear to him that Pavey was the main suspect. After dispatching
some constables to guard the murder house, and to search for
Pavey and other suspicious persons locally, Inspector Savage went
to the wanted man's last known lodgings, No. 31 Manchester
Street, Notting Hill. Neither Pavey nor his wife were at home,
however, and although the canny Inspector kept watch until 1 am
in the morning, the suspect did not make an appearance.

The following morning, Inspector Savage ordered a general
search for George Pavey, instructing that all hospitals and
workhouses should report any suspicious new inmates, and that
all low-class boarding-houses should be searched. It turned out
that a young man had seen Pavey absconding from the murder
house at 3.20 in the afternoon, heading towards the Uxbridge
Road. Ada Shepherd had last been seen alive at 2 pm, by a
confectioner from whom she had purchased a sugar-stick for her
little sister, and at 2.10 by a greengrocer, from whom she had

5.4 George Pavey, and other images from the Acton Atrocity, from the
Illustrated Police News, *November 13 1880.*

purchased halfpennyworth of nuts, obviously as a treat for herself once she had dispatched the younger children at their school. And indeed, some nuts had been found underneath one of Ada's lifeless hands. Inspector Savage suspected that Pavey had raped and murdered Ada soon after she had arrived home around 2.20 in the afternoon. He had then broken open the door to Mr Shepherd's office, and searched it for the money his employer had spoken of receiving for the sale of a house. Finding none, since Mr Shepherd had not cashed the cheque but brought it with him to Norwood, he had stolen a pair of boots and various other articles, before skulking away towards the Uxbridge Road.

The days after the murder, there was much uproar in Acton and its surroundings. Crowds of people stood gawping at the murder house. Rumours were abounding that all Mr Shepherd's children had been murdered, or that the entire family had been exterminated in a bloodbath. Still, the true facts of the case were horrific enough: nothing even remotely like the Acton Atrocity, as the rape and murder was called, had ever occurred in this quiet suburban neighbourhood. Rumours were flying about Pavey being arrested in Croydon, or with his parents in Brighton, possibly disguised as a woman. Unamused by such idle speculation, the police retorted that although several people had been taken into custody in different parts of London, they had all been able to explain themselves. Watch was kept at the railway stations, and at the main roads out of London, and all cheap hotels and lodging-houses were being searched by the police. The description of George Pavey, five feet five inches in height, of sallow complexion, clean shaven face, and walking stiffly due to being partially paralysed in the left side, was widely circulated. Local feeling against the suspect as greatly inflamed, and Inspector Savage was fearful that Pavey would be lynched if he was captured by the Acton vigilantes. The funeral of Ada Shepherd, at Hanwell Cemetery, was very well attended in spite of rainy weather conditions.

On the evening of Sunday October 24, two days after the murder of Ada Shepherd, a sore-footed vagabond came tramping into Hendon Workhouse. He was given some bread and butter, which he devoured with the rapidity of extreme hunger. The workhouse superintendent, who of course knew about the Acton Atrocity, came to see him. Since the tramp was lame in one arm and leg, and very much resembled the description of George Pavey that had been issued by the police, he gruffly called out 'Your name is Pavey!' The vagabond, who was chewing hard at the bread, swallowed convulsively, before meekly admitting 'Yes, it is.' He was promptly taken to the Paddington police station, where he was confronted by Inspector Savage. The detective showed him a large handkerchief, the one found covering the face of the murdered child, and Pavey said 'Yes, it is mine, I put it there!' He kept eating ravenously, consuming an entire loaf of bread, and drinking enormous quantities of tea, but he did not sleep all night.

On October 25, Pavey was charged with the wilful murder of Ada Shepherd at the Hammersmith Police Court. A short, clean shaven man, he looked younger than his 29 years. His story was that around 2 pm the day of the murder, an unknown man had come to No. 3 Herbert Villas, to say that Mr Shepherd wanted Pavey to go to the Uxbridge Road railway station at once. Without asking why, Pavey set off, but since he could not find his master, he returned to find that Ada had been murdered. Since Pavey has a criminal record for child molestation, he realized that he himself would become the main suspect, and absconded from the murder house. He had tramped round London for two days without anything to eat, and was in a state of near collapse, due to hunger and mental anxiety, when he decided to take refuge in Hendon Workhouse.

The police could soon verify that George Pavey had indeed "been repeatedly convicted and imprisoned for horrible offences". He came from a respectable Brighton family, and there was much sympathy for his poor parents. The police were working overtime to find additional evidence against him, and they soon had success: a pawnbroker's assistant named Henry Cross picked him out as the man who had pawned Mr Shepherd's boots, stolen from the murder house, for seven shillings. Pavey's shirt and trousers had been found to be stained with blood, and the forensic specialist Dr Thomas Bond declared that these stains came from human blood. The coroner's inquest on Ada Shepherd, held at the Station Hotel, Churchfield Road [it still stands, but is today the Rocket public house], returned a verdict of wilful murder against George Pavey. According to a local newspaper, Pavey was quite optimistic about his chances at the Old Bailey, even making plans for his wife to sell his clothes to Madame Tussaud's when he had been acquitted.

On trial for murder at the Old Bailey on November 23, things did not look good for George Pavey. His previous career of child molestation, the forensic evidence, and the clear and damning witness testimony all helped to bring the noose round his neck. He was prosecuted by the eloquent Harry Poland and Montague

5.5 George Pavey is sentenced to death, from the Illustrated Police News, *December 4 1880.*

Williams, and his own barrister Mr Frith could do little to combat the relentless witness testimony against him. The jury found Pavey guilty, and the far from bonhomous Sir Henry Hawkins put on the black cap, and delivered the following address:

> George Pavey, it is impossible to conceive a more atrocious or a more cruel crime than that of which you have been convicted by the jury, who have listened patiently and very attentively to all that has been said on your behalf. God knows what can have possessed you to have committed that atrocious cruelty in violating the person of this poor little helpless unprotected child, and afterwards murdering her, as unquestionably you did, in the most cruel and brutal manner. It is difficult to find

language to express one's sorrow at the barbarity of the act which you committed. For the crime of murder of which you have been convicted the law knows no sentence but that of death, and you must, young as you are, prepare to die, for your crime is of so barbarous a nature that I dare not hold out to you any hope that any mitigation of your sentence can be expected.

Sir Henry then pronounced sentence of death, and the prisoner, who remained perfectly calm during its delivery, was removed to the cells. While awaiting execution in Newgate, Pavey was twice visited by his wife, who brought their young child along. He is recorded to have made statements to the warders that after he had been left alone in the murder house together with Ada Shepherd, he felt strong urges to molest her sexually. Angered by her stubborn resistance, he then raped and murdered her. A garbled

5.6 A postcard showing the western part of Cowper Road, stamped and posted in 1910. The murder house is the third house on the right hand side.

account of his dying speech and confession was widely hawked around the Acton streets. George Pavey was hanged at Newgate on December 13 1880, and a dark chapter in London's criminal history was at an end.[2]

Both Harry Poland and Montague Williams, who prosecuted George Pavey at the Old Bailey, wrote memoirs, but neither made any mention of their part in the conviction of the Acton child murderer. Instead, the famous Detective Superintendent Percy Savage, the son of Frederick Savage, pointed out the arrest and conviction of George Pavey as one of his father's greatest cases, instrumental in securing him the post as detective inspector in personal attendance on Queen Victoria. Just as the murderer himself had once planned, his effigy made an appearance at Madame Tussaud's, dressed in a suit of his own clothes, sold to Tussaud's establishment by Pavey's wife.

The key question for the murder house detective, namely whether the house at No. 3 Herbert Villas, Cowper Road, is still standing today, was not immediately easy to answer. The reason for this is that all trace of the various 'Villas' and 'Terraces' in Cowper Road has disappeared, and the houses have been renumbered in a more conventional manner. Situated not far from Acton Central station, the houses in Cowper Road are numbered from the Churchfield Road end to the Shakespeare Road end, with even numbers on the eastern side, and odds on the western one. The houses closest to Churchfield Road on the eastern side are older in character, indicating that this part of the road was first developed. There is a terrace of four houses, and then a pair of semi-detached houses in a similar style. The third house in the terrace, formerly No. 3 Herbert Villas and now No. 6 Cowper Road, is the only house in Cowper Road to exactly fit the drawing of the murder house in the *Illustrated Police News*; not even the windows appear to have been changed.

MURDER IN FLORENCE TERRACE, 1910

In 1910, the house at No. 1 Florence Terrace, Uxbridge Road, Ealing, was owned by Charles Frederick Wright, who held a doctorate in dentistry from Harvard University. He had one dental practice in his house, and another in the Edgware Road. The doctor employed a housekeeper named Mary Ann Covell, and a young page-boy named Harold Reese. Mrs Covell's husband Edward, a retired police sergeant, and their 27-year-old daughter Annie, also lived in this large, end-of-terrace house.

Annie Covell had a boyfriend, the 27-year-old former soldier George Henry Perry, who had become a window-cleaner in civilian life. Annie, who worked as a housemaid at No. 1 Florence Terrace, was very keen to marry George, but he was morose and taciturn, and frustrated by his menial, low-paid job. To save some money, he moved into No. 1 Florence Terrace himself, and in spite of the occasional quarrel with ex-Sergeant Covell, he got on well with the remainder of the large household. But the months kept ticking by without George making any preparations to marry Annie.

On January 8 1910, Annie Covell was to be bridesmaid at a wedding in Hanwell, but George Henry Perry was not invited. George resented this snub very much, and there was an angry quarrel between them, which ended with Sergeant Covell ordering George to leave the house. Annie left the house alone in a cab, dressed in her best bridesmaid's attire. When George returned to No. 1 Florence Terrace a few hours later, hoping that all had been forgotten, he found that the irate Sergeant had packed up all his belongings in a box, and sent it to his parents. There was yet another quarrel, during which the furious George threatened to bash Sergeant Covell's brains in.

On the morning of January 10, George Henry Perry returned

to No. 1 Florence Terrace, asking Mrs Covell to see his girlfriend Annie. She let him into the house and gave him some breakfast. But a few minutes after Annie herself had gone into the breakfast-room, Mrs Covell heard a scream. When she ran into the room, she saw George kneeling on the prostrate Annie, and screamed out 'Man, what are you doing? You are killing my daughter!' She saw that Annie's throat had been cut, and that she was bleeding badly. George stabbed Annie twice in the side, and then rose up, exclaiming 'It is finished!' Seeing that Annie was surely dead, Mrs Covell screamed 'You bad man, you have killed my daughter!' Without any reply, George calmly walked out of the house. But Dr Wright's page-boy Harold Reese had also seen him stab Annie. The quick-witted boy ran out into Ealing Broadway, where he alerted a police constable. When they were returning to No. 1 Florence Terrace, Reece saw George Henry Perry walking away, and pointed him out to the constable. When Constable Brown seized him, George did not resist, but quietly gave himself up for the murder.

There was a fair amount of newspaper publicity about the Ealing Murder, with headlines like 'Bridesmaid Killed!' or 'Shocking Love Tragedy!' The coroner's inquest on Annie Covell returned a verdict of wilful murder against George Henry Perry, and he stood trial at the Old Bailey in April 1910, before Mr Justice Coleridge. There was no doubt that he had murdered Annie, and since evidence indicated that he had purchased the knife purposely on January 8, there was also premeditation. All the defence could do was to refer to George Henry Perry's previous good character, and suggest that he might have been a victim of 'impulsive insanity'. But due to the evidence of premeditation, this was not believed: Perry was found guilty of murder, sentenced to death, and executed at Pentonville Prison on March 1 1910.[3] The executioner was Pierrepoint, and death was instantaneous. The Covells stayed in the murder house at least until 1915, and Dr Wright kept the house until his death in 1931.

There is no Florence Terrace today, but the relevant Post Office Directories show that it was a terrace of eight large houses in what was then Uxbridge Road, with No. 1 at the corner with Florence Road, and the remainder of the terrace running down towards Ealing Common. It turns out that when The Mall was extended to the east, the houses in Florence Terrace were renumbered and incorporated into this thoroughfare; the murder house is today No. 39 The Mall, and home to a firm of solicitors.

MURDER BY AN EALING WEIRDO, 1912

The two middle-aged spinster sisters Sarah and Sophia Baker kept a small lodging-house at No. 5 Kingsley Avenue, West Ealing. In early 1912, they acquired a new lodger: the 49-year-old Arthur James Benbow. Described as a short, stooped man with a dark and sullen countenance, he possessed independent means, and did not work. Since he was fond of reading, he brought with him twelve large boxes full of books, mainly about natural history. In the past, he had several times been asked to leave other Ealing lodging-houses, for behaving in a very strange manner. A confirmed hypochondriac, he was very fussy about his food, and removed various items from the larder if he believed them to be noxious, or deliberately poisoned. He was very jealous of his boxes of books, and accused the other lodgers of tampering with them. Another landlady was spooked by his strange habit of never speaking to, or acknowledging the presence of, her little daughter.

The Misses Baker could not afford to be choosy about their lodgers, so they allowed Benbow a bedroom on the first floor, and a sitting room on the ground floor. He liked to take long, solitary walks around Ealing, or to sit in an armchair reading his books. Occasionally, he made expeditions to central London, and the prim spinsters told him, either in jest or in earnest, that they hoped he was not visiting young ladies of dubious virtue. The weirdo Benbow did not like this allegation at all, protesting that he had in fact been going to the Natural History Museum in South Kensington.

Perturbed by the Misses Baker's unbecoming interest in his [probably non-existent] sex life, Benbow developed the delusion that in order to curb his revelling in London, the spinsters had drugged him and performed some kind of operation to render him impotent. This disagreeable thought remained with him night and day. Intent on revenge against his landladies, he purchased a small pistol, with plenty of ammunition.

On April 2 1912, Sarah Baker left No. 5 Kingsley Avenue at 9 am. When she returned at 12.45, she found Sophia lying on the kitchen floor. The weirdo Benbow, who sat grinning at the kitchen table, made no exertion to help her. Sarah gave a scream and ran next door for assistance, believing that her sister had fainted. But when the recumbent Sophia was examined more closely, Sarah saw that she was lying in a large pool of blood, and that her clothes were stained with gunpowder.

Sarah Baker sent a neighbour for the local doctor, who arrived at 1.45 and promptly declared Sophia dead, since she had been shot through the heart. But when the young doctor looked out of the window, he saw the sinister Benbow sneaking off through the front gate. The doctor pursued and collared the weirdo lodger. When Benbow tried to take something out of his pocket, the brawny young medical man seized hold of his hand. This turned out to be very fortunate for him, since that very pocket contained a small Colt breech-loader pistol, cocked and ready for use!

At the coroner's inquest on Sophia Baker, Benbow appeared quite confused. He said that he had just tried to frighten his landlady by 'snapping' the trigger of his empty pistol in front of her, but this was not believed, since it was quite easy to see if the weapon was loaded or not. Benbow seemed to realize that all was not well with his mind and intellect. He belonged in Broadmoor, he said, and when he was on trial for murder on April 24, the Central Criminal Court agreed with that statement. Benbow was found to be guilty but insane, and he was detained at the asylum for the duration of His Majesty's pleasure.[4] A harmless old lunatic, he lived on at Broadmoor until 1946.

MURDER IN CLOVELLY ROAD, 1917

In 1917, the 49-year-old canteen porter Thomas Whitehouse Fielding lived in a terraced house at No 32 Clovelly Road, Acton, with his wife and four children. On August 22, he complained of feeling unwell, having been off work for two days. He was unable to eat any breakfast, apart from a cup of tea. When Mrs Fielding went to do the laundry, she left her husband reading in a small ground floor bedroom, with his three-year-old daughter Doris. She returned at 10 am, and found little Doris lying dead on the bed with her throat cut. Her husband's lifeless body was lying on the floor: he had murdered his daughter and then cut his own throat as well. At the coroner's inquest on Doris Fielding, there was no question that she had been murdered by her own father; the question was why this quiet family man had suddenly and unprovokedly cut his daughter's throat. He had recently suffered from pneumonia, and was worried about tuberculosis. The verdict was murder and suicide while of unsound mind.[5]

WIFE MURDER IN CONWAY CRESCENT, 1936

Alfred George Gilbert, a young Ealing labouring man, worked as a porter at Mr Pearcey's wine shop in Pitshanger Lane. He lived at No. 211 Conway Crescent, Perivale, with his wife Catherine. On March 3 1936, when he was 22 years old, Gilbert got into serious trouble at work: Mr Pearcey caught him pilfering money, and fired him out of the shop. Gilbert, who seems to have reasoned that thieving was fully acceptable, but *being caught thieving* was a disgrace, returned home in a distraught condition. His wife tried to calm him down as best as she could. She offered to go to the shop and repay the stolen money, but this suggestion made Gilbert furious. A strong, sturdy man, he seized hold of her and strangled her to death.

The dazed Alfred George Gilbert then returned to the wine shop, where he tried to persuade Mr Pearcey to call the police, but the gruff manager just told him to get lost. Instead, Gilbert managed to flag down a police car in the road, telling the constables that he had just killed his wife. They drove him to No. 211 Conway Crescent, where they found that he had been telling the truth.

On trial for murder at the Old Bailey on March 19 1936, before Mr Justice Hawke, Alfred George Gilbert was well defended by the eloquent Mr Christmas Humphries. He called several witnesses, including Gilbert's brother-in-law, to testify that the Gilberts had always been a very devoted couple during their short marriage. Gilbert lacked any reasonable motive to kill his wife, and he had no financial gain from her demise. Mr Humphries suggested that Gilbert had seized his wife by the throat without intention to injure her, but she had fallen down, and the strength of his hands had been enough to kill her. This does not sound particularly likely, but nevertheless, the jury found

Alfred George Gilbert guilty of only manslaughter. The bonhomous Mr Justice Hawke sentenced him to three years penal servitude, the minimum sentence possible.[6]

MURDERED BY HIS BEST FRIEND, 1936

Mr Linford Derrick, the son of an impoverished Somerset country squire, went straight from his public school to the Somerset Light Infantry, serving as a young officer throughout the Great War. While in India, he married a much older woman and had two sons with her. After being demobilized in 1919 with the rank of captain, Derrick joined an insurance company, but he was not up to the job and was asked to leave. Instead, he became the travelling representative of the Liverpool Borax Co., a job he found more congenial. In 1928, he returned to his wife in India, but an attempt to join the Indian police was not successful, and Derrick left his wife for good in 1930 and returned to London. He had always been a useful tennis player, albeit far from championship quality. Fed up with various dull and menial jobs, he became a tennis coach, teaching at various schools and clubs. This job suited the rather indolent Derrick to perfection: he could work when he wanted to, and yet live in comfortable lodgings at No. 7 Lammas Park Road, Ealing, and keep a motor car.

Mr Arthur Earle Wheeler, a middle-class young Londoner, had also served in the Great War, as an officer in the Machine Gun Corps, seeing active service and being wounded on duty. Surviving the war, he married his sweetheart Kathleen, and they had two young daughters. Arthur got a job as an insurance agent, and the Wheelers settled down at a comfortable suburban house at No. 16 Winscombe Crescent, Ealing. But although he worked long hours and tried his best to gain advancement, he was stuck in this dead-end job, beavering away ceaselessly for low wages in the understaffed insurance office. The main family friend of the Wheelers was the dashing tennis coach Linford Derrick. Wheeler used to discuss his wartime experiences with his ex-service friend, and they often went out to have a drink together. The only thing was that he was becoming fearful that his wife was becoming rather too fond of the good-looking Derrick.

But nevertheless, this strange relationship between Linford Derrick and the Wheeler family continued. The overworked Wheeler often had little time for his family, but the easygoing 'Uncle Lin', who had plenty of spare time, took Mrs Wheeler shopping in his car, and played with the children. They often took their summer holidays together, and in 1936, when Wheeler was too busy to take his wife and children to the seaside, he suggested that Derrick should go instead. There were some distinctly dangerous elements in this Ealing 'eternal triangle': whereas Wheeler was obese and unfit, his wife Kathleen was still attractive, and Linford Derrick remained quite fit and handsome in his late thirties. He no longer had anything to do with his wife, and his teenage sons were at school. He must have had some kind of private income, since a few tennis lessons would hardly have paid for his comfortable and indolent lifestyle.

On the morning of August 5 1936, a shaken and dishevelled Linford Derrick came into the Ealing police station with a remarkable story to tell. The evening before, he had driven his best friend Arthur Wheeler back to London from the Felpham holiday cottage. They had a glass of port each at a hotel in Ealing Broadway, and then purchased a quart bottle of whisky, which they emptied at No. 16 Winscombe Crescent. As he sat swigging from his whisky glass, Wheeler became increasingly morose and aggressive. He very much resented that he was unable to take a proper summer holiday, and told Derrick that he did not want

5.7 Wheeler is found dead in the murder house, from the
Illustrated Police News, *August 13 1936.*

him anywhere near his wife. The tennis coach left, driving off in
an angry temper.

But in the middle of the night, Derrick had second thoughts
about quarrelling with his friend, and walked back to No. 16
Winscombe Crescent to patch things up. Wheeler answered the
door, walking downstairs dressed in his pyjamas, and carrying a
large truncheon he used to keep handy for use against burglars.
He did not seem particularly pleased to see Derrick again, and
they soon began quarrelling. When Wheeler said that his friend
would surely fancy spending a night in his wife's bedroom,
Derrick called him a swine. Wheeler returned the insult, before

striking out with the truncheon. Derrick dodged the blow, and after a furious fight, he managed to gain control of the truncheon and deal Wheeler a series of heavy blows. He then collapsed next to his lifeless opponent.

Regaining consciousness, Linford Derrick saw that while defending himself from Wheeler's onslaught, he had killed his best friend. In desperation, he got the idea to stage a burglary, and stole some money and jewelry from the murder house. But when the distraught tennis coach returned home to his lodgings, he felt remorse for killing his friend, and decided to give himself up to the police.

When they investigated Derrick's story, the detectives found a number of discrepancies. Firstly, the tennis coach was practically uninjured from what he had described as a desperate and furious fight. Secondly, this keen motorist could not explain why he had walked all the way to No. 16 Winscombe Crescent, in the middle of the night, when his car had been in good working order. Thirdly, his socks were found to be heavily blood-stained, although his shoes were not, indicating that he had in fact opened the door to the murder house with his own key, taken off his shoes, and sneaked upstairs to Wheeler's bedroom to murder him while he was still asleep. The bloodstains on the walls were no higher than three feet, indicating that Derrick had struck his opponent when he was already on the ground.

On trial for murder at the Old Bailey, before Mr Justice Greaves-Lord, Linford Derrick made a good impression in court. His blameless past and worthy military record was highlighted by the defence, as was the lack of a credible motive. A number of character witnesses described Derrick as the perfect gentleman, and Mrs Wheeler denied ever having an affair or flirtation with him. Using the arguments quoted above, the prosecution suggested that Derrick's story was a pack of lies, and that he had

5.8 Winscombe Crescent, from an old postcard.

deliberately returned to No. 16 Winscombe Crescent with the intention to murder Wheeler. After deliberating for an hour and twenty minutes, the jury found the tennis coach guilty of manslaughter, and Mr Justice Greaves-Lord sentenced him to ten years in prison.[7]

There is reason to believe that Linford Derrick served his sentence and was released from prison in due course. There is nothing to suggest that he married Mrs Wheeler, but his later movements are difficult to follow, since he might well have changed his name after the sentence. Was the verdict a fair one? The police detectives thought not, since the technical evidence, which the jury had quite possibly not been able to entirely grasp the importance of, spoke in favour of premeditated murder. But on the other hand, a cool, calculating murderer would surely have been able to think of a better plan than to bludgeon his rival to death in the middle of the night. It does not appear as if the police made any estimate how much Derrick had been drinking the evening of the killing: a glass of port, part of a quarter bottle of whisky, and then how much when he came home and wanted a nightcap or two? The sentence from Mr Justice Greaves-Lord may well, in the end, have been a fair one.

MURDER IN SOUTHALL, 1937

Frederick Priddle was a young Welshman, born in Thomastown, Glamorgan, in 1913. Growing up during the Depression in the 1920s and early 1930s, he moved away from his native land to find work. He went to West London, where he trained as an acetylene welder. In 1937, he was active at the Acme Works, Southall. He was doing reasonably well: although too badly paid to be able to save money, at least he had a steady job, and lodgings at No. 25 Gordon Road, Southall. He also had a steady girlfriend named Eunice Wiggins, a native of Pontypridd, and they hoped to marry one day.

On December 31 1937, Fred and Eunice went to a jolly New Year's party. Although normally a teetotaller, Fred drank three glasses of wine. They left the party at half past midnight, and after escorting Eunice home, Fred went back to No. 25 Gordon Road. He let himself in using his key, and went into the living room. The electric light did not work, and Fred was alarmed to see a man standing in the dark room, just by the fireplace. Before the startled Welshman realized what was happening, the intruder attacked him ferociously, kicking him in the stomach, and stabbing him in the head and chest. Fred fell unconscious, and his assailant made his escape. After regaining consciousness, Fred lurched out into the small front garden, groaning with pain. His landlord, the foreman David Walker, came to his aid and made sure an ambulance was called. But Fred's chest wound was four inches deep, and he died from various complications after two weeks in hospital. The case was now one of murder.

Frederick Priddle had described his assailant as a thin man of middle size, wearing a light coat and a cap. The police concluded that Fred must have disturbed a burglar at No. 25 Gordon Road, and that this individual had panicked and murdered the young Welshman. Two boxes of matches, eight shillings and sixpence, and a light-bulb had been stolen. There was (and still is) a gap between No. 23 and No. 25 Gordon Road, which would have been very useful for a burglar wanting to access the rear of the property, where he could break into the house unseen. A burglar named Edward Hooper soon became the prime suspect. Fingerprint evidence identified him as the burglar who had broken into No. 65 Hanger Lane the very same night, and stolen three eggs and some roast pheasant. Had he struck again at No. 25 Gordon Road?

The 21-year-old Edward Hooper, a native of Scotland and a deserter from the Cameronians, became very frightened when he realized that he was a murder suspect. He confessed to a string of West London burglaries, and claimed that when Fred Priddle was murdered, he was actually in the process of burgling Shepherd's Bush Vicarage. This Caledonian thief was wholly incredulous when it was suggested that he would bother with breaking into a house in such a poor neighbourhood as Gordon Road. A blood-stained handkerchief and a clasp knife had been found in Hooper's pockets, but this knife could not be the murder weapon since it was too short to fit the wound. His story about burgling the vicarage turned out to be nothing but the truth, and the handkerchief actually belonged to the Vicar! Hooper had been at the Vicarage well into the wee hours, and this building was located far away from Gordon Road. In the end, Hooper was written off as a murder suspect, but he was instead awarded twelve months hard labour for his burglarious exploits.

For a while, Priddle's landlord David Walker was a suspect, but in the end, it was concluded that he was definitely innocent. Nor did Walker have any qualms about living in a murder house, since he is recorded to have remained at No. 25 Gordon Road until the late 1970s. A number of other burglars were briefly suspected, but in spite of some vague leads, nothing worthwhile was concluded, and the murder of Frederick Priddle remains unsolved.[8] It had been a motiveless crime, and the young Welshman had just been in the wrong place at the wrong time. It is very likely that he had disturbed an inexperienced young thief who had broken into the house to do some petty pilfering, and been the subject of a murderous assault.

THE STRANGE CASE OF SIDNEY GEORGE PAUL, 1938

Sidney George Paul was born in Battersea in 1892, but emigrated to Australia at an early age, to work in the pearl fishing industry. In the Great War, he served in the Australian Army from 1915 until 1919. He moved to Belgium in 1920 and married his wife Claire there; they went on to have four children alive. Sidney was a clever, industrious man, who had success with various business ventures in Belgian Congo. He could afford to live in some style, and to educate his children at expensive schools.

In 1938, Sidney George Paul and his family moved into a small semi-detached house at No. 19 Rosebury Vale, Ruislip. He tried to establish himself as a salesman, but without success. This did not seem to worry him unduly, and the neighbours got the impression that the Pauls had a good deal of money. Sidney was a personable man who spoke four languages, whereas his wife Claire was a poor linguist who could barely make herself understood in English. Two of their children attended a convent school in England; the other two remained in Belgium.

In May 1938, there was a mishap when No. 19 Rosebury Vale caught fire in the middle of the night. The Pauls were evacuated with tall ladders, but the contents of one of the downstairs rooms were completely destroyed by the fire. Strangely enough, valuable paintings and antiques had been stockpiled in this very room, and it was only with reluctance that the insurance company eventually paid out. The day before the fire, the Pauls had visited a certain concert hall. On October 15 1938, they again went to this concert hall, and a friend heard them joking that surely, another disaster would happen the day after. But on the morning of October 16, all seemed well. The Paul children went to attend Mass, and Sidney and his wife had some tea, before she went out into the veranda to do some cleaning.

Sidney George Paul later said that he had heard an intruder in one of the upstairs bedrooms. Then his wife suddenly gave a scream, and when he went out to the veranda, he could see her lying motionless on the floor. At the same moment, the intruder attacked him, and he received a series of hard knocks to the head. The intruder was a tall, clean-shaven, dark-haired man wearing a blue jacket, a black cap, and rubber boots and gloves. He had a scar on the right cheek. After his assailant had run off, Sidney knelt down by his wife's side. She spoke to him, saying that she wanted her father's crucifix, which was hanging on the wall. Sidney gave it to her, before running out of the house to seek assistance, shouting 'Come quickly, there is a man in my house!' The neighbour Mr W.G. Cooper was startled to find the wild-eyed Sidney George Paul on his doorstep, exclaiming 'Oh, Mr Cooper, there is a terrible man in my house with a blue coat on! Take this, and write!' But all

Sidney could dictate was 'Mr H. Paul, care of...' before he fell prostrate on the floor, exclaiming 'My poor, dear wife!'

Claire Paul died later the same day, from severe head injuries inflicted by a large axe. Surprisingly, this axe was found hidden inside the house, showing signs of having been cleaned after the murder. Sidney George Paul discharged himself from hospital the very same day and went back to No. 19 Rosebury Vale. Although he had told the police that the intruder had repeatedly struck him on the head with what seemed like a stick, his injuries were very superficial, like if they had been inflicted with a razor. He had handed the police a button which he claimed to have torn from the murderer's jacket, but although this was an uncommon button, four others matching it were found when the murder house was searched. The intruder had stolen £150 from a wardrobe where Mrs Paul had been hoarding her spare cash, Sidney George Paul claimed, but it turned out that he himself was penniless and in debt. There was no technical evidence that there had been an intruder at all, and on October 19, Sidney George Paul was arrested and charged with the murder of his wife.

When the trial of Sidney George Paul began on November 28, it was quite a media event. Medical witnesses described Paul's trifling injuries, which were not consistent with him being beaten up with a stick. Due to her severe head injuries, it did not appear possible that Mrs Paul would have been able to speak about crucifixes, or anything else, after being attacked. The aforementioned neighbour Mr W.G. Cooper had seen Sidney George Paul stoop over his wife, and strike at her; there had not been any other person present. For the defence, it was pointed out that the Pauls had appeared to be a happy and devoted couple. She did not have any life insurance policy, and it would hardly have made any sense, they argued, for Sidney to kill her to gain £50 or £60 that she had saved. The house at No. 19 Rosebury Vale had been up for sale, and an estate agent was hopeful that it would have fetched £1100, a sum that would have enabled the Pauls to start again. There had been little interest in the murder house recently, the agent testified, since "houses within which recent murders have taken place were often difficult to sell". Remarkably, Mrs M.G. Cooper, wife of the star prosecution witness, gave evidence for the defence: she had heard Sidney George Paul groaning, and seen a person in dark clothes leaning over him. Paul had tried to push this person away. Mrs Cooper was not certain if it had been a man or a woman. Another witness claimed that he had seen gumboot footprints in the R.A.F. sports ground behind the Pauls' house, leading to a gap in the boundary hedge of No. 19 Rosebury Vale.

The jury was out for fifty minutes before returning a verdict of Guilty. Mr Justice Asquith sentenced Sidney George Paul to death, and the execution date was fixed for December 20 at Pentonville Prison. On December 16, the Home Secretary, Sir Samuel Hoare, recommended a reprieve, and the sentence was commuted to imprisonment for life.[9] Several experienced Scotland Yard detectives, including Chief Inspector Leonard Burt and Chief Inspector Frederick Cherrill, were convinced that Sidney George Paul was the guilty man: a cunning murderer who had done his best to falsify evidence to support the intruder theory. Sidney George Paul's story of the murderous intruder is unlikely to have much truth in it, and he definitely lied about his activities the day of the murder, but would an educated man, described as a devoted husband, really be capable of murdering his wife of 18 years, and the mother of his four children, in such a brutal and sordid manner? Had the person in black seen by Mrs Cooper in fact been an accomplice, or perhaps rather 'the woman in the case'? As for the later activities of Sidney George Paul, it is notable that a man of that name, born in 1892, emigrated to Melbourne, Australia, in 1948.

TRIPLE MURDER IN EALING, 1941

In late 1941, Gunner Philip Joseph Ward, who served in an anti-aircraft unit battery, was pondering an old slight that still rankled: his unceremonious expulsion from the Brentford & Chiswick Junior Conservative Association back in 1937, for behaving obnoxiously to one of the female members. Intent on teaching the Conservatives a hard lesson, the long-minded Ward got hold of a shotgun and plenty of ammunition, and rented a motor car.

His first victim was the solicitor Leslie Ludford, the former chairman of the Conservative Committee, who was gunned down outside his house in Foster Road, Chiswick. A woman who looked out from her house was also shot at and wounded by the gunman. Ward drove on to No. 1 St Mary's Grove, Chiswick, the home of the former secretary of the Association, who was not at home. Instead, Ward shot her mother, and another woman who answered the door. He then drove on through the Ealing streets, shooting two women at random in Hamlet Gardens and Bollo Lane, before travelling to No. 33 Bruton Way, where he murdered another woman who was completely unknown to him, Mrs Edith Baringer.

The demented Ward drove on in his rented Hillman saloon car, but by now, it had been described to the police. The Hillman was spotted and rammed by armed police in Watford Way, and Ward's three-hour killing spree was at an end. Three of his victims were dead: Leslie Ludford, Mrs Baringer, and also Mrs Crisp of St Mary's Grove. It turned out that the triple murderer had a long history of serious mental trouble; he had been certified insane already in 1932. He had changed his name in the late 1930s, and the army had accepted him as a fully fit wartime recruit. But it was clear to the psychiatrists who examined Ward that he suffered from schizophrenia with paranoid delusions. He was found insane and unfit to plead, and was incarcerated in Broadmoor, where he would live on for many years.[10] Of the murder houses he left behind, those at No. 1 St Mary's Grove and No. 33 Bruton Way still stand.

WIFE MURDER IN ACTON, 1941

William Alfred Deane, a young Acton man, became a van driver. In 1930, he married Nancy Helen Holden, and they soon had two children. In 1932, Deane was caught and fined for dangerous driving. He then had to spend a month in prison for refusing to pay the fine. Emerging from jail, he was dismayed to find out that his wife had been unfaithful to him while he had been behind bars. This led to much marital disquiet, and for a while, Nancy left her husband and made a living as a prostitute. Still, William Alfred Deane took her back, and at the outbreak of World War II, they were living together at No. 55 Newton Avenue.

William Alfred Deane was not considered fit for military service, so he continued driving his van. Nancy got war work at the Ultra Radio Co. in Western Avenue. Here, this 'modern woman' found yet another lover, a bloke named Charles Bilby. She made no secret of her attachment to him, openly taunting her husband. Once, William Alfred gave her a hard knock in the face after he had found the guilty pair together. But even this ill-treatment did not induce Nancy Deane to leave the little house at No. 55 Newton Avenue, or to give up her lover for that matter. In the evening of October 3 1941, things came to an end between this mismatched couple: after yet another angry quarrel, William Alfred Deane stabbed his wife to death with a toolmaker's file. He then went to his father's house nearby and confessed that he had just killed Nancy after she had taunted him about Bilby.

On trial for murdering his wife at the Old Bailey, William Alfred Deane pleaded guilty. There was a good deal of sympathy for him, and even Nancy's relatives had little good to say about her constant infidelity. Only the interloper Bilby, who was also present in court, described her as a good woman, and declared that he had wanted to marry her. The jury found William Alfred Deane guilty of murder, but strongly recommended him to mercy, and he received a late reprieve.[11]

MURDER IN GORING WAY, 1941

Lionel Rupert Watson was a 30-year-old bakelite moulder, who lived in the ground floor flat at No. 9 Goring Way, Greenford, with his wife Phyllis and her illegitimate daughter Eileen. It is not known what stratagem he had made use of to avoid conscription into the military. Their upstairs neighbour, the widow Mrs Lilian Bounds, was a friend of Phyllis but did not care much for Lionel, who seemed like something of a bounder.

Mrs Bounds, who was retired, spent much of her time observing the habits of her neighbours. She was pleased to find that in April 1941, Lionel Rupert Watson moved out of No. 9 Goring Way, preferring to live with his parents. Phyllis seemed genuinely sad to see him go. On May 20, both Phyllis and her daughter disappeared. When asked what had happened to them, Lionel said they had gone on a holiday to Scotland.

On May 26, Mrs Bounds saw the lazy Lionel, who had never been a keen gardener, digging frantically in the garden. 'Hullo! What are you doing? Are you digging for victory?' she called out, but he replied that he was just burying some cabbage leaves and other rubbish. Some days later, Mrs Bounds and the other neighbours noticed a very noxious smell emanating from the garden. She decided to investigate. Had this awful Lionel Rupert Watson murdered his wife and her child, and buried their remains in the garden?

When Lionel Rupert Watson was at work at the bakelite factory, Mrs Bounds sneaked into the garden with a shovel. She did not dig long before she found what looked very much like putrid human flesh. Mrs Bounds called in the police, and Watson was arrested. It turned out that Phyllis and her little daughter had both been poisoned with cyanide. The lazy murderer would have been well advised to have dug a deeper grave for his victims (it was just two feet deep!)

On trial for double murder at the Old Bailey, things were looking bad for Lionel Rupert Watson. The motive for the murder seemed obvious, since he already had a wife, and four children, before bigamously marrying Phyllis. Recently, he had met a 17-year-old girl who worked at the bakelite factory. He wooed her by giving her presents of margarine coupons, hardly the most romantic of presents, but they had the desired effect, from his point of view. He also gave her some of Phyllis' clothes.

Watson's colleagues gave evidence about his interest in cyanide, and his purloining some of this poison from the bakelite factory. Lionel Rupert Watson gave a poor impression in court, due to his cold-blooded callousness, and his lack of remorse. He was convicted of murder and sentenced to death, and in spite of an appeal, on grounds of insanity in the family, he was hanged at Pentonville Prison on November 12 1941.[12]

THE CROCK OF GOLD MURDER HUNT, 1957

Mrs Amy Sarah Bridges was a veteran resident of Selby Gardens, Southall, having moved into No. 12 at this quiet suburban cul-de-sac soon after the house had been constructed in 1934. She had been married twice, once to a man named Clarke, and then to the labouring man Frank Bridges, whom she had left long before his death in 1957. She lived alone at the house in Selby Gardens at least since 1942, becoming increasingly bitter and reclusive as the years went by. When tradesmen approached her house, she shouted at them for being too expensive. A convinced paedophobe, she very much disliked children, sometimes raising her stick to discipline them if they made a row outside the house. In August 1957, when Amy Sarah Bridges was 88 years old, and crippled by hip osteoarthritis, she still lived alone at No. 12 Selby Gardens. There was a good deal of local gossip that this eccentric and cantankerous old woman was very wealthy, and that she hoarded banknotes and gold sovereigns in her small suburban house.

On August 28 1957, the milkman Stanley Keys was doing his rounds in Selby Gardens. He noticed that old Mrs Bridges at No. 12 had not picked up her half-pint of milk, something she always used to do. Although Mrs Bridges was known for her antagonistic attitude towards tradesmen, she had once invited Keys inside her house, to grumble about the high cost of food and supplies, and to show him her family album. The kind, public-spirited milkman told his helper, the ten-year-old David Hill, to have a look through the windows at No. 12, to make sure Mrs Bridges was not ill, or stuck after falling down. The lad returned saying that the old woman was lying motionless on the floor. When having a look himself, Keys noticed that her hands and head were covered in blood, and he swiftly called the police. They broke into the house through a window, but Amy Sarah Bridges was dead and cold, having been brutally beaten to death with a heavy, blunt instrument. A blood-stained iron colander was lying nearby, and also a flatiron. The murderer had left no obvious clues behind after leaving the murder house.

There was immediate newspaper interest in the Selby Gardens murder. Since the motive was thought to be robbery, and since there were rumours that Mrs Bridges had been hoarding gold sovereigns in her house, the headline of the *Daily Mail* exclaimed 'The Crock of Gold Murder!' The *Daily Express* instead interviewed and photographed the young milkman's helper David Hill, under the headline 'Recluse Widow Murdered! Her gold hoard looted... Boy gives alarm!' The neighbours in Selby Gardens were clearly no believers in the 'De mortuis nihil nisi bonum' principle: when interviewed by the journalists, they gave a realistic view of the reclusive and cantankerous murder victim. She had often been rude to the tradesmen who came calling, and had once emptied a bucket of water over a man who had offered to clean all the windows of her house for three shillings. In spite of her age and arthritis, she had still been capable of locomotion using a stick, which had doubled as a useful weapon to keep children and dogs at a respectful distance. Miss Rachel de Liew, who introduced herself as the niece of the murdered woman, told a *Daily Mail* journalist that her aunt Amy had always been "a very stubborn and self-willed old woman". She had kept a boarding-house in Bognor for many years, with considerable success, and made a large amount of money, which she had looked after very carefully. She had hoarded a bag full of gold sovereigns in the house, and also a large wad of banknotes.

Led by Detective Chief Superintendent Stephen Glander and Detective Superintendent Edward MacKenzie, the Scotland Yard detectives began their murder investigation. The problem was that no person really knew the reclusive Amy Sarah Bridges. One of the neighbours had seen a man in a peaked cap enter the murder house through the back door the day before Mrs Bridges was found murdered. Another neighbour had seen two workmen arguing with Mrs Bridges on her doorstep. The autopsy showed that Amy Sarah Bridges had died from repeated heavy blows to the head, presumably from the blood-stained iron colander. The killer had left plenty of blood-stained fingerprints behind, something that is notable; a professional thief or contract killer would surely have had the sense to wear gloves.

Since Mrs Bridges had been murdered the day before the milkman had found her, the sighting of the man in the peaked cap became very interesting. At first, the police believed that he might have been a chauffeur, but another witness had seen a man matching his description riding an old-fashioned bicycle into Selby Gardens: a slightly built, neatly dressed young man in a cap with a shiny peak, carrying a parcel on the handlebars. Thus he might have been a delivery man, or at least posed as one. But would the suspicious Mrs Bridges, who had no liking for tradesmen, have admitted a complete stranger from the street into her house? And was it wise for an intended robber or murderer to approach the house of his intended victim on an old bicycle, in broad daylight? In excess of £280 in cash was found in the murder house, as well as a P.O. savings book with more than £281 credit. It was a strange kind of robber not to have made a better effort to find this money, although the murder house did give the impression of having been searched for *something*. Interestingly, the police found nothing to verify the claim that Amy Sarah Bridges had ever been hoarding gold sovereigns in the murder house.

Amy Sarah Bridges was something of a woman of mystery. How could she have earned so much money from running a simple lodging-house, surely not the most profitable of occupations? The only source for her Bognor career as a landlady was the niece Miss Rachel de Liew, whom the police suspected of having been 'telling porkies' about the gold sovereigns. As for the reclusive murder victim's private life, a little research shows that the neighbours were right that her husband Frank Bridges had died earlier in 1957. He had been just 64 years old when he expired, and thus 24 years younger than his wife! They had married in 1939, when he was 46 years old and she 70; surely a remarkable age difference. On their marriage certificate, she is called 'Amy S. Clarke', and it turns out that an Amy Sarah Ames had married a man named Frank Ernest Clarke in Bethnal Green in 1898. Thus it would appear that Amy Sarah Bridges had been telling the truth about her two marriages, neither of which had resulted in any children.

Dr Jonathan Oates has unearthed some further spicy stuff about Amy Sarah Bridges and her strange affairs.[13] Miss Rachel de Liew, who claimed to be looking after her elderly father in a house at Peel Poad, Woodford, told a journalist that shortly before the murder, Mrs Bridges had asked her to put the old man in a home, and come to look after *her* at Selby Gardens instead! When Miss de Liew refused, Amy Sarah Bridges promptly changed her will, cutting the niece out altogether. Not long after, the mean-spirited old woman relented, and agreed to change the will back, or so at least Miss de Liew claimed, but she had not had time to do so at the time she was murdered! And thus Amy Sarah Bridges left a total of £2590 to Miss Mercy Emma Ames, who might well have been her spinster sister [or cousin], born in Shoreditch in late 1877. Had the murderer found out about these testamentary shenanigans, and decided to silence Amy Sarah Bridges, for good, to prevent her from changing her will again, and to destroy the will that was presumed to be in the house? It would have been highly interesting to find out what the Scotland Yard detectives thought of these matters, but regrettably, this is not possible, since the relevant case file was never deposited at the National Archives, where it ought to have been today. Although police record-keeping was quite lackadaisical in Victorian and Edwardian times, it was much more strictly regulated in the 1950s, and very few Metropolitan Police files from that era have gone astray. Was the loss of the police file about the murder of Amy Sarah Bridges simply the result of incompetence, did some detective pilfer it to be able to ponder the case after retirement, or did this mysterious murder victim possess some other dark secrets that some personage decided should remain hidden forever?

CHAPTER 6

NORTH LONDON

And now they try'd the deed to hide;
For a little bird whisper'd, 'Perchance you may swing;
Here's a corpse in the case with a sad swell'd face,
And a 'Crowner's Quest' is a queer sort of thing!'
 Richard Harris Barham, The Lay of St
Gengulphus *(from the* Ingoldsby Legends*).*

This chapter will deal with the remainder of the North London
suburbs: Finchley, Hendon, Edgware, Walthamstow, Northwood
and Barnet. Of these suburbs, Walthamstow was the site of some
terrible tragedies of the past. In 1883, the 26-year-old blacksmith
William Gouldstone murdered his five children in a small,
recently built terraced house at No. 8 Courtenay Place, opposite
the St James's Street railway station. He was tried for murder and
sentenced to death, but received a late reprieve and was sent to
Broadmoor. The murder house was shunned for many years, and
the entire terrace of houses had a very bad reputation, particularly
after Louisa Jane Pope had drowned her two daughters at No. 13
Courtenay Place in 1905.[1] There is still a Courtenay Place today,
just by the St James's Street railway station, but no older houses
remain.

 Mr Edmund Hamilton's chemist's shop at No. 17 Markhouse

6.1 Gouldstone murders his five children at No. 8 Courtenay Place, Walthamstow, from the Illustrated Police News, *August 18 1883.*

6.2 The double murder at 'Marcroft', from the Illustrated Police News, *April 3 1930.*

Street, at the corner with Prospect Road, was the site of the Walthamstow Mystery of 1888: the assistant chemist William Barber stood accused of poisoning a certain Mrs French, but was acquitted.[2] In 1903, Mr Clarence Marshall murdered his wife and child, before committing suicide, at No. 89 Griggs Road, Walthamstow.[3] There is still a Griggs Road today, but a large school stands on the part that once contained the murder house. No. 30 Raynham Road, Edmonton, where Sarah Alice White murdered her two children in 1912, has fallen victim to the Developer. The detached house 'Marcroft' in Penshurst Gardens, Edgware, where William Tuke murdered his wife and son in 1930, no longer frowns upon the passer-by.[4]

But still, North London is home to a healthy population of murder houses. Highlights include Donald Hume's murder flat at No. 620 Finchley Road and No. 768 North Circular Road, once home to the murderous Graham Frederick Young. For a visitor to the old Newspaper Library in Colindale Avenue, where a good deal of the work on this book has been carried out, over a period of seventeen years, it is curious to know that two murder houses stand in its absolute vicinity: the former wine shop at No. 62 Colindale Avenue, where the manager John Thomas Gregory was killed in 1919, and the former surgery at No. 98 Sheaveshill Avenue, where Dr Johannes Pulfer was murdered by one of his patients in 1957.

THE WALTHAMSTOW TRAGEDY, 1892

Frederick Arthur Harknett, a young London lad, became a private soldier in the Royal Engineers. In 1890, when he was 21 years old, he purchased his discharge from the military and married the 15-year-old music hall artist Adelaide Louisa Raymond. Fred became a carman, working long hours for a meagre salary. He had to lodge with his mother-in-law Mrs Elizabeth Raymond, at No. 51 Buxton Road, Walthamstow, occupying the first floor front room, with his pretty young wife.

In 1892, Fred Harknett was becoming increasingly gloomy and morose. He disliked his boring and menial job, he did not get on with his mother-in-law, in whose house he lodged, and his marriage was on the rocks. Fred had hoped that after Louisa had given birth to their little baby, her giddy and immoral tendencies would cease, but encouraged by her mother, she resumed performing in the music halls, singing and dancing in front of a raucous crowd. Fred did not like this at all, and threatened Louisa that he would leave her if she kept performing. But young 'Louie Raymond', as she called herself on the stage, showed no inclination whatsoever to obey her husband. Fred told his brother, the hairdresser Walter George Harknett, that he was fed up with his wife's loose morals, and that he was leaving her. In a maudlin and self-pitying manner, he exclaimed 'I am only 23, and a poor miserable man I am! If anyone knew of my life they would pity me!'

On July 18 1892, there was once more discontent in the little house at No. 51 Buxton Road. Mrs Raymond told Fred that he was 26 shillings in arrears with his rent, and he promised to pay it, although she did not believe that he had any money. All of a sudden, there was a terrible scream from upstairs, followed by the report of a gun. Mrs Raymond ran upstairs, to find Louisa lying on the floor, bleeding badly from the head. Fred stood over her, with a smoking revolver in his hand. When he saw the mother-in-law staring at him, he took aim at her, but Mrs Raymond leapt out of the way and ran downstairs screaming 'Murder! Murder!' As she did to, there was the report of another gunshot.

The outcry of 'Murder!' had caused a large crowd to

congregate outside No. 51 Buxton Road. A police constable went upstairs, where he found Frederick Arthur Harknett dead from a self-inflicted gunshot wound to the head, and Louisa mortally wounded; she died in the hospital soon after. The coroner's inquest returned a verdict of murder against Frederick Arthur Harknett, who had then taken his own life while his mind was unhinged by his marital troubles.[5] Remarkably, the jury also saw fit to censure Mrs Raymond for not dissuading her daughter from returning to the stage.

A FATHER'S TERRIBLE DEED, 1902

William Henry Downes was a specialist maker of music stools, employing several workmen and doing quite well in business. He lived at No. 180 Forest Road, Walthamstow, with his wife Susan and several children. He had previously lived at Bethnal Green, and was known as a respectable and industrious man. Since his music stool factory was situated in the City, Mr Downes had a lengthy daily commute from Walthamstow, involving several changes of omnibus. On one of these expeditions, he fell off the 'bus in December 1901 and injured his ankle. After a week in hospital, he seemed 'on the mend', but then he took another dangerous tumble off a vehicle of some description, and landed on his injured ankle. Laid up in bed, he cursed his bad luck.

In January 1902, the 40-year-old William Henry Downes was still in bed. His wife instead went to work, since she managed a shop belonging to them, in the Tottenham Court Road. They had a 17-month-old baby named Alice Lucy, and although this baby was supposed to be looked after by a niece, Mr Downes hobbled downstairs and took Alice Lucy upstairs with him. At mid-day, the elder daughter Annie came home, and had a look for her father.

She saw a clothesline tied to the outside handle of the bedroom door, and tried to open it without success. She ran downstairs, where she saw her aunt, who also lived in the house, and exclaimed 'Come quick, Auntie! I believe father's hung himself!' And indeed, this prediction turned out to be nothing but the truth, once the bedroom door had been forced open; on the bed lay little Alice Lucy, also dead from being smothered with the bedclothes. On the mantelpiece was a letter from William Henry Downes to his wife, saying that he "had done this for the best", although there was no logical explanation how anything good could come from the senseless murder of an innocent babe. The coroner's inquest returned a verdict of murder and suicide whilst of unsound mind.[6]

THE EDMONTON FRATRICIDE, 1912

John and Charles Mansfield, two young North London lads, both joined the Rifle Brigade in the 1890s. They served for 12 years, as bandsmen in two different companies, before being discharged after their term of service had expired, both still private soldiers. John became an attendant at the Edmonton District Council Baths, and Charles became a casual labourer. In 1912, the brothers moved into the small terraced house at No. 25 North Road, off the Hertford Road in Lower Edmonton, sharing it with their drinking-companion George Gledhill.

John Mansfield was a reliable workman, and his record at the Council Baths an impeccable one. But his brother Charles seldom held down a job for very long. In August and September 1912, he had left one job as a tram conductor, and two jobs as a barman, either because he was dissatisfied about the pay, or because he was simply fed up with working. John was not at all amused by these shenanigans, since all three inhabitants of No. 25 North Road were supposed to contribute towards the rent, something Charles was unable to do with he was out of work.

On Sunday September 15 1912, John and Charles Mansfield went to a drinking-party at the Houndsfield Club, situated at No. 396 Hertford Road [it still stands, but is today the Edmonton Working Men's Club]. They each had quite a few drinks, but were not intoxicated. People noticed that they kept some distance apart, and did not speak to one another. Nor did they leave the party together: Charles went back to the house at No. 25 North Road before his brother, and went to bed in the middle bedroom on the first floor. John arrived home at 10.30 pm, and the neighbours could hear him shouting abuse at his girlfriend Annie Page, because she had spent the evening with another man. He then went upstairs, in a very angry temper, and the neighbours could soon hear the brothers quarrelling angrily. John shouted 'I pay for everything in this bleeding house, In fact I keep you!' Charles replied 'You keep me? You would bloody starve me!' 'Starve you? I will, too, you ___ bastard!' screamed the furious John. Further bad language ensued, and then the loud report of a revolver.

The neighbours saw John Mansfield leave No. 25 North Road. He went to see his friend Alf Jones, who lived nearby, to tell him he had just shot his brother. Alf persuaded him to return to No. 25 and give himself up. When they came up to the house, a doctor and two police constables were already there. The volatile Annie Page told them that Charles had shot himself by accident, and that John had not been in the house at that time. Remarkably, the badly wounded Charles agreed that he had been playing with a defective old revolver they had, and that it had suddenly gone off by mistake.

Charles Mansfield died a few days later, and the case was now one of murder. The medical evidence spoke against accident or suicide, and when Annie Page admitted that she had made up her story to the police constable, things did not look good for the Edmonton bath attendant. The coroner's jury disregarded the dying Charles Mansfield's statement that he had shot himself by accident, and returned a verdict of murder against his brother John. On trial for murder at the Old Bailey on November 7, he was found guilty by the jury, who strongly recommended him to mercy. The Edmonton Fratricide was reprieved twelve days later, his sentence commuted to imprisonment for life.[7]

THE COLINDALE WINE SHOP MYSTERY, 1919

In 1919, the Colindale Wine Spirits and Wine Stores at No. 62 Colindale Avenue, Hendon, were kept by Mr John Thomas Gregory, a rather furtive-looking, middle-aged man who lived separated from his wife. He had been a grocer in Devon, but had separated from his wife and come to London in 1915. Gregory did not live on the premises, but shared a flat in Warwick Road, Ealing, with his daughter Sybil. In spite of this lengthy commute, he was conscientious in his duties at the wine shop. Since the shop had to be closed from 2.30 pm until the evening, due to the archaic licensing laws of the time, Gregory spent these hours in a small sitting-room, accessed from the shop's side entrance.

On Friday July 4 1919, Gregory closed the wine shop at 2.30 as usual. But just after five in the afternoon, two young women who were passing by the wine shop heard the sound of breaking glass, and a violent quarrel. When one of them tried to peer inside through a side window, she was startled when a young man in a blue coat pulled a red curtain across, particularly since she saw that he also wiped some blood off the window with the curtain as he went along. A passing metal worker saw the startled girls and heard glass breaking

BRUTAL MURDER MYSTERY AT HENDON.

6.3 Dramatic scenes from the Colindale Wine Shop Mystery, from the Illustrated Police News, *July 10 1919.*

and a series of heavy thuds from inside. He tried the shop door but found it locked and instead went for a police constable. Another passer-by managed to break open the side window; when he had a look inside, he saw a groaning man lying on the floor.

At that very moment, the police constable arrived. When he climbed in through the window, he saw Gregory lying on the floor, his head terribly battered with some blunt instrument. The unfortunate wine shop manager expired a few seconds later. A variety of blood-stained blunt instruments were found in the murder room: a pair of tongs, a bent poker, and two heavy broken bottles. There were two empty glasses on the table, indicating that Gregory had invited his killer for a drink or two, before he had been assaulted. In the garden was an empty suitcase marked 'J.W.B.' – were those the initials of the killer? The police issued a description of the wine shop murderer: a clean-shaven young man wearing a neat blue suit and a grey hat. A witness had seen him on a bus going towards Golders Green, and noticed bloodstains on his forehead and collar. The motive for the murder was initially presumed to be robbery, but the detectives were surprised to find that Gregory had already packed up the day's takings, and put them in a bag that was found on the premises.

The inquest on John Thomas Gregory was held in the Hendon Town Hall on July 8. The next door neighbour to the wine shop had seen Gregory walking with a man exactly fitting the description of the killer, about a fortnight before he was murdered. Several other witnesses had also seen the clean-shaven, youthful suspect. One of them had seen Gregory boarding an omnibus with him; they had talked and laughed together, and appeared to be good friends. The wine shop manager went off at Edgware Road, but the suspect had gone on to Tottenham Court Road, alighting near the YMCA. The detectives smelt blood. There was a man at the YMCA with the initials J.W.B. but he have a good account of himself, and stated that he had lent his suitcase to a fellow lodger named Arthur John Biggin. This individual, described as youthful-looking, clean shaved and wearing a blue suit, had left the YMCA the day after the murder, presumably to return to his home town of Sheffield.

This sounded promising, the detectives thought, and the Sheffield constabulary was corresponded with, but it turned out that a young man had already been found in Whiteley Wood, one of the city parks of Sheffield, claiming to have attempted to destroy himself by drinking potassium cyanide. He was said to have 'quickly recovered from the effects of the poison', if he had taken any in the first place, and was returned to London to be charged with the murder of John Thomas Gregory.

Arthur John Biggin's father was a respectable Sheffield builder, and he had received a good education. The police thought he looked like a decent lad, and he freely told them about his relations with Gregory. The 18-year-old Biggin had gone to London with a girlfriend of his, but she had left him and he ended up at the YMCA looking for a job. When he attended an interview at the Hendon Aerodrome, he was invited into the wine shop at No. 62 by the jovial manager, for a free drink. Biggin did not like the looks of Gregory, and gave him a false name and address, but he liked the wine. A few days later, when he went for another interview, Gregory again invited him in for a drink, and offered him to have a few bottles of wine for free if he brought a bag along when he came next time.

On July 3, Biggin had once more made his way to the Colindale Wine Stores, where Gregory treated him to some wine and port. The lecherous wine shop manager said that he often slept alone at the shop, and offered the young man to share his bed, but Biggin was not having any of that, he said. Nevertheless, the two men parted friends, and Biggin returned with a suitcase the next day. Gregory gave him a lavish luncheon, with plenty to drink. He then offered the young man a glass of a reddish yellow liquid, which made him feel drowsy. But when Gregory tried to unbutton his flies, and pull up his shirt, Biggin pushed him away. Exclaiming 'You young viper, you won't, will you? I will make you!', the furious wine shop manager seized up a poker and aimed a blow at Biggin. The young man avoided it and struck Gregory a series of hard blows with a bottle, and some tongs, but the wine shop manager kept attacking him. Finally, Biggin managed to seize hold of the poker himself. After delivering some crushing blows to the head of the older man, he fled the shop in a panic.

Although Biggin assured them that Gregory would have murdered him if he had not fought back fiercely, the police were far from convinced by his story. Why, if there had been such a furious fight, had Biggin escaped with hardly a scratch, whereas his opponent's head had been literally beaten to a pulp? On trial for murder at the Old Bailey on September 16 1919, before Mr Justice Darling, things were not looking good for young Biggin. The prosecution was led by Sir Richard Muir, who exposed that Biggin had run away to London with a girl, and led his and her parents to believe that they were married. Back in Sheffield, he had swindled a firm of stockbrokers out of £150, all of which he had spent on his amusements in London.

Mr Justice Darling and Sir Richard Muir both pressed Biggin hard about his lack of injuries from the alleged fight, but the young man stood by his story, and gave the jury the impression that he was telling the truth. Mr Valetta, defending, then played his trump card. A sergeant from the Devon constabulary testified that when Gregory had kept a wine and spirits business in Kingbridge from 1912 until 1915, he had been ordered to keep observation on him as a predatory homosexual. Several young Londoners were then called, to give evidence that Gregory had invited them into the wine shop for some 'fun', and that he might become quite furious if rebuffed. In his summing-up, Mr Justice Darling said that there was no doubt that Gregory had been a vicious and odious person, and that the jury might well think that by his death the King had not lost a good subject. Arthur John Biggin was found guilty of manslaughter and was sentenced to twelve months of hard labour.

There was a fair amount of newspaper publicity about the Colindale Wine Shop Mystery. 'Death Drama in a Wine Shop!' was the headline of the *Daily Express*, and 'Sentence in Wine Shop Drama!' exclaimed the *Daily Mirror*. Both these newspapers had a good deal of sympathy for Biggin, and quoted Mr Justice Darling's harsh verdict on the hapless murder victim with approval. Gregory's wife and son had not even turned up in court, and the only person to stand by him was his daughter Sybil, a plain young woman who nevertheless got her photograph into the *Daily Mirror*. The normally reliable Sir Richard Muir had certainly had an 'off day' when prosecuting Biggin. His crowing that the prisoner had been exposed as a habitual liar, due to the dishonesty about the girl and the Sheffield swindle, had not had the desired

6.4 A newspaper photograph of the murder house in Colindale Avenue.

effect, since Biggin withstood a very hostile examination in court. Moreover, Sir Richard had acted with blameworthy carelessness when he had introduced the Sheffield evidence into the case, since it could be constructed to show that Biggin had committed an offence other than that he had been charged with. Quite rightly, from a technical viewpoint, a Court of Criminal Appeal quashed Biggin's conviction on October 20, and astonishingly, the Colindale wine shop killer was a free man.[8]

There is no doubt that Arthur John Biggin killed Gregory, and then got off practically scot-free. But was this deserved? Mr Justice Darling may well have been right when he claimed that the wine shop manager was a vile street pest, but this would hardly give any young thug a free-for-all to kill and murder him. Biggin was clearly a thoroughly immoral young man, who lied and cheated, and who was well-nigh destitute at the time of the murder. He surrounded himself with a dodgy crowd of unemployed young London men, and it is a pity that their activities were not properly investigated by the police. It does not take a close student of the music of the Village People to suspect that the YMCA was occasionally the site for various unwholesome activities. Was the set of young men surrounding Biggin in fact queer in more ways than one, and had the young man from Sheffield decided to emulate them and get some freebies from the odious old wine shop manager, only to attack him in a furious rage after some provocation or other? As for the former wine shop at No. 62 Colindale Avenue, it is today home to a small taxicab firm, but the side entrance remains.

MURDER IN HUTTON GROVE, 1925

In his youth, George Frederick Miles had been a Trooper in the 8th Hussars, before serving 25 years as a mounted police constable

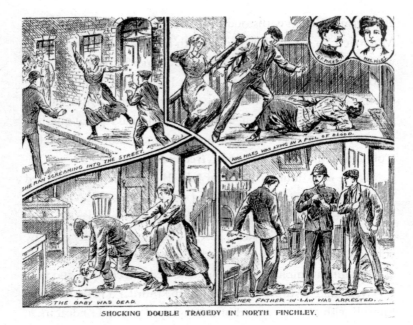

6.5 Shocking Double Tragedy in North Finchley, from the Illustrated Police News, *September 17 1925.*

in Finchley. In 1924, he fell ill with 'neurasthenia' and had to retire. Plagued by headaches and abnormal tiredness, he could spend three weeks in bed. He shared a small house at No. 22 Hutton Grove, Finchley, with his wife Agnes Charlotte and their three daughters, and also his son George and daughter-in-law Selina, and their baby Mary Agnes. There had once been a quarrel between George Frederick and his son George, after Selina had complained that the 'dirty old man' had put his arm around her waist and tried to kiss her, and the relations between the neurasthenic householder and his long-minded daughter-in-law remained very bad.

On the morning September 7 1925, Mrs Agnes Charlotte

Miles heard a muffled scream emanate from the kitchen. Going downstairs to investigate, she saw Selina come running out of the room, with blood gushing from her throat. George Frederick emerged, with a blood-stained razor in his hand, saying 'I have killed Lina and the baby too!' And indeed, the little baby was lying dead on the floor. Mrs Miles managed to calm down her husband, and to persuade him to give her the razor. The coroner's inquest returned a verdict of wilful murder against George Frederick Miles, but the case never went to court. It turned out that at the time of the murder, George Frederick had been waiting to be committed to the Wellhouse Hospital for neurasthenia and cerebral degeneration. Had this hospital's routines involved more speedy committals, much mischief would have been averted. In the end, George Frederick Miles was found insane and unfit to plead, and incarcerated in a lunatic asylum.[9]

A WEST SIDE MURDER STORY, 1931

Alfred John Humphries was born in 1876 and joined the army as a boy, fighting in the Boer War. He married his wife Emma while still a private soldier, and they had a son named Charles Henry. Alfred Humphries was discharged from the army in 1913, but he rejoined the army in 1914 and served throughout the Great War, once being blown up by an explosion and landing on his head. He returned home in 1918 and became a clerk, but by this time, he was a changed man. In a furious temper, he beat up his wife and son, and Charles Henry moved out in 1920, for good.

In 1925, Alfred and Emma Humphries had a second son named Ernest. But in early October 1931, she left her angry, violent husband, taking Ernest with her and moving into the house at No. 12 West Side, Watford Way, Hendon, where Charles

Henry was living with his wife. Alfred Humphries, who had been such an indifferent husband and father since leaving the army in 1918, greatly missed his wife and little son once they were gone, however. He suspected that his estranged son Charles Henry was hiding them, and once waylaid him outside his office, threatening to beat it out of him unless he provided his address. Charles Henry did not give it to him, but the demented ex-soldier found the West Side address by some other means, with lethal effect.

On October 19 1931, a workman heard an outcry from No. 12 West Side. Going to investigate, he found Alfred Humphries at the gate of the house, bleeding from deep wounds to the throat and wrists. 'I have killed my wife! She had run away and left me!' he exclaimed. And indeed, Emma Humphries was found dead in the kitchen, with her throat cut. Alfred Humphries was found sane and fit to plead, and he stood trial for his crime at the Central Criminal Court in November 1931. His adult son testified as to the extreme change in his father after the Great War, a doctor confirmed that the prisoner suffered from epilepsy, possibly secondary to head trauma, and a Harley Street specialist said that epileptics could be prone to extreme fits of violence. Alfred Humphries was found guilty but insane, and was incarcerated in Broadmoor.[10]

WIFE MURDER IN SOUTH WOODFORD, 1936

Claude Ivor Vaissiere was born at Stoke Newington in 1900. His father, the plumber Frederick George Vaissiere, was a drunkard who died at an early age, so he was taken care of by his uncle Richard Vaissiere. After leaving school in 1914, he became an office-boy with George Thompson & Co. Shipowners. A quiet, industrious man, he advanced to become a senior shipping clerk, handling the wages for the entire firm of ship-owners. In 1936, when he was 36 years old, he lived at No. 49 Onslow Gardens, South Woodford, with his wife Ethel. In November that year, he got into trouble with his employers after being caught red-handed pilfering some insurance stamp money, and was told off for this unbecoming dishonesty. For some reason, he took this extremely badly, and became convinced that he was a ruined man.

The following morning, Claude Ivor Vaissiere took his wife's little dog to a dispensary, asking for it to be painlessly destroyed. He then drove on the police station to confess that he had murdered his wife. At first, the officer on duty thought that the dapper, elegantly dressed Vaissiere was joking, but back at No. 49 Onslow Gardens, the dead body of Ethel Vaissiere was found in bed with 67 injuries inflicted by a chopper and a knife. Even the experienced pathologist Dr Keith Simpson was appalled by the extent of her injuries, declaring that death was due to shock and haemorrhage from multiple wounds, inflicted with considerable force.

Claude Ivor Vaissiere told the police that the evening after his petty thefts had been exposed, he had decided that his wife ought to be spared the disgrace that would follow once he had been dismissed from his position. After he had at first felt incapable of murdering the sleeping woman, something had suddenly snapped in his brain, as he expressed it, and he made lethal use of the chopper and knife. The police did not believe a word of this story, due to Ethel Vaissiere's extensive injuries. What kind of man, or rather monster, could go to bed quietly, brutally murder his wife in a bloodbath, and then calmly make sure that her dog was destroyed? But Claude Ivor Vaissiere did not have a criminal record, his marriage had always been happy, and his employers declared that in spite of his recent lapse into dishonesty, he had given them many years of valuable service.

When he was on trial at the Old Bailey for murdering his wife, nobody had a bad thing to say about Claude Ivor Vaissiere. His father-in-law and brother-in-law both declared him a model husband, and his employers added that he had handled £400 000 in wages in the last seven years, and never stolen a penny. As for the insurance stamp money he had pilfered, this was considered a trifling matter, and they would never have prosecuted him. If Vaissiere had confessed to his wife about the theft, instead of brutally murdering her, his quiet suburban family life would probably have continued just like before. A tall man of gentlemanly bearing, Claude Ivor Vaissiere made a good impression in court, and he appeared to be genuinely distraught about the tragedy he had brought about. Appearing for the defence, the psychiatrist Dr Hopewell Ash expressed the opinion that the murder had been committed in a state of mental confusion, and amazingly, this was accepted by the prosecution. Accordingly, Vaissiere was found guilty but insane, and he was committed to Broadmoor during his Majesty's pleasure.[11]

It turns out that Claude Ivor Vaissiere did not remain incarcerated for very long, however. In 1945, he was certainly out and about, because in that year, he married a woman named Lillian D. Bradley in Southampton. The detectives who had investigated the Onslow Gardens mystery back in 1936 must have been surprised and dismayed by the occurrence of the uncommon name Vaissiere in the 'marriages' column of the newspaper. Perhaps they wondered if Vaissiere had been acquainted with his second wife already back in 1936. They had never been convinced by the 'insanity defence' and considered the Onslow Gardens murderer fully sane. But still, this mysterious Claude Ivor Vaissiere seems to have led a blameless existence with his new wife, and there is reason to believe that he died in Gloucester in early 1985. Either he was really the victim of some strange mental quirk, or a cold-blooded psychopath who was also a very good actor.

HUSBAND MURDER IN EDMONTON, 1937

The 44-year-old Mr Jesse Edward Etheridge lived at No. 149 Chichester Road, Edmonton, with his wife Alice and their five children. He worked long hours as a porter at Covent Garden market, and had a lengthy commute to his humble terraced North London home. He had been married to Alice for 16 years, but since the birth of their youngest child, she had been behaving oddly at times. She complained of incessant headaches, and told a lady doctor that she had been hit on the head by a man in Paris. Mrs Etheridge's mother Mrs Alice Bryan was certain her daughter had never visited the French capital in her life, however.

On September 21 1937, Alice Etheridge came running out of No. 149 Chichester Road, screaming 'Hide me! Hide me! He is after me!' After a neighbour had taken care of her, she made a confused statement that she had struck down her husband in a fight. When the neighbour went into No. 149 Chichester Road, she met Mrs Bryant, the aforementioned mother-in-law, who also lived in the house. She had heard sound of a scuffle upstairs, heard her daughter leave the house, and found Mr Etheridge on the upstairs landing, lying in a pool of blood.

A doctor was called, but Jesse Edward Etheridge was dead, stabbed through the heart with a pointed bread knife. The tragic nature of the crime meant that it achieved some newspaper coverage: 'Mother of Five Accused of Murder!' exclaimed the *Daily Express*, and the *Daily Mirror* added that the four youngest children had not been told that they were fatherless and that their mother was in prison accused of his murder. When the 39-year-old Alice Etheridge stood trial for murdering her husband at the Old Bailey, on November 17 1937, she was found insane and unfit to plead, and Mr Justice Humphreys ordered her to be detained in Broadmoor until his Majesty's pleasure be known.[12] The little house at No. 149 Chichester Road still stands, and looks almost unchanged from the plans and drawings in the Etheridge police file.

THE MURDER OF A NORTHWOOD BARMAID, 1937

Mrs Lilian Maud Chamberlain worked as a barmaid at the Northwood Hotel in Green Lane, and lived in a small second-floor flat directly opposite the hotel at No. 47 Green Lane. In 1937, when she was 25 years old, she had been pulling pints at the hotel for four and a half years. She was married to the railway dining car attendant Ivan John Chamberlain, but he might be away for days on end, working on the express trains. Mr Arthur Albert Fisher, licensee of the Northwood Hotel, described Lilian Maud Chamberlain as a model employee: reliable, sober, and punctual. Dark-haired and pretty, she was very popular with the customers.

On August 25 1937, Lilian Maud Chamberlain closed the bar at the Northwood Hotel at 10.45 pm and returned to her flat across the road. The following morning, she failed to turn up for work, so Mr Fisher sent a waiter named Lammas across the road to wake her up; he found her dead in the flat's blood-spattered bedroom. She had been brutally beaten with a blunt instrument, and then strangled to death. Ivan Chamberlain had been away on the trains, so he had a cast-iron alibi. Nor did Lilian Maud Chamberlain possess any enemies, or any skeletons in the cupboard for that matter: Mr Fisher described her as "a woman of the highest character".

Instead, suspicion soon centered on a certain John Thomas Rodgers, a barman at the Northwood Hotel. He was known to have a criminal record for shop-breaking, and had spent most of his teenage years in Borstal. The day of the murder, he had enjoyed his afternoon off, drinking hard at various pubs. At 10 pm, he had been spotted alighting from a motor-coach near the Northwood Hotel. After midnight, he had turned up at Northwood Station in a dishevelled state, missing the last train to central London. He had been wearing a coat and a pair of trousers belonging to Ivan Chamberlain. Rodgers later went to Southend, where he bought a shirt and a pair of socks. He had not reported at work, or been seen again.

This sounded promising, the detectives thought, and the description of the fugitive barman was widely circulated. At mid-day on August 27, Rodgers was recognized by a bus-driver at Golders Green Station, and restrained until a police constable was fetched. When questioned at the police station, Rodgers said that on August 25, he had been having a few drinks at two

6.6 Lily Chamberlain is found murdered, and a view of the murder flat at No. 47 Green Lane, from the Illustrated Police News, *September 7 1937.*

Rickmansworth pubs on his afternoon off. He was going to sleep rough, but did not find it agreeable, so he went back to Green Lane and walked up to Ivan Chamberlain's flat, hoping that he would be allowed to sleep on the kitchen floor. But he found that Lilian Maud Chamberlain had been assaulted inside the flat: the room was full of blood, and she was in a dying condition. Worried that he would become a murder suspect, Rodgers took Ivan Chamberlain's trousers and coat because his own were severely blood-stained. When he had left, Mrs Chamberlain had still been alive.

The police thought that Rodgers looked like a very nasty piece of work, and his story was not believed. Fingerprint evidence indicated that he had been the only intruder inside the Chamberlain flat, and his story did not explain how his clothes could have become so extensively stained with blood, if he had not been the attacker. Rodgers knew both the Chamberlains, and the detectives presumed that in his drunken condition, he had entered the flat with lustful intent, knowing that the railwayman would be away. When Lilian Maud Chamberlain objected to his intrusion, he had attacked her in a furious rage, and then strangled her to death.

On trial at the Central Criminal Court on October 18 1937, John Thomas Rodgers gave a very unfavourable impression. Albeit just 22 years old, he seemed like a hardened and callous wretch. He repeated his story of finding Lilian Maud Chamberlain in a dying condition inside the flat, but again he was not believed. When asked why he had not tried to obtain help if the woman had still been alive, he obnoxiously responded "With me it is always self first, self last, and self always!" After deliberating for two and a half hours, the jury returned a verdict of Guilty, adding a recommendation to mercy on account of the prisoner's age. Mr Justice Charles sentenced Rodgers to death,

6.7 Rodgers is executed, and other vignettes from the murder of Lily Chamberlain, from the Illustrated Police News, November 25 1937.

and since his crime had been a brutal and dastardly one, the recommendation to mercy was not acted upon: John Thomas Rogers was executed at Pentonville Prison on November 18 1937.[13] The bus driver and conductor, who had been instrumental in capturing the murderer, received a reward of £5 each.

The *Daily Express* provided an unexpected and macabre postscript to the Northwood murder case. After first describing how Rodgers' 17-year-old girlfriend had wept when he was sentenced to death, this newspaper calmly reported that in 1919, Rodgers' mother Mildred had stood in the dock at Gloucester Assizes, accused of murdering her husband Matthew, the father of John Thomas. When Matthew Rodgers had been holding his four-year-old son, his wife had cut his throat with a razor, and young John Thomas had fallen down, landing on his head. Mrs

6.8 A postcard stamped and posted in 1968, showing the former site of the Northwood Hotel to the left, and the murder flat at No. 47 Green Lane to the right.

Rodgers had been sentenced to five years in prison for manslaughter; she was released after serving three years and nine months of her time, and went to Canada leaving John Thomas behind. She later turned up in Bristol, where she died in 1924.[14]

A MURDEROUS EDGWARE FISHMONGER, 1937

Walter Ernest Smee was a working-class London lad, born in 1900. He left school at fourteen to become a fish fryer, but in 1915, he lied about his age and became a private soldier in the Royal Field Artillery. He left the army with a good character in 1919, and carried on fish-frying for various shops. He married his wife Rose in 1923, and they soon had three young children. In 1931, Smee opened his own fish shop at No. 178 Lillie Road, Fulham [the house no longer stands]. There was a flat above the shop, which was large enough for the Smees to take in some lodgers: the recently married couple George and Alice Hand. Not long after they had moved into No. 178 Lillie Road, Mrs Smee had to go into hospital for an operation. Mrs Hand was to look after the children while their mother was away, but soon she looked after the needs of their father as well: it did not take long for the amorous Walter Smee to roger the lodger in the flat above the fish shop.

Walter Smee became quite obsessed with Alice Hand, and as their illicit affair progressed, it changed the brave young soldier and industrious tradesman into a bounder and a cad. He sold the fish shop, deserted his wife and children, and kept pursuing his beloved Alice. Although the dim-witted George Hand had belatedly removed his wife to other lodgings, the unemployed Smee visited Alice there when her husband was at work. The disgusted Mr Hand decided to obtain a separation order, but in 1935, his volatile wife broke with her favourite fish fryer and returned to the marital home. The same year, the long-suffering Rose Smee summoned her husband before the South Western Police Court, for deserting her and failing to support her and the children. The cad Smee did not have a leg to stand on in court, and the magistrate Mr Mullins was severe with him: he ought to be in prison for 'carrying on' with another woman when he was unemployed, and failing to support his family. Smee was ordered to pay his wife twelve shillings per week, and an additional two shillings for each of the three children.

It is sad but true that after this disastrous appearance in court, the bounder Walter Smee found it much more economical to move back in with his wife and family. Poor Rose Smee, who was genuinely fond of her husband, willingly took him back. Smee soon deserted her once more, however, taking care that she would not find out his whereabouts and summon him again. He remained unemployed, and sent her no maintenance money. Finally, in 1937, he managed to get a job as an assistant in Mr Isaac's fishmonger's shop at No. 8 Handel Parade, Edgware [it is still standing, in Whitchurch Lane near Handel Way]. Smee moved into the ground floor flat at No. 37 Prescelly Place together with his mistress Alice Hand, who had once more left her husband. For a few months, this arrangement worked well, until Mrs Smee managed to track down her husband through a solicitor, demanding her maintenance money. With his usual caddishness, Smee suggested a compromise: what if Alice went back to her husband for a few months, so that Rose Smee and her children could move into the house at No. 37 Prescelly Place?

Understandably, this suggestion made Alice Hand quite furious, since she had no intention to return to her long-suffering husband, but the Edgware fishmonger did not budge: he was the

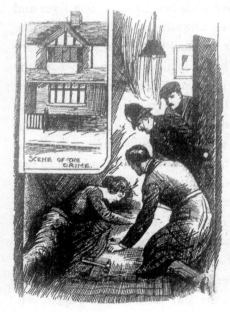

6.9 Alice Hand is found murdered at No. 37 Prescelly Place, from the Illustrated Police News, December 2 1937.

one wearing the trousers at No. 37 Prescelly Place. On the very day the family were to move in, November 24 1937, Walter and Alice quarrelled angrily. A removal man named James Hughes, who was bringing some extra furniture for the wife and children, heard a woman scream. Peering through the dirty window, he could see a man throttling a woman. Hughes ordered his assistant to remain at the house, and himself went off to alert the police. When the constable arrived, Smee feigned surprise, saying that all was well inside his flat, but the excited Hughes described what he had seen through the window. Smee then said 'Take me, guv'nor, I've done her in!' callously adding 'The bitch has caused me a good deal of trouble!' And indeed, Alice Hand was found brutally beaten to death, with a wire tied in a knot around her neck.

The Prescelly Place murder made it into the national newspapers: the journalists marvelled at the immorality of Smee and Mrs Hand, the plight of poor Mrs Smee, and the callous behaviour of the murderous Edgware fishmonger. On trial for murder at the Old Bailey on January 17 1938, before Mr Justice Goddard, things were not looking good for Walter Smee. His defence team emphasized their client's great passion for Alice Hand, which had led to him deserting his wife, family, and fish-frying career. Smee gave evidence in his own behalf, claiming that Alice had attacked him with a hammer, and that he had defended himself, snatching it from her and hitting her twice on the head. The jury was urged to reduce the charge to one of manslaughter, but Smee's story was not believed. He was found guilty of murder, and Mr Justice Goddard sentenced him to death. But with what must have been an extremely narrow margin, the Edgware fishmonger was reprieved, and sentenced to imprisonment for life.[15] He is said to have emerged from prison in the 1950s, changed his distinctive name, and got on with his life as well as he could.

THE FRANCKLYN GARDENS MATRICIDE, 1938

The 47-year-old spinster Miss Jean Mitchell worked as a a telephone supervisor at the Golders Green post office. In October 1936, she purchased a small semi-detached house at No. 30 Francklyn Gardens, Edgware, for herself and her recently widowed mother Jessie. The seller of the house probably laughed all the way to the bank, because the naïve postmistress had paid significantly more than it was worth. The spending of her life's savings, and the responsibility of owning a house, soon took its toll on Jean Mitchell's mind: she tried to sell it, but there were no interested buyers. She worried about bankruptcy and poverty in old age, and stopped eating lunch because she thought she could no longer afford it. Her married sister Mrs Jones thought her a changed woman after the unfortunate purchase of the house: she constantly worried about her finances, when she in fact still had money saved, and was also unduly concerned about the health of her 75-year-old mother, who was in fact still hale and hearty.

In April 1938, Jean Mitchell became increasingly depressed and delusional. She thought it best to end her own existence, and that of her mother as well. On April 27, she strangled her mother to death, and then put two shillings and sixpence into the gas meter, turned on the oven and put her head inside. But her sister had called the police, and when they arrived at No. 30 Francklyn Gardens, they found Jessie Mitchell dead, and Jean Mitchell unconscious in a gas-filled room. Jean Mitchell was charged with murder, but was found insane and unfit to plead, and she was detained at Broadmoor during the King's pleasure.[16]

MERCY KILLING IN HENDON, 1942

In 1942, the 85-year-old Frederick Mills lived with his family at

No. 5 Rowsley Avenue, Hendon. Worn out by senility and disease, he had become bedridden. He often implored other family members to put an end to his misery. In April 1942, his son, the 38-year-old Sapper Sidney James Mills came home on leave. The unfortunate old man begged for euthanasia, and on the morning his leave expired, Sidney killed him. On trial for murder at the Central Criminal Court on April 27, he pleaded guilty and was promptly sentenced to death. This was one of the shortest murder trials on record. His defence council pointed out that Sidney James Mills was a man of blameless character and an excellent service record. In an impossible situation, he had committed the crime hoping to give his father peace and rest from suffering. Mr Justice Oliver agreed that in this tragic case, he would give a recommendation to mercy. And on May 14, sanity prevailed and Sidney James Mills was reprieved.[17]

WIFE MURDER IN BALLARDS LANE, 1942

The North London working-class lad Reginald Irvine Chandler, who left school, had a fascination with the military. He enlisted in a number of regiments, only to desert after a short period of service. In April 1939, when he was twenty years old, he had served in the Rifle Brigade, the Royal Scots Fusileers (twice), the Royal West Kent Regiment, the Bedfordshire and Hertfordshire Regiment, and the East Surrey Regiment. He had been arrested while on the run from the East Surrey ranks, illicitly carrying a loaded Mauser pistol he had purchased from another soldier. At the Great Marlborough Street police court, it was commented that this extraordinary serial deserter certainly seemed to have a strong liking for military life. Reg Chandler had probably hoped that he would be tried by a civil court, and get away from the army, but the magistrate was wise to this trick, and Private Chandler was dealt with by the military authorities for his various misdeeds.[18]

After the Second World War had broken out, Reg Chandler once more joined the army, becoming a Sapper in the Royal Engineers. Now when there was a war on, he took his duties much more seriously, and his superiors considered him a very useful soldier. He had married his sweetheart, the 27-year-old Victoria Page, back in 1939, and they had two children. When Reg rejoined the army, his wife and children took lodgings at No. 21 Nether Street, Finchley. But when Reg came home on leave unexpectedly, he found his wife and her friend Mrs Edith May Ling in the company of two soldiers! Since it was obvious what was going on, the furious Reg evicted them all from the flat. He put the two children into Barnardo's Home, stopped his wife's allowance, and applied for a separation order on grounds of adultery. Victoria Chandler moved into her friend Edith May Ling's flat at No. 365B Ballards Lane, Finchley. When on leave,

6.10 An old postcard showing Ballard's Lane.

Reg Chandler used to stay with his mother-in-law Mrs Annie Page. She knew Edith May Ling as a very bad woman, and feared that her daughter, who had given her much trouble in recent years, was going the same way.

In June 1942, Reg Chandler could not stand the situation any longer. He brought with him a Lee-Enfield rifle and went straight to the flat at No. 365B Ballards Lane, where Edith May Ling let him in without any demur. Victoria was sitting in the second-floor kitchen, and although she must have been frightened when her short-tempered husband came marching in with a rifle, but she probably thought she could control him. For a while, all went well, as the three sat chatting at the kitchen table, but then the returning soldier sternly asked Mrs Ling to make herself scarce, since he wanted to say a few words to his wife in private.

Edith May Ling went downstairs, where she minded her own business for a while. She heard a sharp bang from upstairs, which she presumed to be a door slamming shut. A few seconds later, Reg Chandler came downstairs, looking quite grim. He glared at Mrs Ling and exclaimed 'If I were your husband I would shoot you too!' before absconding. After Reg had left, Mrs Ling went upstairs, where she found Victoria Chandler dead on the floor, from a gunshot wound to the head.

After leaving the murder flat at No. 365B Ballards Lane, Reg Chandler went straight to the Finchley police station, where he surrendered his rifle and confessed that he had just shot his wife dead. The motive was that he was certain that she was unfaithful to him, and that he feared that she was becoming a prostitute, something he could not abide. When he was on trial at the Old Bailey for murdering his wife, there was no question that Reg Chandler had gunned Victoria down, and that there had been some degree of premeditation, since he had brought the rifle along. But even Mr Christmas Humphries, prosecuting, said that the prisoner was a man who had a good reason for jealousy. Some spicy letters had been found inside the murder flat, clearly indicating that Victoria Chandler was 'carrying on' with various men. Major Carter, of the Royal Engineers, testified that the prisoner had been an excellent soldier. The defence alleged that Reg Chandler had fired his first shot to frighten his wife, and that the second had been an accident. Remarkably, Mrs Annie Page wrote to the Judge to express her regard to the man who had gunned her worthless daughter down, and to urge his immediate release.

In the end, the jury found Reg Chandler Not Guilty of murder by Guilty of manslaughter. After reminding the returning soldier that army rifles were intended for use against the enemy, and not against wives, the bonhomous Judge sentenced Reg Chandler to just five years in prison for manslaughter. He is said to have served his time, and then led a law-abiding life for many years. The murder flat at No. 365B Ballards Lane has not changed much since 1942, and a recent author on the case has even reproduced a photograph of a ricochet mark from a factory wall nearby, likely to have been the result of one of the returning soldier's bullets.[19]

MURDER IN MAURICE WALK, 1943

Mr Maurice Stuart Horner was an established London journalist, working as technical editor of 'Commercial Motor' magazine. In 1943, when he was 49 years old, he lived at No. 6 Maurice Walk, Finchley with his wife Nora. Apart from his work at the magazine office, he was a lance corporal in the Middlesex Home Guard. Although Horner was a jovial, popular man, there were those who disapproved of his heavy drinking, and who found his habit of consorting with younger men quite unwholesome. He and his wife had no children, and they slept in separate beds.

Mrs Horner worked part time as an auxiliary ambulance driver, and when she was driving the ambulance late in the evening, her husband took the opportunity to go partying in London, and to try to persuade some young male companion to come with him back to No. 6 Maurice Walk. April 1 1943 was no exception: the bibulous editor went for a prolonged pub crawl, ending up at the Fitzroy Tavern in Great Windmill Street, where he bought a round of drinks although he himself was quite inebriated.

The following morning, the Horners' daily help came to do the chores. She found the house in much disarray, with bloodstains and broken furniture, and many of Mr Horner's belongings strewn about on the floor. Horner was lying in the heavily blood-stained bed, with a towel wrapped around his head. He said that he had been attacked by a Canadian soldier, whom he had invited home for a cup of tea. He refused to allow her to call a doctor, clearly thinking the entire episode should remain forgotten. When Mrs Horner returned home from the ambulance garage, she contacted the police and the local doctor straight away, since her husband was clearly badly injured. Horner was taken to the University College Hospital, where he was later fit enough to make a statement to one of the doctors.

Horner said that after his prolonged drinking session, he had met a good-looking young Canadian soldier at the Goodge Street station platform. The soldier said that his name was 'Rex' and that he had once been a sergeant before being demoted. He spoke of the University of Winnipeg and said that he had been at Oxford. The drunken Horner invited his friend back home to No. 6 Maurice Walk for a cup of tea, and they seemed to get on very well for a while, but all of a sudden, Horner had been violently assaulted with a blunt instrument. The day after, Horner became comatose, and he died on April 5. The case was now one of murder.

It was clear to the Scotland Yard detectives that Horner had been a homosexual, who had made a habit of asking younger men back to his house for some 'fun'. They got the impression that Mrs Horner knew all about this. It was speculated that the Canadian might have become disgusted when Horner made advances towards him, and murdered his host in a rage; on the other hand, the drawers in the lounge had been searched, and Horner's wallet stolen, indicating that robbery might well have been on his mind. Unfortunately, there were no witness descriptions of the Canadian, except that a local police constable had given a young private soldier directions to the Beaver Club near Golders Green at 12.45 the night of the murder, without asking for his identification documents. A number of fingerprints from the killer were found at No. 6 Maurice Walk.

The further police investigation of the murder of Maurice Horner concentrated on investigating his movements the evening and night of the murder, but nothing was found to suggest that the Canadian was anything but a casual acquaintance. Efforts from the Royal Canadian Military Police to find the elusive 'Rex' were wholly unsuccessful. All Canadian soldiers arrested in London had their fingerprints taken, but none fitted those of the killer, and the murder of Maurice Horner remains unsolved.[20]

MURDER IN NEW BARNET, 1943

Gerald Elphinstone Roe was a 41-year-old man of mixed Indian and English heritage. His real name was Minvalla, but when he moved to London, he took his mother's surname. A clever, industrious man, he worked at the Signals Research Development

Department during the Second World War. His wife Elsie Roe, whom he had married in Nairobi, was also employed by a government department. They had two young daughters alive. On May 17 1943, a woman doing a milk round smelt gas escaping at Roe's house at No. 9 Greenhill Park, New Barnet. She called the police, who broke into the premises, and found Mrs Roe in the scullery, her head severely battered by a blunt instrument. She died later the same day.

Gerald Elphinstone Roe was the main suspect, since earlier in the morning, a neighbour had seen a woman in a blue pyjamas struggling with a man at one of the windows of No. 9 Greenhill Park. She had given a scream when he pulled her back into the room and closed the window. When Roe was arrested by a detective at Christchurch, near Bournemouth, he said that his wife had been in good health when he had left in the morning. But his suitcase was found to contain a heavily blood-stained dressing-gown, and there was also blood on a pyjamas, a sheet and a pillow-case found in the suitcase. Several witnesses testified that although a respectable, educated man, Gerald Elphinstone Roe had been very jealous of his wife, and she had been fearful that one day he would murder her.

Convicted of wilful murder at the Hertfordshire Assizes on June 18, Gerald Elphinstone Roe appealed against his conviction on grounds that the judge had misled the jury by telling them that the person who caused the head injuries was the murderer. His defender argued that Elsie Roe's death had been accelerated by the gas escaping from the cooker, and that there was no evidence that Roe had turned it on. But Mr Justice Oliver responded that it did not matter who had turned on the gas, or whether it had been done deliberately or accidentally. There was abundant evidence that Roe had caused his wife's injuries, intending to do serious bodily harm to his wife. The appeal was dismissed, and

Gerald Elphinstone Roe was hanged at Pentonville Prison on August 3 1943.[21] The two little Roe daughters had been left orphans, in the most dismal manner imaginable.

MURDER IN WOLSELEY ROAD, 1948

In 1948, the small detached house at No. 21 Wolseley Road was home to the 49-year-old painter Christopher Brendon McCormack and his two years younger wife Annie. With them lived their married daughter, her husband and infant son, and not less than eight male lodgers. Mr McCormack was a steady, reliable man, and his wife a very house-proud, industrious housewife, who prided herself on looking after the domestic needs of the many lodgers. They used to get on quite well, and none of the lodgers had anything bad to say about them.

On June 24 1948, the McCormacks and their lodgers followed their normal routine. The following morning, one of the lodgers knocked on their bedroom door at 6.20 am, annoyed that his breakfast was not ready. Mr McCormack said that his wife was ill and prepared the meal himself. Later in the morning, McCormack went out drinking, indulging himself to such an extent that a police constable arrested him for being drunk and incapable. As he was awaiting bail at the police station, the local detective inspector received a message that McCormack was a wanted man: earlier in the day, his wife Annie had been found lying in bed, her head brutally bashed in with a blunt instrument.

When taken to Wealdstone police station for further questioning, the drunken McCormack freely admitted murdering his wife, since she had annoyed him with her incessant nagging. When she had been complaining about the amount of work she had to do in the crowded little house, and that she never had a moment's peace, he had seized a large hammer and hit her with it several times. He told the astonished detective that he had resented his wife for quite some time: she neither smoked nor drank, and all she cared about was pounds, shillings and pence.

On trial at the Old Bailey for murdering his wife, McCormack pleaded guilty and was sentenced to death in a trial lasting less than two minutes. 'Two Murder Cases Last Seven Minutes!' exclaimed the *Daily Mirror*, impressed that the mills of justice were sometimes grinding on apace. Bur McCormack was fortunate in that in the late 1940s, there was much debate about the death penalty and its application. The Home Secretary, Mr James Chuter Ede, paid close attention to the debate in the House of Lords about the abolition of capital punishment, and he was reluctant to allow any further executions to be carried out while the debate continued. As a result, Christopher Brendon McCormack received a reprieve in September 1948; he disappeared into a prison cell, and obscurity.[22]

MURDER WITHOUT MOTIVE, 1949

In 1948, the 23-year-old advertising agent Daniel Raven married a young lady named Marie Goodman. She was the daughter of the wealthy Jewish businessman Leopold Goodman and his wife Esther, of No. 8 Ashcombe Gardens, Edgware. The Goodmans were not entirely happy with Marie's choice of a husband, since Daniel Raven had no wealth to boast of, but at least he was a fellow Jew. Daniel had served in the RAF during the war, not without merit, and had once been the sole survivor of a plane crash. The Goodmans made sure that the Ravens got a house of their own, in Edgwarebury Lane. Relations between Daniel Raven and his parents-in-law were not always good; in particular, he was annoyed by his mother-in-law's constant nagging and interfering.

On October 6 1949, Marie Raven gave birth to a son at a nursing home in Muswell Hill. Four days later, the Goodmans came to visit her there. The normally taciturn Jews were very pleased to have a healthy grandchild, and behaved in a bonhomous manner, congratulating Daniel and his wife. In the late afternoon, they left the nursing home in their own car, Daniel following in his own vehicle, before he went on to his own house, situated just a minute's drive away. The same evening, just before 10 pm, the Goodmans were visited by his brother-in-law Frederick Fairman. He found them brutally murdered, by repeated heavy blows to the head.

The police were promptly called, and arrived just minutes later. They could find no signs of a forced entry. Nor did it look like if anything had been stolen. As they were examining the scene of crime, Daniel Raven turned up. He seemed quite shocked that his parents-in-law had been murdered, and kept repeating that before he had parted with the Goodmans, he had offered to stay behind at No. 8, since they had been very fearful of burglars. If only they had taken him up on his offer, then they would still have been alive! The police found his behaviour more than a little odd. Since he was, by his own admission, the last person to see the murdered couple alive, he immediately became a suspect. When his house was searched, a suit of clothes with some lurid-looking stains was found in the boiler. Daniel's shoes looked like if they had been recently cleaned. As a result of these findings, Daniel Raven was taken into custody, and later charged with the murder of his parents-in-law.

On trial at the Central Criminal Court from November 22 until 24, the evidence against Daniel Raven looked impressive. He had lied to the police, he had disliked the Goodmans, and he had previously stolen from them. Both Mr and Mrs Goodman had belonged to blood group AB, and blood of this group had been found on Daniel's suit and shoes. There were also indications that he had unsuccessfully tried to destroy evidence by burning the suit in the boiler, and cleaning the shoes. The likely murder weapon, the blunt end of a TV aerial, was found in the scullery of his house. Although Mr Goodman had kept plenty of valuables in his house, nothing had been stolen, and wads of banknotes in the murder room were left untouched.

Daniel Raven's defence team made a valiant effort to save him from the gallows. They alleged that Daniel had been so concerned about his parents-in-law that he had returned to No. 8 Ashcombe Gardens, to make sure there were no dangerous burglars about. He had found them murdered, and had got splashes of blood on his clothes when he examined the bodies. The horrible sight of the corpses had quite unhinged him, and fearful of becoming a suspect himself, he had cleaned his shoes and tried to burn his clothes. Mrs Raven and others testified that Daniel had always been respectful to his parents-in-law, whose undoubted generosity he had appreciated. When Leopold Goodman's wallet had been examined, it had contained the business card of Inspector Herbert Hannan, a detective specializing in currency offence investigations. Hannan testified that Mr Goodman had been a police informant. A Russian Jew, Goodman had hoped to get naturalized as a British citizen, and the Inspector had promised that this could be arranged, in exchange for some information about financial criminals. Now, had these dangerous City crooks come back to get even with the 'squealer' who had denounced them to the police? But the jury found the case against Daniel Raven too impressive to give him the benefit of the doubt. After deliberating for 50 minutes, they returned a verdict of guilty, and Mr Justice Cassels sentenced him to death. After an appeal had failed, although it was supported by a petition with 15 000 signatures, Daniel Raven was hanged at Pentonville prison on January 6 1950.[23]

In a newspaper interview, Mrs Raven said that although she had moved into the murder house at No. 8 Ashcombe Gardens, she had changed her name, and she was determined that her little son would never learn about the tragedy that occurred when he was just four days old.[24] In December 1950, she remarried, and moved out of the murder house, for good. In 2009, local authors Jeff Grout and Liz Fisher published *Murder without Motive*, a re-examination of the Daniel Raven case. They argued that Daniel Raven was guilty, but found it troubling that the exact motive for the murders had never been elucidated.[25] Raven had a history of mental problems, and was known for his fierce and angry temper. Had his mother-in-law had to pay a very high price for one of her snide remarks about the penniless young Jew who had married her daughter?

MURDER IN FINCHLEY ROAD, 1949

Donald Hume was the illegitimate son of a schoolmistress, born in Swanage in December 1919. He was abandoned by his mother and sent to the West Country orphanage, an institution run by Victorian standards by three sadistic old women. The place was bleak and forbidding, and lacking in any compassion for the children. The proprietors even kept a parrot that screamed 'Bastard!' at regular intervals, to remind the young residents of their lowly position in life.

Donald Hume's miserable life at the orphanage came to an end at the age of eight, when he was adopted by his grandmother. But she soon sent him to live with his mother's sister, Aunt

6.11 Finchley Road, from a postcard stamped and posted in 1904.

Doodie, who was the headmistress of a small Hampshire school. She treated him badly, and made sure he knew that she preferred her two daughters to him. He was worked hard from an early age, and sometimes left at home to look after the house and chickens when the rest of the family went on holiday. One day, he found out, from the family maid, that Doodie was in fact his real mother and not his aunt. Not long after, he escaped to London, where he got a job as an apprentice electrician. When he went to Somerset House to find out the truth about his parentage, the birth certificate indicated that Aunt Doodie was indeed his mother, but there was only a blank where the father's name should have been written. Hume wrote her an angry letter, telling this unnatural mother what he thought of her, in no uncertain terms.

In 1939, Hume enlisted in the Royal Air Force, but he fell ill with meningitis and nearly died. After recovering, he was invalided out of the R.A.F. He realized that there was an immense market for counterfeit gin making, to supply to nightclubs and

231

6.12 A contemporary photograph of the murder flat at No. 620 Finchley Road.

bars in London which suffered from a shortage of liquor. Hume sold 'Finlinson's Old English Gin', consisting of diluted surgical spirits laced with a small amount of gin. He did odd jobs when he felt like it, swindling his customers by fitting their houses with piping made from bicycle inner tubes instead of expensive lead. When one of them expressed concerns that her pipes might be damaged by the frost, the cheeky Hume assured her that with the quality materials he supplied, this was never a risk! When he had enough money, he set up a flourishing electrician's business at No. 620 Finchley Road. At one stage, he had more than forty workmen employed. During this brief period of prosperity, Hume bought the premises next door, and himself lived in the large maisonette flat on the second and third floors, over the electrician's shop.

In 1948, Donald Hume married a respectable woman and

moved to Hay-on-Wye where he set up a factory for electric toasters. The factory soon burnt down, however, and he was once more in financial dire straits. He got involved with a Warren Street car dealer named Stanley Setty, stealing cars that the cunning motor dealer provided with log-books from wrecks from his workshop. Setty, who had been born as Suleiman Seti in Baghdad in 1903, was a wealthy scoundrel and a kingpin of London's seedy second-hand car underworld, who treated the 'spiv' Hume with contempt. A stout, foreign-looking cove, he liked to dress in flashy suits and flamboyant ties. Hume did not like Setty at all, but he realized that the wealthy car dealer was a very useful business contact. The former R.A.F. Aircraftman Hume belatedly learnt to fly an aeroplane, which he used for various smuggling operations.

Donald Hume had a large mongrel dog named Tony, of which he was very fond. One day in September 1949, Setty kicked the dog for scratching the paintwork of one of his cars. Hume made no attempt to retaliate at the time, but when Setty came to No. 620 Finchley Road some weeks later, the long-minded Hume was ready for him. He attacked the sturdy Arab with an SS dagger he had procured, murdering him after a furious fight. He disposed of Setty's car, dismembered his body, and dropped the various body parts into the English Channel from his aeroplane. On one of these expeditions, Tony the dog came along as well, to witness the dismal end of the dog-kicking Arab first hand. Hume did his best to eliminate the bloodstains in his flat, and had the carpet thoroughly cleaned and re-dyed at Burtol Cleaners at No. 618 Finchley Road next door. Setty had carried £1005 in £5 banknotes in his pocket at the time of the murder, and the cautious Hume destroyed most of these, although he could not resist making use of some as well. This was not wise, since the bank knew the serial numbers. Setty had planned to go to Watford to purchase a Jaguar motor car, and after he had disappeared, the Jaguar seller of course

6.13 The living-room of Hume's flat at No. 620 Finchley Road.

6.14 A newspaper photograph of Hume holding an SS dagger.

became a suspect. For a while, Hume was pleased that nobody suspected him, but then Setty's torso turned up on the Essex mudflats, and the Scotland Yard detectives soon realized the significance of Hume and his aeroplane.

On trial for murder at the Old Bailey, Hume admitted having disposed of Setty's body, but he claimed that three gangsters named Mac, Greeny and The Boy had employed him to do so, after this disreputable trio had murdered Setty in his flat. He had been paid £150 in £5 notes, which he had spent quickly. Hume was a reasonably clever and resourceful man, and he gave a good account of himself in court. Although a well-known 'spiv' and smuggler, he had no prior conviction for violent crime. Not knowing of the dog-kicking incident, the police could discern no motive for him to have murdered the car dealer. In the end, Hume was acquitted of murder, but sentenced to twelve years in prison for being an accessory after the fact.[26]

Emerging from Dartmoor in 1958, having served eight years of his sentence, Hume promptly sold his confession to the *Sunday Pictorial*: 'I Killed Setty!', the newspaper headlines screamed out. The *Pictorial* paid him handsomely and gave him ten days to leave the country. Hume changed his name to Donald Brown, and booked a ticket for Zürich to start a new life, with a bogus passport and £2000 he received from the paper. He got a girlfriend named Trudi, impressed her with his lies, and treated her to expensive gifts and meals in gourmet restaurants. Soon, the *Pictorial's* money was gone, and Hume decided to go back to London and rob a bank. On August 1 1958, he walked into Brentford branch of the Midland Bank, shot the cashier Frank Lewis in the stomach, and made off with £2000.

Hume decided to rob another bank, this time in Zürich. The bank he chose was the Gewerbe Bank, one he was already familiar with. Carrying a cardboard box with a gun hidden in it,

Hume entered the bank and marched straight up to one of the counters. He aimed the gun at cashier Walter Schenkel and fired, before jumping over the counter. But Schenkel was not badly wounded, and he managed to set off the alarm. Hume ran out, pursued by a crowd of Swiss vigilantes, who thought nothing of chasing a desperate, armed man. In a cul-de-sac, Hume turned around and fired at the crowd, mortally wounding the 50-year-old taxi driver Arthur Maag. Soon after, he was overpowered by vigilantes and police.[27] Hume was committed to the Regensdorf prison, where he stood trial for murder and was sentenced to life imprisonment. He was a notoriously difficult prisoner, and even became known as the 'Beast of Regensdorf' for his habit of manufacturing weapons to assault the prison warders, or other prisoners. A special strong-room cell had to be constructed for him.[28] In 1976, the Swiss authorities sent Hume back to Britain, where he was incarcerated in Broadmoor.[29] He died in 1998, aged 79.

The ground floor of No. 620 Finchley Road is today home to the 'Dixy Chicken' fast food outlet, but the upper floors look not dissimilar to old photos of the murder house from 1949. The building's sinister history with regard to knife-related violence has continued into the present time. In October 2008, some young yobs visiting the chicken bar complained about the quality of the 'Dixy Chicken' chips, and demanded a full refund. After an angry argument, one of the thugs attacked the chips vendor, stabbing him six times with a large knife. The yob was sentenced to just 12 months in prison, but in a crackdown on mindless knife violence, the Lord Chief Justice saw fit to treble this sentence.[30] None of the journalists writing about this case saw anything sinister about the words '620 Finchley Road'. Fortunately for proprietors of murder houses, the 'gentlemen of the press' forget very quickly.

THE 'MEMORY GAS' MAN OF WEMBLEY, 1953

In 1953, one of the flats at No. 20 Second Avenue, Wembley, was home to the middle-aged draughtsman Derek James and his wife Beatrice. They had married in 1947, and outwardly seemed quite content. But the 42-year-old Mrs James, a housewife with too much time on her hands, also had a younger lover, the 37-year-old ex-RAF man Raymond Harold Barker, who was working in a factory. Barker was an alcoholic who drank like the proverbial fish, and Mrs James shared this predicament to some degree. In September 1953, she left her husband and moved into Barker's lodgings for a fortnight, but then she quarrelled with him and went back to Second Avenue, where her forgiving husband allowed her back into the house. She continued her association with Barker, and often had a few drinks with him at a hotel when her husband was away.

On Monday December 15 1953, Raymond Harold Barker went on a drunken 'bender', drinking more than a gallon of beer, half a bottle of cherry brandy, and some whisky and liqueurs. With his luncheon the following day, he drank ten pints of beer, some wine, and a couple of glasses of gin and whisky. Amazingly, he was still capable of locomotion, lurching out of the pub for a few hours of rest before it was time to meet 'Betty' James for a late afternoon drinking party at No. 20 Second Avenue, while her husband was away. The jolly Raymond Harold Barker drank with his usual thirst, but Mrs Brown was in an angry temper. She disapproved of his constant drunkenness and reckless spending, and spoke of ditching him for another lover. This remark sent Barker into a furious rage, and he stabbed her with a small kitchen knife. As she ran away to get to the telephone, he stabbed her again and again, before knocking the telephone handset against her head until she lay still.

When the police came to No. 20 Second Avenue at 4.50 pm, they found Mrs James dead in the hall. She had been stabbed more than sixty times. The hue and cry was soon on for Raymond Harold Barker, whose association with Mrs James was known by some of the neighbours. He had not returned to his lodgings, nor had he gone to work. On December 17, some police constables found a drunken tramp in a bombed building. He looked very much like the suspected killer Raymond Harold Barker, and when he was searched, Mrs James' purse and wallet were found in his pockets. At the police station, he willingly confessed to murdering his beloved Betty in a drunken rage, after she had hit him and spoken of finding another man.

Raymond Harold Barker was committed for trial at the Central Criminal Court, and granted legal aid. The prospects for his defence team looked far from bright, since the use of drunkenness as an excuse for murder had not been successful in the past. But on the other hand, this was the early 1960s, when there was a great reluctance to send murderers to the gallows. Barker's defence team chose a controversial strategy to save him from the hangman's noose: the Harley Street specialist Dr Arthur Rossiter Lewis, who had some ideas of his own about the workings of the human memory, was allowed into Brixton Prison to administer a 'memory gas' of his own concoction to Barker, allowing him to recall what had happened the afternoon of the murder. After dosing the prisoner with an admixture of oxygen and carbon dioxide, Dr Rossiter Lewis concluded that Barker's mind must have been so severely deranged at the time of the murder that he could not describe these events at all. This was the first time any such approach had been used on a prisoner facing a capital charge, said Dr J.M. Matheson, the principal medical officer of Brixton Prison, adding that in his opinion, Barker had deliberately been holding back information after being dosed with the 'memory gas'.

The distinguished psychiatrist Dr Arthur Spencer Paterson also appeared as a defence expert witness, testifying that in his opinion, the prisoner suffered from something called 'mania-à-potu', namely hallucinations resulting from chronic alcoholism, and that his mind had been severely deranged at the time of the murder. Again, both Dr Matheson and the psychiatrist Dr Desmond Curran disagreed: they had found nothing to suggest that Barker had suffered from a disease of the mind at the time he committed the murder. In his summing-up, Mr Justice Cassels was severe against Dr Rossiter Lewis and his 'memory gas' experiment, adding that the jury ought to dismiss it from their minds, since it had yielded nothing. After deliberating for three hours and a half, the jury found the prisoner guilty but insane, and Mr Justice Cassels directed that he should be detained as a Broadmoor patient.[31] He may well have emerged from its walls at some later date, since a Raymond Harold Barker is recorded to have died at Westminster in 1990.

MURDER OF A DOCTOR IN SHEAVESHILL AVENUE, 1957

Johannes Pulfer, a young German doctor, watched the rise of Hitler's Third Reich with considerable anxiety, since he was of Jewish origin. Wisely, he left Germany in 1933, taking his wife Gertrude with him to London. He learnt English and obtained a license to practice as a general practitioner, from consulting rooms in his small semi-detached house at No. 98 Sheaveshill Avenue, Colindale. Dr Pulfer had a cousin named Rudi Bamberger, who had changed his name to Bamber, a more English-sounding name that by that time had not been sullied by the murderous Jeremy, of White House Farm notoriety.

Rudi Bamber lived with the Pulfers for a while, but he quarrelled with the doctor in the early 1940s, and was evicted from the house in Sheaveshill Avenue. In 1947, Rudi married the psychotherapist and human rights campaigner Helen Balmuth. They got back on good terms with the rather gloomy, isolated Dr Pulfer, and often visited his house to enjoy some good old-fashioned German food.

In 1957, Dr Pulfer still lived at the little house in Sheaveshill Avenue. In March that year, the Bambers came to visit. They were entertained by Gertrude Pulfer in the upstairs sitting-room, as the doctor saw a patient downstairs. All of a sudden, there was an outcry, and the doctor's little dog began barking furiously. Rudi Bamber ran downstairs, followed by the two women, but he wisely retreated when a foreign-looking young man came bursting out from the consulting room, foaming at the mouth and brandishing a large knife. Behind him, Bamber could see the doctor lying dead on the floor. Rudi Bamber ran out of the house, followed by the two women. The murderer pursued them, seized hold of Helen Bamber and put his knife to her throat, before releasing her and running off.

When the police and a doctor arrived at No. 98 Sheaveshill Avenue, they found Johannes Pulfer dead from a knife wound to the throat. The doctor who had saved himself from the Nazis had been murdered by a London maniac instead. The identity of the murderer was not in doubt, since the case notes dropped to the floor had the name Elias Georgiou, a 25-year-old Cypriot who was employed at the Phoenix Telephone Works nearby. He kept complaining of feeling unwell, but Dr Pulfer found nothing physically wrong with him, and he instead suspected that the Cypriot was suffering from severe psychotic delusions. The murder weapon, a formidable ten-inch stiletto, was found in a hedge not far from the murder house. The police soon arrested Georgiou, and he was identified by the Bambers as the Sheaveshill Avenue assassin. No motive for the murder was obvious, except that the Cypriot was clearly quite insane: he had interpreted one of the doctor's remarks as a suggestion that he should marry another young man, and reacted with intense fury. Since Georgiou spoke very bad English, and the doctor retained his German accent, it may well be that an unintentional *faux entendre* had triggered the murderous attack.

Georgiou was found to be insane, and incarcerated in Broadmoor.[32] Dr Pulfer's selfless service to the local community was praised in his obituary in the *Hendon & Finchley Times*. His tragic death sent a clear message to London's other GPs: it was foolhardy and unwise to see dangerous lunatics alone and unprotected, in a small suburban house. Helen Bamber, who came so very close to becoming the murderer's second victim, lived on to become a distinguished authority on human rights violations, and the founder of the Helen Bamber Foundation to support and rehabilitate their victims.

THE NAUGHTY MR PIETERSEN, 1960

On October 5 1960, the 17-year-old labourer Douglas Aves was late for work at the Wood Green building company where he was employed, and he was sacked, on the spot. When he was walking home, presumably in a gloomy frame of mind, he was approached by a swarthy, middle-aged man he had bet before. This individual, who called himself Cecil and worked on the buses, said that he knew a decorator who lived in the flat below his own at No. 257 Green Lanes, Palmers Green, and that this neighbour needed a labourer. Douglas Aves accompanied Cecil to his tiny second-floor flat in the converted house, but it turned out that the decorator was not at home. Instead, Cecil made Douglas a cup of tea, and showed him some framed foreign banknotes on the wall. Then, all of a sudden, he instead showed him some very obscene postcards, grabbed hold of his arm, and said 'I like you!'

Douglas Aves, a strong and sturdy young man, replied with a powerful blow in the face, which sent his opponent sprawling, and then another blow to the head with a milk bottle. Cecil started screaming for assistance, and Douglas Aves rapidly made himself scarce. There was a dental practice on the ground floor of the house, and the nurse saw Douglas come running downstairs, saying that there was a 'queer' in the top room, and that the white-coated nurse ought to attend to him. But since the nurse was needed at the dental practice, it was in fact the first floor neighbour who found the semi-comatose Cecil later in the afternoon. He expired from his head injuries soon after.

Since Douglas Aves had been spotted both by the nurse and by a lavatory attendant who saw him bandage his hand, which had been injured when he knocked his opponent down, he was soon arrested. Douglas Aves made a full confession of what had happened at No. 257 Green Lanes, and the police found that his story was corroborated by both technical and fingerprint evidence. They also knew that the 45-year-old bus conductor Cecil William Pietersen, a native of South Africa, was a well-known street pest who liked to approach young men with indecent proposals, although this of course did not exonerate any person who decided to put an end to his existence. On trial at the Old Bailey, Douglas Aves was found Not Guilty of murder but Guilty of manslaughter, and he was sentenced to twelve months in prison.[33]

THE POISONER OF NORTH CIRCULAR ROAD, 1962

Graham Frederick Young was born in 1947, the son of the Neasden labouring man Fred Young and his wife Margaret. She died from tuberculosis when Graham was just three months old, and the boy was taken care of by his aunt and uncle. When Graham was three years old, his father remarried, and took his son back. Graham Young grew up at No. 768 North Circular Road, Neasden, with his father Fred, stepmother Molly and elder sister Winifred. This humble little terraced house faces the Neasden Recreation Ground, but between the house and the park are six lanes of busy traffic; a less attractive position for a house is difficult to imagine. Graham was a thoroughly nasty little boy, who kicked old ladies shopping bags over, was cruel to animals, and enjoyed various cowardly pranks. He was disrespectful to his stepmother, and although his father tried various stratagems to discipline him, they did not have the desired result.

Although an indifferent performer at school, Graham Young was both intelligent and precocious. He read books about Hitler and the Third Reich, and became a self-proclaimed Nazi and anti-Semite. Another, equally sinister interest of this strange teenager was medicine and pharmacology: he read textbooks on toxicology, and took great interest in the action of various poisons. He set up a small laboratory at No. 768, and found no difficulty in securing considerable amounts of various dangerous poisons from gullible chemists. He impressed them with his scientific knowledge, saying that he needed chemicals for his experiments, and signing the register with a false name. When a number of cats died in the neighbourhood, Graham was accused of poisoning them.

Already in his early teens, Graham began making experiments on human beings. When another schoolboy knocked him down in the playground, Graham threatened to murder him. Not long after, the other boy was struck down by severe vomiting; he would probably have died had he not been taken into hospital. Graham did not like his stepmother, so he dosed her with increasing amounts of antimony. For more than a year, she continually complained of malaise, stomach pain and back ache. Fred Young had several similar attacks, which often occurred after he had tried to discipline his thirteen-year-old son. Winifred suffered a fainting-fit and was taken to the Middlesex Hospital, where a doctor diagnosed her with belladonna poisoning. Graham was scolded for his carelessness with his chemicals, but unbeknownst to his family, he had now built up a small pharmacy of dangerous poisons, including arsenic, antimony and thallium.

In April 1962, Graham murdered his stepmother by giving her a hefty dose of thallium. When Fred Young returned home from work, he saw his son stand gloating at the rear window, watching Molly Young writhing in agony in the rear garden. The poison was not detected at the time, and her death was thought to be from natural causes. Graham then set about to murder his father with antimony. Fortunately for the stalwart Fred Young, he was taken into hospital after suffering debilitating attacks of vomiting and stomach pains, and competent doctors made the correct diagnosis: he was being systematically poisoned. This time, suspicion fell on the sinister Graham, and he was taken into custody and his stockpile of poisons confiscated. A psychiatrist considered him a malevolent young psychopath, who showed no regret whatsoever for his murderous actions. In July 1962, he was committed to Broadmoor for an indefinite period of time.[34]

And here the story should have ended. At Broadmoor, the sinister Graham amused himself by various pranks, like putting Harpic in the nurses' drinks, or topping up their coffee with carbon monoxide from a gas-stove lighter. After another lunatic had died, from cyanide poisoning, Graham was suspected of having picked laurel leaves in the hospital grounds, and extracted the poison from them, to conduct yet another of his lethal 'experiments'. But as the years went by, the North Circular Road poisoner made up his mind to get out of Broadmoor. For several years, he tried to be on his best behaviour, to impress the psychiatrist Dr Unwin that he had 'recovered'. Although his detention had been subject to a restriction meaning that subsequent discharge would have to be approved by the Home Secretary, and although the Hospital Order initially stipulated that he should be detained for at least 15 years, Graham was released after just nine years. This was a decision that Dr Unwin, who had been the prime mover in this attempt to rehabilitate the Poisoner of North Circular Road, would one day bitterly regret.

After his release from hospital in 1971, Graham Young began work as a stock-keeper at John Hadland Laboratories in Bovingdon, Hertfordshire. Through gross malpractice from the Broadmoor authorities, his employers were not informed of his past as a convicted poisoner. Soon after Graham started work at Bovingdon, his foreman Bob Egle fell ill and died unexpectedly. The former Broadmoor inmate had been making tea laced with poisons for his colleagues. A sickness swept through his workplace and, mistaken for a virus, was nicknamed the 'Bovingdon Bug'. A few months after Egle's death, another of Young's workmates, Fred Biggs, was admitted to London National Hospital for Nervous Diseases. After suffering agony for several weeks, he became Young's third and final victim.

Graham Young took a vigorous interest in the havoc caused by the Bovingdon Bug. Boasting of his knowledge of chemicals and poisons, he asked the company doctor if the investigators had considered thallium poisoning. When he told a colleague about his collection of poisons and noxious chemicals, this individual became suspicious and called in the police, who uncovered Young's criminal record. Young was arrested on 21 November 1971. Police found a stockpile of antimony, thallium and aconitine in his flat. They also discovered a detailed diary that Young had kept, noting the doses he had administered, their effects, and whether he was going to allow each victim to live or die.

On trial for murder at St Albans Crown Court, Young was convicted and sentenced to life imprisonment.[35] While in prison, he befriended Ian Brady, with whom he shared a fascination with Nazi Germany, and the armed robber Roy 'Pretty Boy' Shaw. Young died in his cell at Parkhurst Prison in 1990, aged just 42.[36] His death was ascribed to a myocardial infarction, but there have been persistent rumours that he had poisoned himself, or alternatively that he had been murdered by fellow inmates, or by the prison officers.

CHAPTER 7

EAST LONDON

So the Clerk and the Wife, they each took a knife,
And the nippers that nipp'd the loaf-sugar for tea;
With the edges and points they sever'd the joints
At the clavicle, elbow, hip, ankle, and knee.
Thus, limb from limb, they dismember'd him
So entirely, that e'en when they came to his wrists,
With those great sugar nippers they nipp'd off his 'flippers,'
As the Clerk, very flippantly, term'd his fists.
     Richard Harris Barham, The Lay of St
   Gengulphus (from the Ingoldsby Legends)

This chapter will deal with all East London suburbs north of the river, including Leyton, Leytonstone, West and East Ham, Plaistow, Stratford, Canning Town, Barking and Ilford. This has been an area rich in murder ever since these suburbs were constructed in late Victorian times. Perhaps the epicentre of East London murder was Charlie Brown's Tavern, also known as the Railway Tavern, Limehouse. It was situated by the railway bridge on the corner of Garford Street. Charlie Brown, a famous East End character, kept this large and rowdy pub from 1893 until 1932. Charlie was a great collector of curiosities, and he had his own private museum on the premises, with items donated by

THE ONE & ONLY ONE *Charlie Brown*

SOME OF CHARLIE BROWN'S WORLDS TREASURES

7.1 Charlie Brown's Tavern, from an old postcard.

7.2 Charlie Brown's collection.

sailors from all over the world. Already in Victorian times, the Railway Tavern had a fearsome reputation. In 1891, John Alexander Lewis murdered Emily Adams at the Railway Tavern, and seven years later, Charles Truett murdered his sister-in-law Augusta on the premises. In 1944, the American sailor Mathew Smith stabbed another sailor to death on the premises. It is sad but true that London's only triple murder pub was pulled down in the 1980s, for the construction of the Docklands Light Railway.[1]

Decay, wartime damage, and development have meant that Charlie Brown's Tavern is not the only East London murder house to have disappeared. No. 10 Alexandra Street, Plaistow, where William Burrett murdered his wife Ada in 1900, no longer stands. Nor does No. 23 Venour Road, Bow, where the extraordinarily monickered Samson Silas Salmon murdered his cousin Lucy Smith later the same year, nor No. 11 Park Grove Road, Leytonstone, where William Hoffman murdered young

7.3 Another notorious East End address, the burnt-out house at No. 100 Sidney Street, where two armed burglars and murderers died after the 'Siege of Sidney Street' in 1911.

Helen Walden in 1904. No. 10 Biggerstaff Road, Stratford, where George Newton murdered Ada Roker in 1911, no longer frowns upon the passer-by.[2]

In 1897, the drunken docker William John Cronin got into an altercation with Henry Cuthbert, whom he suspected of being a 'blackleg' in the Great Dock Strike. He shouted some abuse to Henry Cuthbert about the strike, and shoved his wife Eliza to the ground when she tried to intervene. Cronin then barged into Cuthbert's house at No. 16 Carr Street, Limehouse, entered the kitchen, picked up a shovel, and struck 10-month-old baby Eliza hard on the head as she lay sleeping in her cot. On trial for murder at the Old Bailey, Cronin was well defended, and he got off with seven years in prison for manslaughter. In 1925, William John Cronin was still at large: he worked in the Docks, and lodged at No. 126 Old Church Street, Stepney, with his equally middle-aged lady friend Alice Garratt. They were both fond of drinking beer and gin, and after they had enjoyed a few, sound of revelling would alternate with angry quarrels emanating from No. 126. But one day, one of these quarrels ended in blows, and Cronin cut his paramour's throat with great violence. The murderer tried to escape, but was tackled by a neighbour, arrested, tried and executed. Neither No. 16 Carr Street nor No. 126 Old Church Street remains today.[3]

Plaistow's House of Horrors at No. 35 Cave Road, where the 13-year-old Robert Coombes murdered his mother in 1895, and left her body to decompose in the bedroom as he went out to amuse himself with his younger brother, no longer frowns upon the passer-by. Ilford's has also lost its most notorious murder house, the Little Shop of Horrors at No. 23 Cranbrook Road, where the demented chemist Harris Cocker poisoned his wife

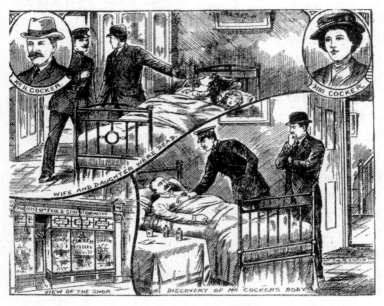

7.4 Incidents from the Ilford mass murder, and a view of the shop of horrors at No. 23 Cranbrook Road, from the Illustrated Police News, August 8 1918.

and four children in 1918. He stored the corpses in a second-floor bedroom and kept the chemist's shop open for business as usual for several days, telling his assistant that his family had gone on a holiday. But since it was July and the weather was very hot, putrefaction set in very rapidly. Driven to distraction by the terrible smell emanating from the bedroom, Cocker committed suicide inside his Shop of Horrors. But still, this shop, and the maisonette flat above it, stood for decades to come, until it was an unlamented victim of the expansion of Ilford Station in the 1980s.[4]

Some famous modern East End murder houses have also perished, notably No. 11 King Edward Road, Barking, where Walter John Cross murdered the crippled watchmaker Percy Busby in 1947. No. 429 Longbridge Road, Barking, where the wealthy businessman Joseph Hayes was gunned down by the robber Ronald Cooper in 1964, has been demolished, along with many other suburban villas, for the construction of a large housing estate. Cooper went on the run for many months, but was hunted down, tried and sentenced to life imprisonment for murder.[5]

But still, East London has many treasures to offer the murder house detective. Read about the Upton Park Tragedy of 1888, ponder the mysterious murder of little Amelia Jeffs in West Ham, and marvel at the meanness of the Leytonstone Baby-farmers and the cruelty of the quadruple murderer of Stukeley Road, who wiped out an entire family in 1919.

THE UPTON PARK TRAGEDY, 1888

Emma Elizabeth Aston was employed at Mr Evans's mantle warehouse at Old Change Buildings in the East End. She avoided the company of wicked men, worked hard and advanced to become a forewoman. But her good looks attracted the attention of the Lothario of the mantle warehouse, the foreman Jack Morris. In 1882, Emma found herself pregnant, and left her situation at the warehouse. After her child had died very young, she got her old job back. Jack Morris was a married man with a family of his own, but he kept making vague promises of marrying Emma, or at least taking good care of her and her future children. In 1886, Emma again became pregnant, and once more left the warehouse; Jack set her up in lodgings at No. 2 The Limes, Gipsy Lane. Here, she gave birth to two sons: Bertie in 1886 and Frank in 1887.

In 1887, Emma Aston was 38 years old, and no longer the good-looking young wench who had once attracted the lustful eye of wicked Jack Morris. He made sure he got a younger and more attractive mistress, and set her up in a comfortable hotel. This cost money, but Jack economized by reducing Emma's weekly allowance. In June 1887, she had to move to cheaper lodgings in a small terraced house at No. 36 Whitfield Street, Upton Park. She called herself Mrs Styles, her mother's maiden name, and pretended that her husband was a commercial traveller who was nearly always away from home. She lived with Bertie and Frank in a bedroom, a kitchen and a scullery, for three shillings and ninepence per week.

The landlady of No. 36 Whitfield Street found 'Mrs Styles' a woman of superior upbringing, and very fond of her two little sons. She suffered much from neuralgia and backache, and found it difficult to work, apart from looking after her children and doing a little needlework. Miss Alice Jones, the landlady's daughter, who had befriended 'Mrs Styles', noticed that she seemed very sad and careworn, and that the letters from her 'husband' came very irregularly. Three of these brief and pathetic missives, with the original stamped envelopes intact, are kept in the police file on the case. In early 1888, the letters ceased to come altogether, meaning that she was quickly becoming entirely destitute. She was three weeks in arrears with the rent, and owed money for a baker's bill, and for a doctor's bill for the children. She wrote to Jack three times, but he did not reply. Alice Jones did what she could to help her friend, giving her an occasional meal, and making sure the children had some milk to drink, but she noticed that 'Mrs Styles' was becoming quite desperate from her distressed situation in life.

Early in the morning of February 20 1888, Alice Jones found 'Mrs Styles' sitting on the kitchen sofa. She exclaimed that she had just killed her two dear little children. And indeed, when Alice Jones and the lodger Nathaniel Boocock went into her bedroom, they found both children lying dead on the bed. 'Mrs Styles' told them that she was not married, and that her real name was Emma Aston. She had thought of going to the man who had supported her, but she knew that he would give her nothing. In desperation, she had then murdered both the children. She had tried to cut Frank's throat, but the knife was very blunt, so she had suffocated him instead. Bertie had taken a long time to kill, since he had struggled terribly when she suffocated him with the bedclothes. Emma Aston then thought of taking her own life, but something made her desists, since it was 'wrong'.

A police constable came to No. 36 Whitfield Street to take Emma Aston into custody. When she was questioned by Inspector Eady at the Ilford police station, she seemed perfectly rational and coherent, describing how Jack Morris had ceased to support her and the children, and how she had been rendered desperate by want and shame. Two doctors examined the children's bodies, finding clear evidence that they had both been murdered. The Upton Park Tragedy attracted a good deal of newspaper publicity, and poor Emma Aston, who had lacked friends and protectors when rendered destitute, now had a dozen journalists pitying her, and naming and shaming Jack Morris for his heartless conduct.

He was said to be sought for by the police, but they had not been able to track him down. He had a salary of nearly £300 a year, so a few shillings to support the mother of his children would hardly have made much impact on his financial situation.

When she was on trial for murder at the Old Bailey on March 19 1888, before Mr Justice Hawkins, there was no doubt that Emma Aston had murdered her children. The Holloway prison doctor had kept her under observation for four weeks, as she was awaiting trial, and he could testify that during her time in the prison infirmary, she had been perfectly sane. Still, he and another medical witness agreed that she might well have suffered from 'moral insanity' or an 'uncontrollable impulse' while committing the deed. Emma Aston was found guilty of murder, but not responsible for her actions at the time she committed the act, and she was committed to Broadmoor. She was discharged from there in 1897, but re-admitted two years later.[6] The last we hear from Jack Morris is that he had absconded from the Metropolis, taking with him his young mistress, but leaving his wife and family behind.

THE ROOM WITH THE SINISTER CUPBOARD, 1890

Charles Jeffs, a native of Gloucestershire, moved to East London as a young man and became a machinist at the London & Tilbury Railway Works. The 1881 Census has him living at No. 75 West Road, West Ham, with his wife Mary Annie and his six-year-old daughter Amelia. By 1890, Charles Jeffs had moved down the road to another neat little terraced house at No. 38 West Road; Amelia, or Millie as she was called, was now fifteen years old. Although very pretty, with blue eyes and fair hair, Millie was a shy, timid girl. She had left school a year earlier, and had two situations as housemaid or nursemaid. Millie was now staying at home, where she could be depended on to look after her two younger siblings, and to perform various household chores. At half past six in the evening of Friday January 31 1890, Mrs Jeffs sent Millie out to buy threepence worth of fried fish at a shop in Church Street nearby. The neatly dressed teenage girl, why was well known locally, took a basket and obediently walked off. The girl Elizabeth Harmer saw her in West Street and spoke to her: Millie said that she was going on an errand to buy some fish up by the West Ham Church. A schoolboy saw her going on her way, walking slower than she usually did, and appearing to be rather preoccupied with something. But Millie Jeffs never arrived at the fish-shop, nor did she return home.

When Millie did not come home, Mr Jeffs went to the fish-shop to ask for her, and after learning that she had not made it there, or returned home, he went straight to the police station. A description of the missing girl was circulated to all stations of the Metropolitan Police, and the local West Ham constables made every exertion to find her, but to no avail. Millie's distraught parents also searched for her, and the district was in quite an uproar, since several other local girls had disappeared without trace in the preceding years. Canon Scott, the influential vicar of West Ham, assured the police that the timid Millie, who had until recently attended the day school he himself supervised, could not have disappeared by her own free will. Foul play must be suspected, and they should make every exertion to search all empty houses, and all other places where a body might be hidden. On February 10, the popular clergyman wrote to the *Times* to issue an appeal to find the missing girl.

In 1890, West Ham was expanding rapidly, and terraces of houses were being constructed in what had once been rural fields

7.5 *Incidents from the murder of Amelia Jeffs, from the* Illustrated Police News, *February 22 1890.*

and pastures. One of these building operations had been ongoing in the newly constructed Portway, facing the West Ham Park. A terrace of ten three-story houses had been constructed about a year earlier, but only one of them had been sold; the others were dirty and unfurnished. On February 14, when a party of police wanted to look through the Portway houses, as part of the search for Millie Jeffs, they found that some of the houses had their front doors open, but others were securely locked. Samuel Roberts, an old man who served as caretaker to the builder of the houses, was able to let Sergeant Forth and Constable Cross into most of the houses, but he claimed to have lost the key to No. 126, and said he could not let them go in there. But since the policemen had strict orders from Inspector Thomson to search *all* the houses, they went round to the back and let themselves into No. 126 through an unlocked window. They felt a noxious smell, and saw that the dust on the floor had been disturbed. Sergeant Forth found a penny, and a small brooch, on the landing, and as he walked upstairs, the smell became stronger and more disagreeable.

7.6 *A portrait of Amelia Jeffs, from the*
Illustrated Police News, *February*
22 1890.

AMELIA JEFFS.
THE WEST HAM VICTIM.

His olfactory sense led him to a cupboard inside a small front bedroom on the second floor, and in there he found the semi-putrid body of Millie Jeffs.[7]

Police reinforcements, and a competent doctor, were soon on their way to No. 126 Portway. Poor Amelia had been brutally raped, before being strangled with a scarf. Since her footprints could be seen in the dust on the floor, she had clearly been dragged or cajoled into the house, and murdered in there. The terrace of houses faced the Portway, but behind them was a field of waste ground awaiting development. Any person could have negotiated the low fence to the small back garden of No. 126, and entered the house through an unsecured ground floor window. After some lead had been stolen from one of the empty houses, old Samuel Roberts had been employed as a watchman to deter thieves and mischievous youngsters out to break some windows. Roberts had keys to all the houses except No. 126, and he could not explain how he had lost them. After the 'West Ham Atrocity' had been described in the press, two witnesses came forward to the police. One of them had seen a man lead an unwilling girl towards the terrace of empty houses in the Portway, but had not taken any action since he presumed it was a father disciplining his

The cupboard in which the body was found.

Amelia Sarah Jeffs.

7.7 *Another portrait of the Portway murder victim.*

daughter. Another individual had seen a man carry a large bag towards the Portway houses; had it contained the body of Millie Jeffs?[8]

On February 17 1890, Mr C.C. Lewis, the South Essex coroner, opened the inquest on Amelia Jeffs at the King's Head tavern in West Ham Lane. Charles Albert Jeffs, the first witness, described how his daughter had disappeared. She had carried a basket, a latchkey, and threepence for the fish. She had often been to this shop in the past. Millie had always been a very good girl, and she had never demonstrated any precocious interest in the opposite sex. Mr Joseph Roberts, the builder who had erected the terrace of houses in the Portway, and lived just a few doors away, did not deny that Mr Jeffs had approached him about a week earlier, asking permission to search the terrace of empty houses. Mr Roberts had helped him to have a look around, although there had been difficulties in finding the relevant keys. He could not explain why the key to No. 126 was lost, except that his elderly father Samuel 'whose memory is very frail' might have left it in another lock by mistake. Joseph Roberts felt certain that Millie

SCENES OF WEST HAM MURDER.

7.8 Useful sketches of the locality of the West Ham murder, from the Penny Illustrated Paper, *February 22 1890.*

Jeffs had been abducted and held hostage elsewhere for some days, however, before she was murdered and put in the cupboard at No. 126, since his son had made a remarkable discovery the day before the murder. James R. Roberts, described as an active, bright-looking fourteen-year-old lad, said that he had made a habit of collecting 'marbles' from empty ginger beer bottles. The carpenters working in the terrace of houses in the Portway used to leave plenty of bottles behind, so he searched these houses at regular intervals. The day before Minnie Jeffs had been found at No. 126, he had made a thorough search of this house, including the cupboard in the second floor front bedroom. It had been empty.

The police surgeon Dr Grogono declared that Millie Jeffs had

Spoken to by a neighbour's child.

7.9 Amelia Jeffs speaks to the other girl in the street, from the Illustrated Police Budget.

He called up the other officer.

7.10 The body of Amelia Jeffs is found, from the Illustrated Police Budget.

been murdered by strangulation. She was likely to have been *virgo intacta* before she was raped. A woolen scarf was tied round her throat, and the deep constriction round her throat contained particles of wool from this scarf. There was considerable signs of putrefaction, and "her appearance was consistent with death having taken place on January 31". Thus the medical evidence spoke in favour of Millie Jeffs being violated and murdered soon after she was abducted, and invalidated Mr Roberts' hypothesis that she had been held captive for a considerable period of time. The police detectives also suspected that the boy James Roberts had been 'telling porkies', since no carpenters had been at work in the terrace of houses for some period of time, and since it would hardly have been possible to have searched the houses for bottles on a dark February evening, without striking a match or using a candle.[9]

The London newspapers reported every detail about the murder of Amelia Jeffs, and the outcome of the adjourned inquest. Mr Frederick Smith, the Mayor of West Ham, offered a £100 reward for the apprehension of the murderer, and two other collections were ongoing among the East London burghers. An anonymous well-wisher had paid all costs for an impressive funeral service for Amelia Jeffs, which was held at West Ham Church on February 19. Canon Scott expressed grief and shame at the circumstances of the blameless Amelia's untimely and shocking death, and prayed that God would bring the elusive murderer to earthly justice. A large crowd had assembled, many of them carrying wreaths; they accompanied the funeral procession to the East London Cemetery in Plaistow, where a freehold plot had been purchased, to enable a monument to be raised. It is sad but true, however, that no gravestone or monument marks the place of the grave of the murdered girl today, however.

Both Mr Lewis the coroner and Mr Foden the foreman of the jury fully shared the police suspicions against the Roberts family, and they faced much more hostile reception when the inquest was resumed on March 3. First, Mr Jeffs was asked whether Amelia had known any person connected with the row of houses in the Portway; he said that she had more than once spoken of 'Daddy

The evidence as to the keys.

7.11 *The coroner's inquest, from the* Illustrated Police Budget.

7.12 *Suspects at the coroner's inquest on Amelia Jeffs, from the* Illustrated Police News *March 1 1890.*

Watchman', as the other children called Samuel Roberts. This individual was the next witness. He said that he lodged with his son James at No. 78 Evesham Road, and worked as caretaker and odd jobs man for his other son Joseph. He denied ever having met Amelia Jeffs, and she had never called him 'Daddy Watchman', as the other children were in the habit of doing. He made a number of confused statements about the missing set of keys to No. 126.

Joseph Roberts testified that although all the Portway houses had been completed, they still needed some attention from the plumber and painter to be fully inhabitable. There had once been two sets of keys for each house, kept in a small cupboard, but one of the sets for No. 126 had been missing for five or six months. The day Amelia Jeffs had disappeared, Joseph Roberts had come home from work at a quarter to six, and not gone out again, he said. The builder then faced a barrage of hostile questions from the jurors, many of which he parried using his father's indifferent powers of memory as an excuse. Mr Lewis said that since Amelia's boots had not been dirty, she could hardly have walked through the mud in the rear garden; had the murderer let her into the house through the front door, using the missing keys to open it? When the adjourned inquest was resumed a week later, the Roberts family again received a proper grilling, which they withstood without any obvious lies or contradictions. In his summing-up, Mr Lewis said that although young James Roberts' story must be false, he believed that this was due to the lad mistaking the days, rather than lying. There was no further evidence to be added, and the jury returned a verdict of murder against some person or persons unknown.[10]

In early May 1890, the murder house at No. 126 Portway was taken for three years by Mr Bitten and Mr Hewitt, two officers of the Essex County Council, although their wives and servants were reluctant to move into this house of horrors. And sure enough, one of the domestics was terrified when she heard ghostly footsteps in the landing just a few days later! Mr Bitten and Mr Hewitt, who did not believe in ghosts, decided to search the house. When they opened a trapdoor leading to the attic, and entered the roof void where the cistern was kept, they saw that some bricks had been disturbed in the dividing wall to No. 125, leaving a small aperture. Here, the two men found two keys with

7.13 Did the Portway killer return to replace the keys? From the Illustrated Police News, *May 24 1890.*

a cardboard label saying '126'! Had the 'ghostly footsteps' been those of the murderer, or an accomplice, entering the house to replace the missing keys? When interviewed by a journalist, Joseph Roberts pooh-poohed these concerns: it must have been the house painter Mr Warren who had left them up there.[11] Nor did the police show any particular interest in this singular discovery, not understanding why the murderer would want to enter a fully inhabited house at night, to put some keys in the attic.

The police file on the Amelia Jeffs case should have been at the National Archives, but I find nothing to suggest that it has ever been there. It might have been lost or mislaid, or stolen by some detective who wanted to keep studying this mysterious murder. In his memoirs, Sir Melville Macnaghten briefly discussed the Jeffs case, with the same obtuseness and carelessness evident in his Memorandum on Jack the Ripper. None of the houses in the Portway terrace was fit for habitation, he pontificated [one was inhabited, and the others ready to be sold], and it was a workman who had found the body, completely by chance [it was the police, as the result of a search]. Macnaghten claims to have been at the scene himself to see the murdered girl: "The body looked as if it had been 'laid out' by loving hands, as for decent burial, the little hands were crossed on the bosom, the frock carefully pulled down, and the hat, which must have fallen off in the house, placed *by*, but not *on*, the head." This is a decidedly strange description of the semi-putrid remains of a raped and murdered young girl. Macnaghten had also seen the marks of Amelia's heels in the dust on the floor, and he presumed that the murderer had decoyed her into the house, the door of which had been left open by accident. He concludes with claiming that there had been "very grave suspicions attached to a certain individual. Legal proofs were wanting, and, there being no sufficient evidence to justify an arrest, it must be classified as an 'undiscovered' crime." The Report of the Commission of Metropolitan Police for 1890 states that the only capital crime left unaccounted for in 1890 was the murder of Amelia Jeffs, since "the evidence against the author of the crime was deemed insufficient to justify his arrest. In respect to this case it is only right to add popular suspicion did grave injustice to an innocent person."[12]

And here the matter might well have ended. The police investigation of the murder of Amelia Jeffs made no further headway, and although a drunk named William Turner gave himself up for the murder in September 1890, he was found to be suffering from the DTs and hallucinosis. But as several commentators have pointed out that in the 1880s, there had been a series of other mysterious crimes, some of them against young girls, in the West Ham area. In April 1881, 14-year-old Mary Seward left her family home at No. 98 West Road, never to be seen again. In January 1882, 12-year-old Eliza Carter disappeared from her married sister's house at No. 70 West Road. Her dress was found in West Ham Park, with all buttons torn off, and there was suspicion she had been raped and murdered. There were many other alleged disappearances of girls, boys and adults, and the legend of the West Ham Vanishings, sometimes stated to involve ten or more people, and to have involved supernatural forces, had begun.[13] Charles Wagner, the son of a well-to-do pork butcher carrying on business at No. 104 Victoria Dock Road, Canning Town, disappeared in April 1882 after being sent to the bank to deposit £150 of his father's money. It turned out that young Wagner had been lured away to Ramsgate by the journeyman butcher James Walter. After Charles Wagner's dead body had been found underneath East Cliff, Walter stood trial for murdering him and stealing the money, but he was found guilty only of the theft, and was sentenced to seven years in prison. It is notable that although many alleged East London disappearances were reported from 1882 until 1884, there were none in the six following years, until Amelia Jeffs was abducted in January 1890. It is also notable that at this time, Mary Seward and Eliza Carter were the only 'official' missing girls; the other alleged 'vanishings' would appear to have been either spurious or eventually resolved.

According to Elliott O'Donnell and other early chroniclers of the West Ham Vanishings, these mysterious disappearances ended with the murder of Amelia Jeffs in 1890. It is not generally known that the eastern and north-eastern suburbs of London were the site of a number of unsolved crimes during the 1890s, all of them with young girls as the victims. In August 1892, the 23-year-old Walthamstow labourer George Herbert Bush confessed murdering Amelia Jeffs, by chloroforming her. He was a known petty criminal, who had also spent lengthy periods in various asylums. Since there was nothing to suggest that chloroform had been administered to Amelia Jeffs, and since the police believed that Bush had been in prison at the time of the murder, he was not taken seriously. In December 1892, the 10-year-old Annie West was found dead in a ditch in Walthamstow. The same evening, George Herbert Bush had returned to his lodgings in a soaking wet condition, allegedly from falling into a ditch. He had been discharged from Brentwood Lunatic Asylum just a few days earlier. Bush later admitted murdering Annie West, and he was taken into police custody once more. The autopsy showed no signs of rape or violence, and Annie West had not drowned in the ditch, since her lungs contained no water. Bush's confession was not believed, and he was once more set at large.[14] In July 1893, 11-year-old Eliza Skinner was assaulted and raped in Walthamstow.[15] In December 1898, five-year-old Mary Jane Voller was found murdered in a ditch in Barking, and just a few months later, five-year-old Bertha Russ was found murdered inside a cupboard in an empty house in Lawrence Avenue, Little Ilford.[16]

The murder of Amelia Jeffs is very likely to have been committed by a pervert with a liking for young girls. He showed impressive coolness and clearly had good local knowledge. And is it not rather peculiar that three adolescent girls disappeared from the same street, West Road, in 1881, 1882 and 1890? And then we have a report of two not dissimilar crimes in Walthamstow in 1892 and 1893; is it just a coincidence that the man confessing to one of them had previously given himself up for murdering Amelia Jeffs? And finally, we have the matter of two more unsolved murders of young girls, in 1898 and 1899; is it not rather queer that one of them was also found inside a cupboard in an empty, recently constructed house? To be sure, it would have been interesting to know the name of the builder of the Lawrence

Avenue murder house, which was still unnumbered at the time of the murder.

As for suspects, one of them is the man James Walters, who was lucky to get off the charge of murdering Charles Wagner in 1882; after spending seven years in prison, he would be emerging from his cell in 1889. This would explain the hiatus between the two abductions in 1881 and 1882, and the murder of Amelia Jeffs in 1890. But Walters does not appear to have been a pervert, rather a mercenary robber who took advantage of his young victim's trust. Then we have the weirdo George Herbert Bush, who actually admitted murdering Amelia Jeffs, but he seems to have been just plain crazy, whereas the true murderer was a cool, calculating man. At the coroner's inquest, Joseph Roberts emerged as the leading suspect, perhaps along with his father Samuel, whose memory failure seemed to happen only at convenient times. In particular, the false testimony provided by the lad James provides food for thought: had his father told him to lie, in order to confound the police and coroner? And might the length of the series of crimes perhaps be explained by the existence of two perverted serial killers of young girls, from the same family?

As for the murder house at No. 126 Portway, the ghost-hunter Elliott O'Donnell wrote that since Portway's House with the Sinister Cupboard had not only witnessed one of the grimmest and most mysterious murders upon record, but it was also haunted by all kinds of superphysical horrors. To disguise its identity, the Portway houses were renumbered, O'Donnell claimed.[17] But there is no contemporary account of No. 126 Portway being haunted, after the episode of the rediscovered keys in May 1890, nor is there any reason to believe that the houses were ever renumbered. The terrace of ten three-story houses is still there today, between Caistor Park Road and Geere Road, and No. 126 looks outwardly virtually unchanged since the time of the murder back in 1890.

CHILD MURDER IN BORTHWICK ROAD, 1892

Mr Thomas Bonner Dixon was a respectable clerk, working at Messrs Roll, tea merchants, of White's Grounds, Borough, and living at No. 14 Borthwick Road, Leytonstone, with his wife Louisa and little daughter Marie. Although he was just 30 years old, his health was far from good, and he was tormented by recurrent ear infections and abscesses.

On the morning of May 4 1892, Thomas Bonner Dixon left home early to catch the 7.15 train, but he returned home at nine in the morning, looking very glum, and complaining that his ear was discharging pus again. Since he had not eaten any breakfast, Louisa cooked him an egg and some toast, but he did not want to eat it. Instead, he asked for a steak, and his dutiful wife went out to purchase one. When she left the house, she could see her husband sitting at the breakfast table, holding baby Marie on his lap.

When Louisa Dixon returned to No. 14 Borthwick Road twenty minutes later, nobody answered her knock, so a neighbour helped her to open a window using a large knife. In the bedroom, she found her husband and baby dead in the blood-soaked bed. He had cut both their throats with a razor.

At the coroner's inquest, it was divulged that the day before the tragedy, Thomas Bonner Dixon had been dismissed from his job. Louisa Dixon testified as to her husband's disagreeable ear disease. In recent weeks, he had seemed distracted and odd, but there had been nothing to suggest that he was losing his mind. In a letter he had left behind, Dixon said goodbye to his dear wife, and asked that his son should not be told about his disgraceful end. The letter provided no explanation why this exemplary family man had murdered his innocent little daughter, who had been just one year and ten months old when he put an end to her existence.[18]

SENSATIONAL LOVE TRAGEDY IN LEYTON, 1906

Mr Walter Harry Sudul worked as a clerk at the Royal Gunpowder Factory in Waltham New Town and lived at Station Road, Waltham Cross, with his wife Edith and his little daughter. In 1904, when he was just 26 years old, he was already something of a pillar of the local community. A strict teetotaller and a young man of impressive integrity, he was secretary of Newham Sports, and treasurer of the Gunpowder Factory's Christmas Club. An enthusiastic footballer himself, he was also secretary of Waltham Glendale FC. Although no stranger to sorrow in his private life – his father had been found drowned, and his first-born child had also died untimely – Mr Sudul was viewed as a jolly good fellow, and as a 'coming man' of great expectations.

And indeed, all would have been well with Walter Harry Sudul and his career, had he adhered to the convention of monogamy. But when out partying with the football club in late 1904, he met the young barmaid Henrietta Howard, who worked at the Abercorn Rooms of the Great Eastern Hotel. He fell in love with her and set her up as his mistress in a newly built house at No. 7 Moyers Road, Leyton, which she shared with her elderly step-parents. Two years went by, and although Mrs Sudul was hardly the most perceptive of women, she was beginning to realize that there must be a rival for her husband's affections. She tried to spy on him, but the canny Sudul had kept the identity of his paramour well hidden. There were some angry scenes in the Sudul household, during which the amorous gunpowder clerk once threatened to destroy himself.

In the meantime, young Henrietta Howard, who had kept her job as a barmaid, was beginning to tire of Walter Sudul. She told a friend that he had once asked her to marry him, but knowing

THE LAST KISS

*7.14 Sudul guns down his sweetheart, and a drawing of the murder house,
from the* Illustrated Police News, *December 29 1906.*

that he already had a wife, she had not taken him seriously. On
December 21 1906, Walter Sudul had supper with Henrietta and
her step-parents at No. 7 Moyers Road. Her stepfather Mr
Crooks, who was not the shrewdest of men, and who did not
know that Sudul already had a wife and child, regarded them as
an engaged couple, and had no objection to Sudul coming and
going like it pleased him. After dinner, Walter and Henrietta went
out for a 'walk', not returning until close to midnight. The
neighbours in Moyers Road were alarmed to hear two shots, and
when they ran outdoors, they found the two lovers dead in the
doorway of No. 7. Walter had shot his mistress with a heavy
Webley revolver, before turning it on himself.

At the coroner's inquest on Walter Sudul and Henrietta

7.15 Other incidents from the Sudul tragedy, from the
Illustrated Police News, *December 29 1906.*

Howard, Sudul's wife and brother testified about his double lives. It also turned out that he had embezzled much of the money entrusted to him by the sports club, to pay for keeping the 'expensive' Henrietta. In particular, the workmen at the Royal Gunpowder Factory, who had entrusted their Christmas savings to this presumed pillar of the local society, were dismayed to find that their £140 had been spent as well. As they sat grinding their teeth at the turkey-less Christmas table, the factory workers were likely to have made some choice predictions about the scoundrel Sudul's destination in the Afterlife. The *Times* briefly reviewed the outcome of the inquest, which ended in a verdict of Walter Sudul wilfully murdering Henrietta Howard, before committing suicide while temporarily insane. The *Illustrated Police News* gave

the embezzling East London Lothario a proper Christmas send-
off, however, with a full-page illustration and the caption
'Sensational Love Tragedy in Leyton!'[19]

THE CANNING TOWN MASS MURDER, 1908

In 1908, the seaman George Cutler Nadin lived at No. 9 Bethell
Avenue, Canning Town, with his wife Margaret and his five
children. He worked on the Royal Mail Steam Packet Company's
tramp steamer between London and Southampton, and had a
good reputation, although he was still an ordinary seaman at the
age of 35. His neighbours thought him a respectable, hard-
working man, and very fond of his family. In November 1908,
George fell ill with a fever and was off work for an entire week.
He suffered from melancholia and sleeplessness, but still he
hoped to go back to work the following week.

7.16 *George Nadin goes on a rampage in Bethell Avenue, from the*
Illustrated Police News, *November 28 1908.*

Early in the morning of November 21 1908, Mrs Adelaide McCombie, living at No. 10 Bethell Avenue, saw ten-year-old Angus Nadin come running out of No. 9 wearing only his nightshirt, bleeding profusely from the throat. She promptly went into No. 9, where she saw Mr and Mrs Nadin struggle in the passage. He tried to cut his throat with a razor, but she did her best to stop him. Mrs McCombie ran up to them and managed to seize the razor, but when the frenzied Nadin took it back, she ran out into the road and sent her husband for the police.

When Inspector Ball and some constables arrived at No. 9 Bethell Avenue, George Cutler Nadin was found in the front room. After wounding both his wife and Mrs McCombie, he had cut his own throat with the razor, but he was still alive. The little boy Angus was lying on the pavement outside the house, quite dead. The demented George Nadin had also cut the throats of his younger sons Johannes and Frederick Charles; their bodies were found in a pool of blood on the bed. He had wounded his eldest son George Jr and his daughter Margaret, but they were still alive. As George Jr expressed it when questioned by Constable Dadson, "Father had his breakfast and came into the bedroom and cut all our throats, but he could not get hold of Maggie and me, since we kicked." The three dead children were taken away for burial, and the five wounded people were removed to the Poplar Hospital.

At the inquest on the three murdered children, held at West Ham Police Court, held on December 30, George Cutler Nadin was fit enough to attend, although he was still in hospital for his injury. He gave no sign of understanding what was said to him when he was charged with wilful murder. When he was on trial at the Old Bailey on February 2 1909, Mrs McCombie and other neighbours gave evidence of the dramatic happenings back in

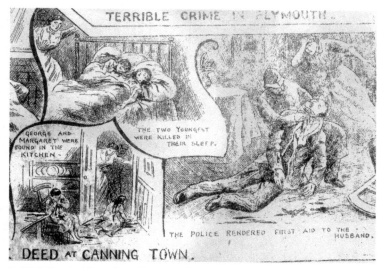

7.17 Other incidents from the Bethell Avenue murders, from the Illustrated Police News, *November 28 1908.*

November. Dr James Scott, the medical officer at Brixton Prison, had examined Nadin and found him suffering from melancholia and great mental depression. When his wife had visited him at the Poplar Hospital, he had asked her why she was wearing black clothes, but she had not had the strength to tell him of his murderous deed. George Nadin Jr told the doctor that when his father had assaulted him, he had exclaimed 'If I am ill any more, I will show you what I will do!' Dr Scott concluded that although George Cutler Nadin had been suffering from melancholia at the time of the triple murder, and thus been insane and incapable of knowing the nature and quality of the acts he was committing, he was sane, and fit to plead and stand trial, at the present time.

When George Cutler Nadin was formally charged with the murders when leaving hospital on December 29, the seaman was

THREE CHILDREN KILLED IN LONDON.

WHERE THE TRAGEDY TOOK PLACE.

7.18 Nadin goes on a rampage, and an image of the murder house, from the Illustrated Police Budget, *November 28 1908.*

horrified. He said that he remembered getting up the day in question, but then his mind had gone blank. In the week before the murder, he had felt very low in spirits, and unable to sleep. Inspector Ball had spoken to Nadin's mother, who told him that he had visited some religious meetings, and that he had got the fixed idea that God would punish him for all his wrongdoings. On trial for murder at the Old Bailey, George Cutler Nadin was found guilty but insane, and he was ordered to be detained at Broadmoor during His Majesty's pleasure.[20]

Due to their uncommon name, it is possible to follow the subsequent careers of the remaining Nadins. Mrs Nadin died prematurely in 1926, and George Jr died in 1932 at the age of just 36. Margaret Jr married in 1918 and may well have lived to be quite old. The murderer himself was released from Broadmoor in 1922; he returned to the West Ham area, where he led a quiet life until his death in 1952, aged 78.

THE STORK ROAD DOUBLE MURDER, 1912

Walter James Limpus was born into an Anglo-Indian family in Calcutta. At school, he lost an eye when another pupil fired a stone at him with a powerful catapult. Young Limpus received a reasonable education and became a mechanic. For some reason, he left India in 1907 and settled in Grimsby, where he married Lucy Clapton the year after. Attracted by the bright lights of London, they soon left the north-eastern fishing metropolis and settled in West Ham.

But Walter James Limpus, who had done very well in India, and reasonably in Grimsby, faced stiff competition in London. He did not possess any skills that set him apart from London's many other mechanics, and as a result found it hard to secure employment. In 1912, the gloomy, unemployed Limpus was living in the ground floor flat at a small terraced house at No. 24 Stork Road, Forest Gate, with his wife Lucy and their two-year-old son Stanley James. He more than once suggested to Lucy that they ought to move back to Calcutta, where his family lived, and where he would find plenty of work, but she was worried that little Stanley, whose health was very delicate, would not cope with the Indian climate.

At 7.30 in the morning of February 11 1912, the newspaper boy Ernest Locke was busy delivering papers in Stork Road. All of a sudden, a half-dressed man came running out from No. 24, screaming 'Murder! Murder! Murder!' and flourishing a blood-stained hatchet, which he struck against the railings. Terrified, the boy Locke took to his heels. Limpus returned to the house, threw away the hatchet, got dressed, and ran up Stork Road to Mr Frederick Pretty's newsagent's shop in Knox Road nearby. Mr Pretty, who had just opened the shop, was surprised when the wild-eyed Limpus, dressed in only his shirt and trousers, blurted

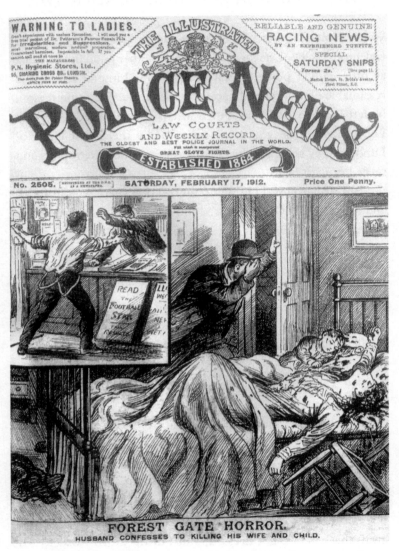

7.19 The Forest Gate Tragedy is discovered, from the Illustrated Police News, *February 17 1912.*

out that he had just murdered his wife and little son. His hands were spattered with blood. 'What shall I do?' the desperate Limpus screamed, as Mr Pretty and his wife tried to calm him down. Mrs Pretty tried to blow a police whistle to summon assistance, but she was too unnerved to master its mechanism. Instead, she dispatched a team of newspaper boys to search for the local constable.

In the meantime, Mr Pretty and Limpus returned to No. 24 Stork Road. In the bedroom, they found the corpses of Lucy and Stanley Limpus lying on the bed, both murdered and mutilated by the hatchet. Police Constable Frederick Short, who had been summoned by the newsboys, came plodding up to No. 24, knowing nothing about what had happened. 'What's the matter, boy?' he said to the distraught-looking Limpus. 'Good God, I have murdered my wife and child! Go in to them, I did it with an axe!' The incredulous constable went inside, to see the blood-stained corpses on the bed. At the police station, Limpus kept babbling about that he had not slept for many nights, and that his little boy had suffered from bronchitis. He ought to have committed suicide, since their lives were worth more than his own, and now he must go to the gallows.

But when Walter James Limpus stood trial at the Old Bailey for the murder of his wife and child, the medical officer at Brixton prison, who had kept him under observation since his arrest, expressed the opinion that he had been suffering from delusional melancholia and that he had been incapable of knowing the nature and quality of his actions. Accordingly, he was ordered to be detained at Broadmoor during his Majesty's pleasure, remaining there until his death in 1966.[21] The hatchet used by Limpus in the Stork Road Double Murder of 1912 was at Scotland Yard's Crime Museum for many years, and may well remain there today. As for the little terraced house at No. 24 Stork Road, it survives in good order, along with the rest of this humble suburban street, although Mr Pretty's newsagent's shop at the corner of Knox Road and Elm Road has been converted into residential property.

MURDER AT THE COOPERS ARMS, 1912

In 1911, the 51-year-old railway boilermaker Tom West moved into No. 15 Station Road, Ilford [it no longer stands] with his wife Bertha. He was a hard-working labouring man, but she drank heavily, and liked to go to the pubs in the evening without her husband. After Bertha had once slept at the house of an admirer, the labouring man Albert Faulkner, it was clear that her marriage to Tom was on the rocks. Although the Wests continued to live together, they quarrelled incessantly. Their oldest daughter Margaret, who was married to a man named Albert Rulten, took Bertha's youngest daughter Lilian into her own house, since she felt that her hard-drinking mother was no longer up to the task of taking care of a child.

In January 1912, the middle-aged Bertha West's behaviour went from bad to worse. When Tom gave her some money to pay the rent to the landlady, she took the money and went to the pub. She sat drinking with Albert Faulkner for half an hour, before going back to his house. But Tom West, who had followed his wife after the landlady had told him that she had not been paid, suddenly barged into the house and gave Faulkner a merciless thrashing, as Bertha looked on.

This clear demonstration of Tom West's violent streak was lost on his drunken wife, however. Margaret Rulten, who was very fond of her father, was fearful that the short-tempered boilermaker would injure her mother, or murder the creature Faulkner. A few days later, when Bertha West was going her lunch break at the laundry where she worked, in Chadwell Heath High Road, Tom unexpectedly arrived and took her to the Coopers Arms nearby, at the corner of High Road and Station Road. They had a couple of pints of beer each, and when Bertha stood up to leave, Tom suggested that they should have a meal as well. When Bertha said that she had brought her own food, Tom attacked her and stabbed her behind the ear with a knife. She fell to the floor, and when one of the pub customers asked Tom to help lift her onto a chair, he refused, saying "Let her lie! I did it, and I will stand by it!"

When Tom West stood trial for murder at the Essex Assizes, things were not looking good for him. But his daughter Margaret Rulton testified that Tom's hobby was shoe repairing, and that he always carried a cobbler's knife. His barrister urged that the killing had not been premeditated, but that it was the result of a sudden impulse. With what must have been a narrow margin, the jury agreed, and Tom West was sentenced to fifteen years penal servitude. He emerged from Maidstone Gaol in 1922, having served ten years of this sentence; it is not known if he ever walked into the Coopers Arms murder pub again.[22]

THE HEYWORTH ROAD MURDER, 1914

Evan Davies was born in West Ham in 1855. As a young man, he had an adventurous disposition, and went to Canada and the United States, but he soon returned to West Ham, where he became a stonemason and married his wife Sarah. They had at least one child, the daughter Lily Jane, who became a general servant.

In 1914, when Evan Davies was 59 years old, he lived at No. 25 Heyworth Road, West Ham. He owned the entire house, but sub-let the ground floor to another family. He still worked as a stonemason, although some disagreeable skin disease affecting his hands meant that he was no longer as useful to his employer. But in early 1914, Evan Davies developed the dangerous fixed idea that his 56-year-old wife Sarah was being unfaithful to him, with a Sunday school superintendent named Scrivener, and perhaps with two other men as well. When he challenged her, she denied all his wild accusations. Lily Jane, who often visited her parents, was amazed at her father's state of furious and groundless jealousy, as she expressed it. She tried to make him see reason, and had the ground floor lodgers testify that there had been no visits from Scrivener, or from other dodgy-looking men for that matter.

Lily Jane Davies hoped that her father had been convinced that he was not being made a cuckold, but the desperate Evan Davies was unable to see sense. Clearly there was a conspiracy against him, involving his daughter and neighbours! He made plans to take his revenge, and purchased a bicycle, a revolver, and a good supply of ammunition. The plan would be first to murder his unfaithful wife, then Scrivener, and then as many as possible of her other lovers.

On May 22 1914, Evan Davies felt unwell. His hands ached, and he did not feel fit for work. Sarah called him a fraud and ordered him to get out of bed, since she could no nothing when he was in the house, constantly grumbling and spying on her. The demented stonemason decided that this was the day for her to die. The lodger Blanche Dyer later saw Evan come downstairs with his bicycle. He carefully inflated the tyres and adjusted the chain. Then he went back upstairs and there was a loud explosion. The old stonemason came running downstairs, jumped onto his bicycle, and made off. When Blanche Dyer went upstairs to investigate, she found Sarah Davies dead on the kitchen floor.

Pedalling furiously, Evan Davies went to look for the man

Scrivener. The revolver was loaded and ready in his pocket. But although he had carefully ascertained where Scrivener was working as a clerk, in Aldgate, the fortunate Sunday school superintendent was not at work that particular day. Old Evan lost heart and decided to give himself up to the police. Since he was fearful of being lynched by the locals for murdering his wife, he took a cab to the West Ham police station.

At the coroner's inquest on Sarah Davies, there was amazement when her husband described his cunning murder plan. Only fate had saved Scrivener from being gunned down as well, and then the furious old man might well have gone on a rampage to murder his wife's other alleged lovers. 'I meant to pop off four! And the other three I intended to do are in court now!' he raved. The inquest returned a verdict of wilful murder against him, and at the Old Bailey, he was found guilty but insane, and sent to Broadmoor.[23]

MASS MURDER IN STUKELEY ROAD, 1919

Mr Walter Frank Cornish, a 42-year-old East London builder and decorator, lived at No. 13 Stukeley Road, Forest Gate, with his wife Alice and his two daughters Alice Jr and Marie. In 1919, Mr Cornish was doing quite well in business, since the war had caused a shortage of builders. He was able to save money, and may well have hoped one day to find more promising living accommodation for his family than the rather mean-looking little semi-detached house in Stukeley Road.

On April 28 1919, Mr Cornish's next-door neighbour heard a scream from the garden of No. 13. Going to his back door, he saw Walter Frank Cornish trying to climb over the dividing fence, screaming 'Look at my head! He has chopped the tip off my

7.20 *An entire family wiped out: incidents from the Stukeley Avenue carnage, from the* Illustrated Police News, *May 6 1919.*

finger!' His head was covered with blood, and he had a kitchen cleaver in his hand. There was a deep cut to the left of his head, and one of his fingers had been cut off. When taken to hospital in a tram, he was able to explain that a man dressed as a soldier had attacked him when he returned home from work, and that he was fearful for the safety of his wife and children. And indeed, then No. 13 Stukeley Road was searched by the police, Mrs Cornish was found dead in the garden shed, and the mangled remains of the children were in the cellar. When Mr Cornish died in hospital later the same day, the Stukeley Road murderer had succeeded in wiping out the entire family.

The police soon found some important clues to the identity of the quadruple murderer. A short-statured young soldier, said to have been Mrs Cornish's nephew, had been staying at No. 13 Stukeley Road for some weeks, but since his conduct had been very unsatisfactory he had been asked to leave. A girl had seen this very individual running away from No. 13 the evening of the murder. His face and hands had been covered with blood, his teeth had been chattering together, and he had worn his army cap the wrong way. The police found out the identity of the absconded soldier, and issued his description:

Private Henry Beckett, Army Veterinary Corps, aged 38, 5 ft. 0.5 in., complexion fresh, hair dark brown, eyes blue, heavy dark moustache (waxed). Dressed in khaki uniform, no overcoat, black leggings and boots.

On May 2, a short man with a waxed moustache entered a shop in Barking Road. Although he was in civilian attire, the alert shopkeeper recognized him as the fugitive Beckett and alerted the police. After Beckett had been taken into custody, he said that his real name was Henry Perry, although he sometimes used the name Beckett. He freely made a detailed confession of his crimes. In 1916, Perry had enlisted in the 3rd Suffolks and served in Palestine for a while, but he had been captured by the Turks and forced to work in a railway building project. Somehow he had caught syphilis in this environment, but he had been liberated in Constantinople and treated at a hospital in Italy, before being repatriated.

Back in London, Perry had made contact with his step-aunt Alice Cornish, and she allowed him to lodge in their house for five weeks. But after Perry had seduced a war widow, and proposed marriage to her, Mr and Mrs Cornish showed him the door. Mrs Cornish had also received information from other relatives that before the war, Perry had been a thief who had spent much of his time in prison. For some days, Perry went round to various military establishments, trying to trick them into giving him his demobilisation payment, but without success. Poor as a church mouse, he was tramping round the West Ham area, when he got the idea to burgle the Cornish house.

It turned out that Mrs Cornish was at home, and she was far from pleased to see him. Perry knocked her down with a kitchen poker and dragged her to the garden shed, where he finished her off with a pickaxe and a carving-fork. He cut off her finger to steal her wedding-ring. As the two children came home, Perry knocked them on the head with a hammer, and threw the bodies down into the cellar. He then waited until Mr Cornish came home. Seeing Perry lurking in the passage, the startled householder exclaimed 'What game are you up to, sneaking back like this? I am going to hand you over to the police!' Perry hit him hard on the head with the axe, and chopped his finger off, but Cornish got away into his neighbour's garden. Carrying with him a good deal of money and valuables he had stolen, Perry swiftly absconded from the Stukeley Road house of horrors. He used Mrs Cornish's wedding ring to pay for the services of a prostitute in Stratford.

When Henry Perry, alias Beckett, was on trial for murder at

THE CALL OF JUSTICE   THE EXECUTION.

EXECUTION OF BECKETT, THE FOREST GATE MURDERER.

7.21 Beckett is executed, from the Illustrated Police News, July 17 1919.

the Old Bailey, before Mr Justice Darling, the only avenue open to his defence team was to play the 'insanity card'. Perry had once been blown up with high explosives, and while he had been in the hands of the Turks, they had disciplined him by whipping him on the soles of the feet, knocking him on the head with a rifle, and throwing him into a dungeon. But the medical officer at Brixton prison found Perry sane, although of a low intelligence and mentality. He belonged to a family of travelling hawkers, and himself looked very much like a Gipsy. Lord Darling, in pronouncing sentence of death, said that he had never heard a case in which the circumstances of the crime were more horrible. After an appeal had been turned down, Perry was hanged at Pentonville Prison on July 10 1919.[24]

LAST OF THE LONDON BABY-FARMERS, 1919

The executions of the notorious baby-farmer Amelia Dyer in 1896, and her equally dastardly colleagues Amelia Sachs and Annie Walters in 1903, did nothing to stop the baby-farming racket. After Leslie James, the Cardiff baby-farmer, had been executed in 1907, the Children Act of 1908 increased state powers to supervise foster care and enforce infant protection. As a result, the baby-farming racket suffered badly in the years leading up to the Great War.

In 1919, the little house at No. 2 Carlton Road, Leytonstone, was home to the 52-year-old clerk Henry Hatchard, and his wife Beatrice. Since the neighbours heard many small children crying at the premises, both day and night, they called in the police. Since it turned out that the local officials were already suspecting that the house was an illicit nursing-home for babies, the premises were inspected on July 2. The house contained ten living babies, aged between six weeks and twelve months. A dead baby was lying in an old perambulator. In addition, the Hatchards' own four adolescent children, and three adolescent foster children, were living at No. 2 Carlton Road. That left a total of nineteen people living in this small house. There was very little furniture, and all the rooms were extremely filthy. The sight of the dead infant, and the dirty, malodorous rooms, was a shock even to the experienced police constables.

The Hatchards were both arrested, and it was debated whether to charge them with murder or manslaughter. Clearly, the house at No. 2 Carlton Road was a baby-farming establishment, since various single mothers came forward to tell that they had deposited their unwanted infants with Mrs Hatchard. But had this sinister, alcoholic harridan deliberately murdered the children, through starvation, or had she just been muddled and incompetent in looking after them? The former view received support when it turned out that another baby had recently expired on the premises. But in the end, it was decided to 'play it safe', and the Hatchards were charged only with manslaughter.

On trial at the Old Bailey, before Mr Justice Darling, Henry Hatchard stated that he had worked as a clerk at the same firm for 38 years, and that he was an active member of the Salvation Army. Accompanied by his children, he had used to sing rousing hymns to cheer the crying little babies up. At other times, Beatrice Hatchard had played the piano loudly to drown their cries. She had often seen drunk during the daytime, and a 79-year-old woman, whose task it had been to clean the house, shared this predicament.

In his summing-up, Mr Justice Darling, who was known for his severity, surprised many people when he gave credence to the creature Hatchard's statement that he had worked so very hard that he lacked the energy to supervise his wife's wholesale adoption of small children. It was not a criminal offence, he pontificated, for a man not to keep his wife in order. The jury duly took the hint: Henry Hatchard was acquitted, and his wife sentenced to five years in prison for two counts of manslaughter, and four counts of neglecting children.[25] The Last of the London Baby-farmers got off lightly; their house of horrors still stands today.

A MURDEROUS EAST HAM BLACKSMITH, 1925

George William Barton, a 51-year-old blacksmith living in Troy Town, Peckham Rye, was engaged to marry his 38-year-old widowed sister-in-law Mrs Mary Palfrey, who lodged in two rooms and a scullery in the ground floor flat at No. 12 Bartle

7.22 Little Teddy Palfrey finds his mother murdered, from the Illustrated Police News, *January 29 1925.*

Avenue, East Ham. Barton had previously been married to her sister Florence, about whom Mary Palfrey had been unkind enough to spread some very unpleasant gossip, both before and after she had died. When George William Barton visited Mary Palfrey on January 22 1925, to upbraid her about her calumnies against poor dead Florence, there was an angry quarrel. When Mary Palfrey told Barton that she had not been faithful to him, the furious blacksmith knocked her on the head with a length of pipe, cut her throat, and walked out of the house. When Mary Palfrey's eleven-year-old son Edward came home and found the body, he ran into the neighbour's house at No. 10, exclaiming 'Come, Mrs Carroll, my mummy is lying dead in the kitchen!'

Two days later, George William Barton came into the Vine Street police station to give himself up for the murder. In a detailed confession, he said 'I admit I have done it. It was partly through jealousy and the way she treated her poor sister. I intended to play the game and go straight with her. I would have married her and treated her all right, but she admitted to me that she had not been straight with me… ' At the coroner's inquest on Mary Palfrey, a pathetic letter from Barton to his son was read: 'Forgive me. I have only revenged Florrie's name. Mary deserved all she got. I am off abroad on Saturday with a friend, so cheer up!'

On February 26 1925, George William Barton stood trial for the murder of Mary Palfrey, at the Old Bailey, before Mr Justice Avory, known as a 'hanging judge' of considerable severity. The evidence against him seemed quite solid: he had been observed leaving the murder house by Mary Palfrey's son, and then there was the matter of the confession, and the letter to the son. His barrister argued that George William Barton had suddenly been seized by a fit of jealousy, and killed the woman in a moment of frenzy. But Mr Justice Avory's summing up was very much against the accused, since he said that the law did not regard jealousy as provocation that would reduce the crime. The jury accordingly found Barton guilty.

When asked by the Clerk of the Court whether he had anything to say, Barton stood up, exclaiming: 'I am very sorry I am not Ronald True. If I were, I would not be convicted. I should be sent to a convalescent home to dig up the garden for the rest of my life. As I am a poor man I have no chance!' Mr Justice Avory paid no attention to the prisoner's socialist rethorics about the 'toff' Ronald True who had been sent to Broadmoor for murdering a prostitute in 1922, but calmly sentenced him to death. Barton replied by cursing the Judge, in a blood-curdling manner, and exclaiming 'May you be hung tomorrow!'

But it was George William Barton who was hung, at Pentonville Prison, on April 2 1925.[26] In spite of the murderer's curse, Mr Justice Avory lived on for more than ten years, dying in 1935 at the age of 84. As for 'Little Teddy' Barton, who had found his mother's mangled corpse, he and his sister were 'fostered out' to another neighbour in Bartle Avenue. The murder house at No. 12 Bartle Avenue still stands.

MURDER IN ILFORD, 1933

Robert James Kirby was born in 1909, one of a large lower-class East End family who occupied various small houses in the Stratford district. They led a rough existence, and Robert's father Charles Kirby had convictions for larceny and for neglect of his family. Once he was charged with attempting to murder his wife Sarah Jane, by striking her hard with a poker, but the charge was reduced to wounding with intent, and he was fortunate to be sentenced to only four years in prison.

In spite of their unpromising childhood and upbringing, Robert Kirby's seven siblings all grew up to become honest and hard-working East Enders. But as for himself, Robert was a dull, sullen schoolboy, who suffered badly with eczema, malnutrition and anaemia. As he grew up, he became a thief, burglar and tramp, serving time more than once for larceny and house-breaking. His brother Charles William tried to help the family black sheep in 1932, getting him a temporary job as a labourer for a telephone company. To the surprise of his brothers and sisters, Robert worked hard for seven months. But his criminal record meant that he was unable to find a permanent job, and for several months, he lived on the charity of his siblings, who soon had enough of this drunken, work-shy fellow.

Although a far from prepossessing specimen of humanity, Robert Kirby managed to get himself a steady girlfriend, the pretty seventeen-year-old Grace Ivy Newing, who worked as an assistant in a confectioner's shop. She lived with her mother and large family in a recently constructed council house at No. 28 Stevens Road, Chadwell Heath. Robert and Grace spent a good deal of time together, and in June 1933, he told Mrs Newing that Grace might well be pregnant. This turned out to be the case, and thus Robert had yet another problem, since he was unable to get a job, or to support a family. And after supporting him for nine months, his brother Charles William had had enough of his sponging off the family, and told him that he must find other lodgings. Depressed and self-pitying, Robert Kirby spoke of committing suicide by taking an overdose of aspirin, but Mrs Newing did not think he was sincere.

In the evening of July 6 1933, Robert Kirby waited for Grace Newing to come home to No. 28 Stevens Road, from her evening shift at the confectioner's shop. When Mrs Newing went to bed, she saw them sitting in the lounge. A few hours later, Robert turned up at the house of one of his married sisters, saying that he had just murdered Grace. And indeed, she was found strangled to death at No. 28 Stevens Road. On trial for murder at the Old Bailey on September 21 1933, Robert Kirby's defence team tried various stratagems to save him from the gallows. The dismal Kirby said that Grace had asked him to kill her, and a doctor testified that the prisoner was a mental defective. The prison doctors had found him sane and fit to plead, however, and his story of a 'suicide pact' was not believed. Robert Kirby was found guilty of murder and sentenced to death, although the jury added a recommendation to mercy. Since Kirby was a nasty piece of work, and his crime a dastardly one, this recommendation was not acted upon, and he was hanged at Pentonville Prison on October 11 1933.[27]

MURDER BY AN ARMY VETERAN, 1936

Ernest Bauckham was born in 1879, into a large working-class West Ham family. His father either died or left the family, so Ernest and his many siblings were brought up by their mother Jane. The 1891 Census has the 12-year-old Ernest working as a 'Match Factory Hand', and living with his mother, brother and two sisters at Canning Town. He later became a workman at a cable factory, and married his Dutch wife Adelaide in 1902. The 1911 Census has the 32-year-old Ernest Bauckham, his 30-year-old wife Adelaide, their 4-year-old daughter Adelaide Maud, and his 60-year-old mother-in-law Mrs Adelaide Bande living at No. 24 Randolph Road, Custom House.

In July 1915, Ernest Bauckham joined the King's Royal Rifle Corps, serving on the Western Front and seeing a good deal of action. In October 1916, he suffered a serious wound to the left thigh, but recovered and joined the Labour Corps in 1918. When he was demobilized in April 1919, with a 'Good' character and the Victory and General Service medals, he rejoined his family and went back to his old job at the cable factory.

But in 1930, all was not well with the Bauckham family. Adelaide Maud had married a man named Lampnell and moved out of the humble family home, but both Ernest and his wife were seriously ill, and he was no longer able to work. He applied to the Rifleman's Aid Society, and was eventually awarded an army disability pension, but by then Adelaide was dead, and Ernest himself had just recovered from an operation for what was thought to be throat cancer.

In early 1935, the 56-year-old army pensioner Ernest Bauckham moved into Mrs Jessie Gymer's house at No. 31 Thurlestone Avenue, Ilford, as a lodger. He lived in a small first-floor bedroom, and soon became very good friends with his landlady. They lived as man and wife, and often went out drinking together. In September 1936, Mrs Gymer was still living with her favourite lodger. Her married son, the motor driver Arthur Gymer, did not approve of their relation, or of his mother's bibulous habits, but he thought her old enough to look after herself.

When Arthur Gymer and his wife arrived back home at No. 31 Thurlestone Avenue in the late evening of September 13 1936, they found Jessie Gymer dead in the bath. She had been knocked down and then drowned. Two hours later, Ernest Bauckham went into the Leman Street police station and confessed that he had just murdered his landlady. He had disapproved of her drinking with other men behind his back, and after an angry quarrel, she had told him to move out of No. 31 Thurlestone Avenue and find another room for himself. When she brought him his clothes after he had had a bath, the quarrel resumed, and in a furious temper, he had drowned her in the bath, before lurching off into the night.

When Ernest Bauckham was charged with murder at the Stratford police court, a woman at the back of the court shouted 'Ta Ta, Daddy!' The prisoner acknowledged this uncouth outcry, which may well have emanated from his daughter Adelaide Maud, with a wave of his hand as he left the dock. But Ernest Bauckham would answer for his crime at a higher tribunal than the Central Criminal Court. The senior medical officer at Brixton Prison had examined him, and found signs that he suffered from advanced cancer of the throat, and was not fit to stand trial. And indeed, the Thurlestone Avenue murderer died in Brixton Prison on October 13 1936.[28]

MURDER IN HILLVIEW CRESCENT, 1937

Frank Arthur Hart was born in 1884 and became a van guard at Messrs Wright & Son, biscuit manufacturers, at an early age. He left the firm in 1903 and enlisted in the Royal Navy, rising through the ranks to become Chief Petty Officer in the sickberth. He left the Navy in 1925 and moved back to the biscuit factory. By that time, he had a wife, Mrs Kathleen Hart, and a niece named Olive Good of whom he was very fond. They lived in a little cottage at No. 1 Hillview Crescent, Ilford. It was a sadness for him and his wife that for some reason or other, they were unable to have children of their own.

In the 1930s, Frank Hart began to borrow money and live above his station. He appealed to Colonel Wright, head of the biscuit factory, for relief, but was snubbed. In April 1937, Frank had become very depressed. Life was no longer worth living, he reasoned, and according to his version of events, Kathleen Hart and Olive Good felt equally suicidal. Frank struck both women by a heavy coal hammer until they were dead, before he went out to pick some daffodils, which he placed near the bodies of the two murdered women. He then opened the gas taps and was unconscious by the time his brother George came to call, but in hospital, the murderer recovered completely. On trial at the Central Criminal Court, Frank Hart pleaded guilty to murder, and was sentenced to death. He repeated that he wanted to die, and refused to accept legal advice. The Court of Criminal Appeal upheld the verdict, but medical experts found Frank Hart insane and he was incarcerated in Broadmoor.[29]

MURDER IN BYRON AVENUE, 1940

In 1940, the small terraced house at No. 46 Byron Avenue, East Ham, was home to the middle-aged newsagent's deliveryman David Crawford and his 60-year-old widowed sister Mrs Jane Potts. They had lived there for fourteen years, and led quiet and contented suburban lives until the war broke out. In 1935, they had taken a lodger, the 33-year-old French polisher William Marden. He was abnormally shy and reserved, and did not like walking in the streets since he imagined that everybody was looking at him. The kind Mrs Potts was fond of both her brother and the lodger Marden, and she used to cook them some nourishing meals when they came home from work.

In early February 1940, William Marden suffered a bad bout of influenza, and he was off work for several weeks. After a fortnight's holiday at Leigh-on-Sea, he returned to No. 46 Byron Avenue, and was back to work on March 18. The following day, David Crawford got up at 5.30 am and started his paper round fifteen minutes later. William Marden and Mrs Potts got up around 7 am, and she served him his breakfast. But at 7.40 am, the neighbour at No. 44 heard terrible screams emanating from next door, and continuing for two or three minutes. She ran out into the street, where she spotted David Crawford returning from his beat. She called out to him, and he ran up to No. 46 and opened the front door with his key. Mrs Potts was lying dead in the scullery with much blood around her face and head. Glass fragments were everywhere, since a large bottle had been used to assault her.

David Crawford saw the weirdo William Marden standing by the kitchen table, next to an empty porridge bowl, and said to him 'You've done a nice thing, haven't you?' but the strange lodger did not react. Mrs Ann Benjamin, the neighbour from No. 48, who possessed some first aid training, felt Mrs Pott's pulse and heartbeat, but detected none. When she cried at Marden 'Whatever made you do it?', the lodger replied 'She ruined my life! She scandalized me!' Dr Isaac Arnott, the local practitioner, found that Jane Potts was indeed dead, from repeated heavy blows to the head with a heavy glass bottle, of which only the head and neck remained intact. The weirdo Marden told the doctor that all of a sudden, Mrs Potts had grabbed the bottle and started hitting herself over the head with it, but he was not believed. When a police constable took him into custody, he muttered 'I done it.'

When William Marden was on trial for murdering Jane Potts at the Central Criminal Court, on April 23 1940, things were not looking good for him. There had been no other person in the house at the time of the murder, and Marden had confessed both to the neighbour and to the police constable. Dr Grierson, of HM Prison Brixton, testified that although Marden had always been very shy and self-conscious, he had no history of psychiatric disease, although several relatives of his had been insane, or committed suicide. Although Dr Grierson found it likely that Marden had suffered from a degree of post-influenzal mental depression, he was fit to plead and stand trial. Both David Crawford and the two neighbour-women testified that Jane Potts had always been very kind and inoffensive, and that she had always been getting on quite well with the lodger Marden. This quiet, unassuming woman was the last person to have scandalized any person. The two neighbours testified, with much feeling, that they had never heard anything more dreadful than the screams from the murdered woman. In the end, William Marden was found guilty but insane, and incarcerated in Broadmoor.[30]

MURDER WITHOUT MOTIVE IN MORNINGTON ROAD, 1944

William Henry Davies, a photographer by trade, lived at No. 27 Mornington Road, Leytonstone, with his wife Catherine, his son William and daughter Evelyn. In 1941, when he was 64 years old, he was diagnosed with prostate cancer, and became an invalid, with a suprapubic drain from the bladder. The hospital doctors also found him very depressed and morose. They suggested that he should be admitted to a nursing home, but the invalid discharged himself and went home to No. 27 Mornington Road.

On April 20 1944, Mrs Catherine Davies brought her ailing husband his tea at 11 am. He was as morose as ever, and refused to drink any. When she returned, he remarked that the chimney needed some repairs. As she bent down to investigate, he hit her hard on the head with a hammer three or four times, and jabbed a broken bottle into her face. The demented invalid then attempted to destroy himself, through drinking disinfectant and drowning himself in the bath, but neither of these stratagems had the desired effect. When Evelyn Davies came home to fetch her mother for luncheon, her wet and dishevelled-looking father just said 'She has gone for a long rest; don't ask me any questions!' Unable to find her mother, Evelyn called the police, who discovered the body in the locked ground floor front room, and took William Henry Davies into custody.

At the police station, William Henry Davies made a full confession, although he did not supply a motive for his rash acts. Nor could his children discern any credible motive for him to brutally murder his wife of many years, who had nursed him devotedly. It turned out that the prisoner's real name was William Henry Jones, and that he had served nine months in prison for housebreaking back in 1912. On trial at the Central Criminal Court on June 27 1944, before Mr Justice Asquith, William Henry Davies was found unfit to plead, and he was incarcerated in a lunatic asylum.[31] The murder house at No. 27 Mornington Road still stands.

MURDER IN RICHMOND ROAD, 1944

On July 31 1944, screaming was heard from the first floor flat at No. 150 Richmond Road, Leytonstone. A police constable was alerted by a neighbour, and he made his way to the house, where he was met by the 40-year-old shoemaker William Kilbey, who explained that he had just murdered his wife Hilda. She was found lying dead in a large pool of blood in the upstairs flat, with a number of stab wounds, and the body pinned to the floorboards by a large ornamental sword. The constable took Kilbey with him to No. 109 Richmond Road, situated opposite No. 150, where he made use of the telephone to summon assistance.

At the police station, William Kilbey explained that his wife had often been unfaithful to him, and that although they had two children, neither had been fathered by himself. Since he feared that she was slowly poisoning him, to get her hands on the life insurance money, he had decided on pre-emptive action. At HMP Brixton, two doctors found it likely that Kilbey's allegations against his wife were the results of insane delusions. He was found fit to plead and stand trial for his crime at the Central Criminal Court, where he was found guilty but insane, and incarcerated in Broadmoor.[32]

MURDER AND ARSON IN RAINHAM ROAD SOUTH, 1944

Frank Sanderson was a young East End labouring man, active as a process worker in Dagenham. In 1944, he had a girlfriend, the waitress Iris Sedgwick. Although Frank liked to visit her in her flat over a shop at No. 535 Rainham Road South, he became quite annoyed when she started telling people that he intended to marry her by Christmastime. This was nothing that Frank had contemplated at all. When he came to see her on December 23, there was an angry quarrel and Frank went berserk. He strangled Iris and set fire to the flat to hide his crime. The fire brigade made sure that the fire was extinguished and the evidence secured, however.

When called to the police station the next day, as the obvious suspect, Frank Sanderson seemed quite unconcerned, making jokes about his workmates pulling his leg about his forthcoming 'marriage'. But all of a sudden, he confessed to the murder, even after being cautioned by the police. After a short trial at the Central Criminal Court, Frank was found guilty of murder and was sentenced to death. The Home Secretary had a difficult choice whether to give him a reprieve. It spoke in his favour that the crime did not appear to have been premeditated, and that he seemed genuinely contrite. But on the other hand, he had actually tried to conceal his activities by burning down the murder house, and Iris had been pregnant at the time she was murdered. It must have been by quite a narrow margin that he was finally reprieved at the end of February 1945, the sentence being commuted to life imprisonment.[33]

THE MAN WHO CANNOT HANG, 1956

In the 1950s, the seaman's outfitters shop at No. 5 West India Dock Road, Limehouse, was kept by Mr Morris Senefft and his wife Betty. A certain Isaac Senefft had been keeping the shop, at the same premises, as early as 1912. It is curious that just across the road from the shop, there had been an unsolved murder at the corner with Rich Street back in 1945: Mrs Lilian Hartney was found dead just by the buildings of the Unemployment Assistance Board, and there was never any useful clue concerning the identity of the culprit.

In early 1956, the 21-year-old Welsh laboratory assistant David Glanville Kemp was becoming seriously dissatisfied with his job.

A native of Ynys-Hir, Rhondda, he wanted to leave Mother Wales and start a new life on the ocean wave. Although he had no nautical experience, and walked with a limp, he thought it would be easy to become a merchant mariner. Having travelled to London by bus, he went into Senefft's shop on February 18 and ordered a merchant service officer's uniform, saying that his own uniform had been stolen. The day after, he was back to order some further items. This strange young Welshman then caught a cab, but he ordered the driver to return to Senefft's shop after a while. After a short absence, the cab driver saw him coming out of the shop, wearing a merchant service uniform. Kemp went to Stepney, where he paid off the cab driver, who had also noticed that he had an injured hand. This injury was severe enough to force him to attend London Hospital, where one of the nurses noticed that his coat still had the price tag on it. When Mr Senefft returned home on the afternoon of February 19, he found his wife dead in the shop, from multiple stab wounds.

There was a fair bit of newspaper publicity about the hunt for the West India Dock Road murderer, who was dubbed 'The Man who Cannot Hang' since three days earlier, the House of Commons had voted to abolish or suspend the death penalty for murder. The police had a good description of the murderer: a young man with a limp carrying a light brown bag. The motive for the murder was presumed to be that this strange killer had such a strong desire to get his hands on a suit of nautical attire. They soon arrested David Glanville Kemp, and the cab driver, the nurse, and other witnesses gave evidence against him when he was on trial for murder at the Old Bailey on April 27. He was found guilty, and Mr Justice Byrne sentenced him to death, but the Home Secretary recommended a reprieve, and the Man who Cannot Hang was instead jailed for life.[34]

WIFE KILLED SON AND HUSBAND, 1958-1968

In the 1940s, Mrs Lilian Myra Giles appeared to live contentedly as a suburban housewife at No. 59 Roll Gardens, Ilford, with her husband Arthur and young son Derek, born in 1942. But as she got older, Lilian Myra sometimes behaved very strangely. She suffered mental breakdowns in 1950 and 1955, being treated with electro-convulsive shocks in Goodmayes Hospital, with what was presumed to be good success.

In 1958, Mrs Giles was becoming concerned about her now 16-year-old son Derek. He ought to be studying to become a teacher, she thought, and she very much disapproved that he had got himself a girlfriend. On March 20 1958, Lilian Myra Giles decided that Derek must die. She laced his tea with sleeping pills, and when the boy seemed quite unaffected by the pills, she seized an axe and beat him to death with 54 blows to the head. Lilian Myra Giles was convicted of murdering her son, although she was declared insane and sent to Broadmoor. No motive for her murderous rage ever emanated, apart from the story about the girlfriend.[35]

Even in the 1950s, it was the custom that murderers sent to Broadmoor should stay there for a considerable period of time. This was not the case for the quiet, benign-looking Lilian Myra Giles, however: as early as 1961, she was released into the care of her husband back at No. 59 Roll Gardens. This was not a good decision. In September 1968, she struck Arthur Giles a heavy blow on the head with a large chamber-pot, and he died ten days later. For the second time, she was on trial for murdering a close relative. Her plea of guilty to manslaughter on grounds of diminished responsibility was accepted, and she was returned to Broadmoor, this time with a recommendation that she should be detained without limit of time.[36]

In 1971, the name of Lilian Myra Giles again hit the news. In his will, Arthur Giles had bequeathed his whole estate to her, but his son from an earlier marriage, Arthur William Giles, of course objected to his father's murderer inheriting his worldly goods. His solicitors contested the will, and Arthur William was granted letters of administration to his father's estate. But from Broadmoor, Lilian Myra also employed a team of solicitors. They objected that she had been found guilty only of manslaughter on grounds of diminished responsibility, and that she should be allowed to inherit the money her husband had bequeathed to her. Her detention for hospital treatment under the Mental Health Act was not in the nature of a punishment, but a remedial order. The legal wrangling went on for several years, until the case was tried in the Chancery Division, before Sir John Pennycuick, the Vice-Chancellor.

Quoting various precedents, among them the fate of the estate of Mrs Crippen after she had been murdered by her husband, Sir John pontificated that it was established legal practice that a murderer should not inherit his victim. The Mental Health Act did not change this principle, and the position of Lilian Myra Giles was exactly the same as if she had been convicted of manslaughter before the introduction of the Act. He declared that Mrs Giles was excluded from any benefit from her late husband's will, and that the plaintiff Arthur William Giles was entitled to his father's estate, including the humble, terraced little murder house at No. 59 Roll Gardens.[37]

CHAPTER 8

DISCUSSION

With regard to the Clerk, we are left in the dark,
As to what his fate was; but I cannot imagine he
Got off scot-free, though unnoticed it be
Both by Ribadaneira and Jacques de Voragine:
For cut-throats, we're sure, can be never secure,
And 'History's Muse' still to prove it her pen holds,
As you'll see, if you look in a rather scarce book,
'God's Revenge against Murder,' by one Mr. Reynolds.
    Richard Harris Barham, The Lay of St
    Gengulphus *(from the* Ingoldsby Legends*).*

For a crime to qualify as murder in this book, it has to have been classified as such during some stage of its investigation and/or prosecution. Thus it remains a 'murder' even if the prisoner is ultimately sentenced to prison for manslaughter, as long as he or she was originally on trial for murder. In the 324 London murders covered by this book and its two predecessors, the murderer committed suicide in 39 instances. Not less than 49 murders are unsolved, but this is a statistical aberration due to the enrichment of 'interesting' murders in these three books. In cases where a suspect was convicted for the crime, he or she was executed in 75 instances, sent to Broadmoor in 65, and imprisoned in 90 cases.

In two instances, namely Gino Ferrari, who absconded to his native land after shooting his brother-in-law in 1913, and Lord Lucan, who was never seen again after the gruesome murder at No. 46 Lower Belgrave Street, the suspected murderer successfully made his escape. Another murderer, Frederick Foster who admitted beating his common-law wife to death at No. 40 Market Street in 1893, was actually taken into police custody, but escaped on the way to the police station, and was never seen again. In twelve instances, the person on trial for murder was freed due to excellent advocacy or lack of evidence. Some of these people, like Alice St John and Arthur Alfred Meader, were lucky to get off so very lightly. In the strange case of Dr Smethurst in 1859, and in the equally peculiar Barber/Randall drama of Clapham Road in 1963, there is the question whether murder was committed at all.

Many people's idea of a historical murder mystery comes from the 'Columbo' TV series and others of that ilk: a wealthy person is killed, there is a quantity of likely suspects, all with credible motives, and it takes the work of a clever and experienced detective to solve it. In real life, murder is very different: as shown in this book and many others, the vast majority of murders are spontaneous rather than planned, and the capture of the culprit an easy matter. Drunken, disturbed husbands murder their wives or take revenge on their enemies, madmen go on the rampage, and deranged women kill their children. There is also the 'autogenic massacre' type of mass murder, in which a desperate individual murders his or her children, and sometimes also spouse, before committing or attempting suicide. The extreme example is of course the Tooting Horror, claiming eight lives in total, and the Else, Manser and Hickman cases also deserve mention. In many cases of both spontaneous and planned murder, the killer gives himself up to the police. Even in cases of planned, premeditated murder, for revenge or for profit, the police usually get their man, or woman in the case of Mrs Pearcey. Richard Brinkley, one of the most cerebral murderers in these books, distributed his poisoned stout with blameworthy carelessness. The butler-killing Moroccan Mustapha Bassaine, who had committed the perfect murder, and successfully absconded to his native land, received a well-deserved come-uppance when he was foolish enough to return to Europe, and the clutches of the Scotland Yard detectives.

Of the 49 unsolved murders in my three 'murder houses' books, not less than 15 involved prostitutes murdered either by casual 'customers', or in some instances perhaps by cunning serial killers. Five involve homosexuals killed by casual partners, six are 'shop murders' committed by desperate or careless robbers, another nine involve elderly and/or reclusive people murdered by intruders, and three are gangster-style executions. Although many other perverts preying on young girls have been successfully brought to book, the murder of Amelia Jeffs in West Ham in 1890 has remained unsolved; it may well be related to other cases of violence against young girls in that part of London. Of the ten remaining unsolved murders, three are household names, namely the Bravo Mystery of 1876, the Harley Street Mystery of 1880, and the unsolved murder of Jill Dando in 1999. The others are known to crime afictionados only, although the mysterious murders of Arabella Tyler, Agnes Jones, Violet McGrath and Amala de Vere Whelan certainly deserve to be better known. The Bravo, Harley Street and Tyler cases would have been deserving of better-quality police work; the murder of Jill Dando remains the greatest mystery of modern London, and I do not expect it to be solved.

It will please [or perhaps not] a feminist to know that although the carnage among London's women has been considerable inside the Murder Houses of London, only 24 female murderers have been inhabitants of these sinister dwellings. Some of the cases have involved child-murder [Elizabeth Rapley, Julia Spickernell, Emma Aston, Emma Symmonds] or vaguely motivated 'mercy-killings' [Edith Wood, Sarah Hudson, Jean Mitchell]. A considerable proportion have involved revenge on an unsatisfactory husband [Emma Aitken, Mme Fahmy, Alice Etheridge], boyfriend [Flora Davy, Maud Eddington, Ruth Ellis] or girlfriend [the Lesbians Marilyn Bain and Norma Everson]. Kate Webster murdered Mrs Thomas for plunder, Styllou Christofi took revenge on her daughter-in-law, and Mrs Pearcey and Lilian James took revenge on their rivals. Then we have Lilian Myra Giles who murdered her husband and son in two separate incidents, the baby-farmers Amelia Sachs and Annie Walters, and the unclassifiable case of the two weirdoes Ralph and Caroline Dyer. Of the six women executed, we can shed few tears for the terrible virago Kate Webster, the cunning Mrs Pearcey, the two baby-farmers or the murderous Styllou Christofi, but Ruth Ellis is the odd woman out, and in my opinion, she definitely ought to have received a pardon.

In the 97 instances where men murdered men, 36 murders were committed for profit or robbery, 12 involved gangsters, and 15 the homosexual underworld of the time. In 20 cases, the motive was hate or revenge, and 14 were random killings committed by obviously disturbed individuals. In not less than 166 of the murder houses of London, men murdered women. In 52 cases, husbands murdered their wives, and in 39 more, boyfriends their girlfriends. In 22 instances, prostitutes were murdered, and in eight, casual sex partners. In 16 of the cases where men murdered women, the motive was profit or robbery, 15 of the murders were committed for hate or revenge, and 14 were random slayings committed by disturbed individuals.

London's history of serial attackers goes all the way back to 1790, when that mysterious figure, the London Monster, was on the prowl in the Metropolis, slashing the buttocks of well-dressed women in the streets. A Welsh artificial flower-maker named Rhynwick Williams was convicted of being the Monster, but the evidence against him is far from convincing.[1] Then we have the Ratcliffe Highway serial killings in 1811, where two families were brutally murdered by an unknown assailant, for reasons presumed to be robbery. A sailor named John Williams was arrested for the murders, and committed suicide in police custody while awaiting trial, but the evidence in favour of his guilt is not very impressive.[2] In particular, it remains unexplained how a short, foppish man who was a laughing-stock among the tough East End sailors could murder several able-bodied people without making an uproar, or being injured himself. Both murder houses involved, the shop at No. 29 Ratcliffe Highway and the Kings's Arms public house in Old Gravel Lane, stood for many years after the murders, but neither remains today.

As for Jack the Ripper, that quintessential Victorian serial killer, he has not received much mention in this book, since his contributions to London's remaining architecture of capital crime are negligible, although the house at No. 29 Hanbury Street, where Jack murdered Annie Chapman in the back yard, stood until 1970. It is not generally known that around the 'Ripper' year of 1888, a number of young girls disappeared in the West Ham area; one of them, Amelia Jeffs, was found murdered in an empty house in 1890. The mystery of the West Ham Disappearances is a mystery still, and it has received comparatively little interest from crime historians and armchair detectives. Nor has it been appreciated that between the years 1903 and 1909, the Bloomsbury and Brixton areas of London were the scene of (at least) six unsolved murders of prostitutes, again suggesting that a serial killer might have been at large.

The Soho Stranglings in 1935 and 1936, claiming three victims, have been suggested to be the work of a previously unknown serial killer, but may well be the by-product of the gangster-related criminality in Soho at the time, culminating in the murder of 'Red Max' Kassel in 1936. The suave, gentlemanly-looking Gordon Cummins, also known as the Blackout Ripper, was a bona fide London serial killer, however. Cummins claimed four victims in 1942, but he may well be guilty of two unsolved murders the previous year. Soho was again the site of a suspected serial killing in 1947 and 1948, three mysterious murders of prostitutes that have left the same number of murder houses behind. The serial killer known as Jack the Stripper, who claimed six victims in 1965 and 1966, chose to deposit the naked corpses of his victims in the Thames. The strangely little-known psychopath Patrick Mackay, a serial killer preying mainly on elderly women from 1973 until arrested in 1975, admitted three murders and may well have been guilty of another five, and holder of the macabre record of leaving five London murder houses behind. As for that monster Dennis Nilsen, he outclasses all his fellow London serial killers with regard to the number of his victims, although he only made use of two murder houses to dispatch them.

The number of historic murder houses in a certain part of London depends on two independent variables: the degree of murderous activity in the area, and the amount of older houses still surviving. Some of the notorious old rookeries of crime, in Westminster, in the East End, and in St Giles's, have disappeared altogether, in large-scale slum clearances.[3] The East End has comparatively few murder houses standing, in spite of its formidable reputation for lawlessness, due to wartime destruction and widespread 'development' in recent times. In contrast, the architecture of capital crime in Paddington and Bayswater is still there to see; although the inhabitants of those parts have usually been well behaved, the solidly built terraces of houses remain to this day. Soho's plentiful population of gangsters, pimps and prostitutes, and its durable Georgian and Victorian architecture, had made sure that that a wealth of historic murder houses survive to this day. The kaleidoscope of respectability is reflected in London's architecture of capital crime.[4] Few murders occurred in the grand, newly built Bloomsbury town houses in Georgian and early Victorian times, but this area became the Murder Neighbourhood in the 1870s, a seedy area of fly-blown brothels and lodging-houses, where the most horrid and mysterious murders abounded. Bloomsbury gradually regained its lost respectability, and few murders take place in its expensive flats today. The long and gruesome criminal history of the great Metropolis is fascinating indeed: it is reflected, in a glass darkly, by the Murder Houses of London.

BIBLIOGRAPHY OF SOME KEY WORKS

M. Baggoley, *Surrey Executions* (Stroud 2011)

F. Barker & D. Silvester-Carr, *Crime & Scandal: The Black Plaque Guide to London* (London 1991)

I. Butler, *Murderers' London* (London 1973)

D. Cargill & J. Holland, *Scenes of Murder* (London 1964)

R.A. Downie, *Murder in London* (London 1973)

M. Fido, *Murder Guide to London* (London 1986)

G. Howse, *Foul Deeds and Suspicious Deaths in London's East End* (Barnsley 2005)

   A-Z of London Murders (Barnsley 2007)

B. Lane, *The Murder Club Guide to London* (London 1988)

J. Oates, *Unsolved Murders in Victorian and Edwardian London* (Barnsley 2007)

   Foul Deeds and Suspicious Deaths in Ealing (Barnsley 2007)

   Unsolved London Murders of the 1920s and 1930s (Barnsley 2009)

   Unsolved London Murders of the 1940s and 1950s (Barnsley 2009)

N. Papadimitrou, *Foul Deeds and Suspicious Deaths in Barnet, Finchley and Hendon* (Barnsley 2009)

E.S. Shaw, *A Companion to Murder* (London 1960)

   A Second Companion to Murder (London 1961)

L. Stratmann, *Middlesex Murders* (Stroud 2010)

   Greater London Murders (Stroud 2010)

MAJOR NEWSPAPERS CONSULTED

DE	Daily Express
DM	Daily Mirror
DMa	Daily Mail
DN	Daily News
DT	Daily Telegraph
ET	Evening Telegraph
Ind	Independent

IPB	Illustrated Police Budget
IPN	Illustrated Police News
LWN	Lloyd's Weekly Newspaper
MC	Morning Chronicle
MP	Morning Post
NYT	New York Times
PIP	Penny Illustrated Paper
RN	Reynolds' Newspaper
Sta	Standard

NOTES

INTRODUCTION

1. The first is J. Bondeson, *Murder Houses of London* (Stroud 2014), the second is *Murder Houses of South London* (Leicester 2015).
2. The five major modern sources on London's topography of capital crime are Cargill & Holland, *Scenes of Murder*, Butler, *Murderers' London*, Downie, *Murder in London*, Fido, *Murder Guide to London* and Barker & Silvester-Carr, *Black Plaque Guide to London*. On celebrated suburban murders, these book receive support from the 'Foul Deeds' series, particularly the useful books by Dr Jonathan Oates.

1. CAMDEN

1. OldBaileyOnline; *MC* 5 and 6 Oct 1814.
2. *MP* Oct 5 1814.
3. Fido, *Murder Guide to London*, 125-6; G. Howse, *Murder & Mayhem in North London* (Barnsley 2010), 2-3.
4. OldBaileyOnline; *DN* March 7 1885, *LWN* March 8 and 15 1885, *Sta* March 12 1885, *IPN* March 28 1885.
5. OldBaileyOnline; *MP* Nov 6 1891, *Jackson's Oxford Journal* Nov 14 1891.
6. NA CRIM 1/65/4; OldBaileyOnline and RootsWeb; *Times* Jan 19 1901 7b, *IPN* March 9 1901.
7. *British Journal of Psychiatry* 47 [1901], 630-1.
8. NA CRIM 1/150/1 and MEPO 20/1; *Times* May 28 1914 3g, *Manchester Evening News* May 27 1914, *Western Daily Press* June 26 1914.
9. NA WO 339/19050 and HO 144/1648/156610; B. Taylor (*Police History Society Journal* 16 [2001], 12-5); *Times* July 27 3e, Sept 20 5a and Nov 9 3d, 1915, *DMa* July 27 1915.
10. Books on the mystery of the Irish Crown Jewels include J.C. Ray, *The Mystery of the Irish Crown Jewels* (Cedar Rapids IA 1944), F. Bamford & V. Bankes, *Vicious Circle* (London 1965), J. Cafferky & K. Hannafin, *Scandal*

& Betrayal (Doughcloune Co. Cork 2002), M. Dungan, *The Stealing of the Irish Crown Jewels* (Dublin 2003) and T. Coates (Ed.), *The Theft of the Irish Crown Jewels* (Dublin 2009). On the two Shackletons, see R. Huntford, *Shackleton* (London 1996), and on Francis Bennett Goldney, see A. Bateman, *The Magpie Tendency* (Whitstable 1999). Articles about the mystery include those by F. Murray (*Age* May 17 1961), T. O'Riordan (*History Ireland* 9(4) [2001]. 23-8). N. Twomey (*Kerryman* July 20 2001), D. McKittrick (*Ind* Dec 11 2003) and L. Kelleher (*Sunday Mirror* June 29 2003), and the useful internet papers by S.J. Murphy, of the Centre of Irish Genealogical and Historical Studies.

11. NA MEPO 3/1678; Shaw, *Companion to Murder*, 214, M. Hastings, *The Other Mr Churchill* (London 1963), 186-9, *IPN* Jan 12 1933. *Times* Jan 4 7a, Jan 5 12b, Jan 7 5b, Jan 14 7c, 1933, *DM* Jan 4, 7, 14 and 21, 1933.

12. The trial was reported on in the *Times* March 15 16a, March 16 11b, March 17 16e, March 18 9c, 1933, *DM* March 16 and 18 1933, *DE* March 17 and 18, 1933.

13. *DE* March 22 1933.

14. NA MEPO 3/1700; TrueCrimeLibrary and RootsWeb; *Times* June 29 16e, July 2 13f, July 3 11f 1935, *DM* June 26, 28, 29, July 1 and 3, 1935.

15. *DM* June 29 1935.

16. *DE* July 1 1935.

17. *Times* Sept 18 7b, Sept 19 9e 1935, *DM* Sept 18 1935.

18. *Times* Oct 15 4g, Oct 22 13g 1935, *DM* Oct 28 1935.

19. *DM* Oct 31 1935.

20. *Times* Aug 21 7d and Aug 24 7e, 1935, *DM* Aug 21 and 22 1935, *DMa* Aug 22 1935, *ET* Aug 23 1935, *Western Daily Press* Aug 23 1935.

21. *DMa* Aug 22 1935.

22. NA CRIM 1/1280; *Times* Jan 16 2e, Jan 17 9e, Jan 25 2d, Feb 11 2e, 1941, *DM* Jan 15, 16 and 17, Feb 11, 1941 *DMa* Jan 15, 16 and 25, 1941.

23. *DT* April 1 1943 and the 'Historic Pentre' homepage.

24. I. Butler, *Murderers' London* (London 1973), 117-8, Lane, *Murder Club Guide to London*, 52-5, Howse, *A-Z of London Murders*, 26-7, Fido, *Murder Guide to London*, 126-7; *DM* Aug 25, Sept 9, Oct 27 and Dec 3 1955, *DE* Sept 2 and Oct 27 1955.

25. The books on the Ruth Ellis case include R. Hancock, *Ruth Ellis* (London 1963), J. Goodman & P Pringle (Eds.), *The Trial of Ruth Ellis* (Newton Abbot 1974), G. Ellis, *My Mother Ruth Ellis* (London 1995) and M. Jakubait, *Ruth Ellis* (London 2005); see also Butler, *Murderers' London*, 118-21, Lane, *Murder Club Guide to London*, 56-8 and Fido, *Murder Guide to London*, 127-9.

26. The Magdala Tavern is featured on various pub homepages, on GeoGraph, and in the *Hampstead and Highgate Express* May 3 2012.
27. *DMa* June 16 2006, *Guardian* Jan 2 2008.
28. *Guardian* Jan 29 2009, *DT* Jan 29 2009.
29. *Camden New Journal* Jan 29 2009 and Oct 14 2010, *Camden Review* Oct 7 2010.

2. HACKNEY, STOKE NEWINGTON AND TOTTENHAM

1. On the Hoxton Horror, see *Famous Crimes Past & Present* 10(125) [1905], 170-4 and G. Logan, *Guilty or Not Guilty* (London 1930), 257-8.
2. On the Morgan case, see Howse, *Foul Deeds and Suspicious Deaths in London's East End*, 103-7; on Emily Newber's crime, see *LWN* Dec 24 1893 and *PIP* Feb 17 1894.
3. G. Logan, *Rope, Knife and Chair* (London 1935), 100-11.
4. P. Stubley, *1888: London Murders in the Year of the Ripper* (London 2012), 208-10; N. Lacey, LSE Law, Society and Economy Working Papers 18/2009; OldBaileyOnline; *Sta* Dec 31 1888, *DN* Dec 31 1888, *MP* Dec 31 1888 and Jan 7 1889, *Times* Jan 7 1889 4f.
5. *Times* April 17 1901 11f, *DT* April 12 1901.
6. NA CRIM 1/68/1; OldBaileyOnline; see also *Times* July 27 13f, July 31 11e and Aug 3 12d, 1901, *DMa* Aug 8 1901, *Star* Sept 21 1901, *IPN* Aug 3 and 10 1901.
7. NA CRIM 1/93/10 AND 1/582/29; OldBaileyOnline; *Times* Oct 3 9E, Oct 5 8b, 1904, *DM* Oct 4, 6 and 14, Nov 23 1904, *PIP* Oct 8 and Nov 26 1904.
8. NA CRIM 1/104/4; OldBaileyOnline; *Times* Nov 19 1906 13d, *DM* Oct 19 and 21 1906, *Western Times* 20 and 24 Nov 1906.
9. NA PCOM 8/17; OldBaileyOnline; *Times* Nov 7 1910 14d, *DM* Nov 3 and 17, 1910.
10. On Robertson, see NA MEPO 2/232; *DM* July 28 1912, *IPN* July 31 1912.
11. On the Ferrari case, see NA MEPO 3/233; the ItalianGenealogy homepage; *Times* July 25 1913 4e and Aug 6 1913 3d, *DM* July 25 1913, *DMa* July 25 1913.
12. *DE* Oct 15 1917, *DMa* Oct 19 1917 and Nov 28 1918, *Liverpool Echo* Oct 15 1917.
13. NA CRIM 1/178/2; TrueCrimeLibrary; *Times* April 28 1919 16c, *DM*

May 22 1919.
14. *Times* Sept 10 1927 12d.
15. TrueCrimeLibrary; *DM* March 22, April 4 and 11 1922, *DT* March 21 1922, *Henley Standard* April 12 2012.
16. NA MEPO 3/1590; *Times* July 11 5f, Aug 3 7d, Sept 21 11d, Sept 22 7f, 1923, *DM* Sept 21 and 22 1923.
17. NA CRIM 1/1145; *Times* Dec 20 1939, Dec 28 1939 3d and Jan 16 1940 3d, *DM* Dec 28 1939 and Jan 16 1940, *DE* Dec 28 1939.
18. NA MEPO 3/2211; *DM* March 19 1942, *Hornsey Journal* March 20 and 27, May 1 1942.
19. NA CRIM 1/2525; *Times* Nov 19 1954 3g and Dec 11 1954 2g, *DE* Nov 18 1954 and Jan 14 1955, *DMa* Nov 17 and 18, Dec 11 1954, Jan 14 1955.
20. *Times* April 2 4e, April 5 8c, April 6 6g, April 22 8g, May 27 9b, 1960, *DM* April 2, 4, 5 and 22, 1960.
21. *DMa* June 8 and 9 1961.
22. *Times* Aug 30 4f, Sept 10 10d, Oct 20 6e, 1960.
23. *Times* July 3 1971 1d, *DM* July 3 1971.
24. NA MEPO 26/152; R. Narayan, *Black Community on Trial* (London 1976), 16-8.

3. KENSAL RISE, WILLESDEN, BRONDESBURY, KILBURN AND CRICKLEWOOD

1. A. Rattle & A. Vale, *Amelia Dyer, Angel Maker* (London 2007), 153-6, 179-81.
2. Stratmann, *Greater London Murders*, 35-42.
3. *Times* Aug 18 7b, Aug 26 3g, Sept 23 3e, 1939.
4. *Times* June 13 4d, June 15 4c and Oct 1 4a, 1955 and March 25 1964 8g.
5. NA CRIM 1/48/9; *Times* Aug 2 1897 4d, *MP* Aug 2 1897, *RN* July 18 1897, *DN* Sept 17 1897, *IPN* July 24 1897, *Hampshire Advertiser* July 17 1897.
6. On the Crossman case, see Shaw, *Second Companion to Murder*, 42-3, Downie, *Murder in London*, 162-3, Fido, *Murder Guide to London*, 129-31, Howse, *A-Z of London Murders*, 39; *Times* March 25 9c, March 29 9e, April 14 10f, 1904, *Star* May 14 1905.
7. L. Snow, *Queen's Park, Kensal, Brondesbury and Harlesden* (Chichester 2006), 65.
8. NA CRIM 1/104/1; *Times* Sept 8 7a and Sept 15 14a, 1906, *DM* Sept 15 1906, *Poverty Bay Herald* Oct 9 1906, *Grey River Argus* Nov 16 1906, *Bay*

of Plenty Times Nov 19 1906.
9. NA CRIM 1/118/2; OldBaileyOnline; *Times* Oct 14 4d and Oct 28 4a, 1910, *DM* Oct 17 1910.
10. Oliver Smith's later tribulations are recorded in NA PCOM 8/304.
11. On the Quarry case, see NA MEPO 3/1699; M. Hamblin Smith (*British Journal of Psychiatry* 81 [1935], 923-4); *Times* June 12 14b, July 15 7d, July 25 16a, July 26 11e, July 30 16e, Aug 15 4g, 1935.
12. NA MEPO 3/1744; Oates, *Unsolved London Murders of the 1940s and 1950s*, 15-9; *Times* April 12 1940 10a, *DM* April 11 1940.
13. NA MEPO 3/2165.
14. Fido, *Murder Guide to London*, 129, *Times* Dec 22 1959 4d, Jan 7 15e, Jan 21 17d, Jan 22 17a, March 5 3f, 1960, *DM* Nov 16, Dec 4, 12 and 24 1959, Jan 21, 22, June 15 1960.
15. NA MEPO 2/11381; *DE* July 20 1968, *Daily Sketch* July 29 1968, *Slough Express* July 19 1968, *Sunday Telegraph* July 28 1968 and Jan 5 1969.
16. *Times* Aug 2 1971 2g and *DE* July 31 1971.
17. On Dennis Nilsen, see J. Lisners, *House of Horrors* (London 1983), B. McConnell & D. Bence, *The Nilsen File* (London 1983) and B. Masters, *Killing for Company* (London 1986); also Lane, *Murder Club Guide to London*, 29-34, Barker & Silvester-Carr, *Crime & Scandal*, 245-8; *DM* Feb 12, Oct 25 and Nov 4 1983.
18. On Nilsen's later vicissitudes, see *DM* Dec 22 1983, April 4 1995, April 25 1998, Dec 26 1998 and Aug 27 2005.
19. *DM* April 29 1994.

4. HAMMERSMITH AND BARNES

1. C. Duckworth, *The d'Antraigues Phenomenon* (Newcastle upon Tyne 1986), M. Grimwade & C. Hailstone, *Murder and Mystery in Barnes and Mortlake*, Barnes and Mortlake History Society Occasional Paper No. 2, 1989; de Loriol, *South London Murders*, 13-6, Oates, *Foul Deeds and Suspicious Deaths in Richmond and Kingston*, 19-23; *MC* July 25 1812, *Caledonian Mercury* July 25 and 27 1812.
2. 'The Dartmoor Suspect' on Casebook; *Times* Feb 27 1896 7e, *RN* Jan 26 1896, *IPN* Feb 1 1896, *Sta* Feb 6 1896, *DN* Feb 27 1896.
3. NA CRIM 1/70/2 and 1/582/21; OldBaileyOnline; *Times* Dec 25 1901 7a and Feb 13 1902 9a.
4. NA CRIM 1/192/3; *Times* April 27 1921 9b, *DM* April 15, 16 and 27 1921, *IPN* April 21 1921.

5. *Times* Dec 5 1922 5e, *DE* Dec 3 1922.
6. *Times* May 23 1924 5g.
7. NA MEPO 3/1626; S. Mazzarella in the internet book *Filson Young*, Chapter 39; *Times* Jan 17 7e and Jan 20 9a, 1927, *DM* Jan 17 and 20 1927, *IPN* Jan 20 1927.
8. *Times* Jan 28 1942 9g, *DMa* Jan 27 1942, *Dundee Courier* Jan 27 and 28 1942.
9. NA MEPO 3/3137.
10. *Times* Dec 2 1954 8f, Dec 3 1954 5b, Jan 20 1955 5c, *DM* Dec 3 and 18 1954, *DE* Dec 18 1954, *DMa* Dec 3 1954 and Jan 20 1955.
11. Oates, *Unsolved London Murders of the 1940s and 1950s*, 125-31; TrueCrimeLibrary; *Times* April 30 5d, May 1 6g, 1956, *DMa* May 22 1956.
12. *Times* Aug 28 6d, Dec 2 7c and Dec 3 7e, 1959, *DMa* Aug 28 and Dec 3 1959.
13. On the Arbaney case, see NA CRIM 1/4166; *Times* July 5 1963 12f, Oct 9 1963 5f, *DM* July 27 1963, *DMa* Oct 9 1963.
14. *DT* Nov 4 2011, *DMa* Nov 4 2011.
15. *DMa* Aug 10 2012.

5. WEST LONDON

1. T. Tullett, *Portrait of a Bad Man* (London 1956), H. McLeane, *Chesney the Fabulous Murderer* (London n.d.); Stratmann, *Greater London Murders*, 77-84. Dr Jonathan Oates informs me that N. 22 Montpelier Road was demolished as late as around 1990. It is curious that there is an [invented] ghost story concerning No. 16 Montpelier Road, said to have been the site of a murder, and many suicides.
2. OldBaileyOnline; Oates, *Foul Deeds and Suspicious Deaths in Ealing*, 77-82; *PMG* Oct 23 1880, *Sta* Oct 26 and Nov 2 1880, *IPN* Oct 30, Nov 6 and 13, Dec 4 1880, *LWN* Oct 31 and Nov 7 1880, *RN* Oct 31, Nov 28, Dec 5 and 19 1880.
3. NA CRIM 1/115/7; OldBaileyOnline; *Times* March 2 1910 3c, *New Zealand Herald* Feb 26 1910.
4. Oates, *Foul Deeds and Suspicious Deaths in Ealing*, 100-5; *Times* April 3 1912 8e, April 18 1912 4a, *DM* April 3 and 4, 1912.5. Oates, *Foul Deeds and Suspicious Deaths in Ealing*, 106-8; *Times* Aug 25 1917 3e.
6. NA CRIM 1/831; Oates, *Foul Deeds and Suspicious Deaths in Ealing*, 113-6; *Times* March 4 4g, March 11 13g, March 20 11d, 1936.
7. On the Derrick case, see NA MEPO 3/1715; Fido, *Murder Guide to*

London, 122, Oates, *Foul Deeds and Suspicious Deaths in Ealing*, 124-9; *DM* Sept 24 1936, *DE* Sept 23 and 24 1936.

8. On the Priddle case, see NA MEPO 3/1728; Oates, *Unsolved London Murders of the 1920s and 1930s*, 184-9 and *Foul Deeds and Suspicious Deaths in Ealing*, 124-9; *Times* Jan 15 7e, Feb 9 4b, 1938, *DM* Feb 9 1938, *DE* Jan 7 1938.

9. On the Paul case, see NA MEPO 1/1735 and HO 144/22665; Shaw, *Second Companion to Murder*, 168-70, Stratmann, *Middlesex Murders*, 125-39; *Times* Dec 1 11c, Dec 2 11a, Dec 9 8f and Dec 16 13e, 1938, *DM* Dec 2 1938, *DE* Nov 29 and 30 1938, *DMa* Dec 1, 2 and 16 1938.

10. Oates, *Foul Deeds and Suspicious Deaths in Ealing*, 141-5, *Times* Dec 4 3e, Dec 11 2e, 1941 and Jan 20 1942 8g.

11. On the Deane case, see NA MEPO 2/2190; Oates, *Foul Deeds and Suspicious Deaths in Ealing*, 137-40; *Times* Nov 14 2e, Dec 16 9d, Dec 27 2e, 1941.

12. Stratmann, *Middlesex Murders*, 140-51; *Times* Sept 16 2e, Sept 17 2d, Sept 18 9c, Sept 19 2e 1941, *DM* July 8, 12, 19 and 30, Aug 2 and Sept 16, 19 and 26, 1941.

13. Oates, *Unsolved London Murders of the 1940s and 1950s*, 154-9. On the Bridges case, see also *Times* Aug 29 5e, Nov 16 4c, 1957, *DM* Aug 29 1957, *DE* Aug 29 1957, Jan 3 and 5 1959.

6. NORTH LONDON

1. On the Gouldstone case, see *Times* Aug 10 1883 12a and Aug 14 1883 8e, *IPN* Aug 18 1883; on Louisa Jane Pope, see *Times* Sept 15 1905 10c.

2. Stratmann, *Greater London Murders*, 153-60.

3. On the Marshalls of Griggs Road, see Howse, *Foul Deeds and Suspicious Deaths in London's East End*, 173-7.

4. NA MEPO 20/1; NA MEPO 3/1653, *IPN* April 3 1930 and RootsChat.

5. The unfortunate Harknetts are on the RootsWeb homepage; see also *Times* July 20 1892 4f, July 22 1892 6d, *Sta* July 22 1892, *Jackson's Oxford Journal* July 23 1892, *New Zealand Herald* Sept 3 1892.

6. *Essex Newsman* Jan 11 1902, *Manchester Evening News* Jan 8 1902.

7. On the Mansfield case, see NA CRIM 1/135/1; *DM* Nov 8 and 20 1912, *DE* Oct 3 1912, *DMa* Oct 3 and Nov 8 1912, *ET* Oct 11 and Nov 7 1912.

8. NA CRIM 1/179/3; Papadimitrou, *Foul Deeds and Suspicious Deaths in Barnet, Finchley and Hendon*, 76-85, Stratmann, *Middlesex Murders*, 63-77; *Times* July 11 9c, July 12 12e, July 14 9a, July 15 7c, July 18 8e, July 26

7c, 1919, *DM* Sept 17 1919, *DE* July 15 and Sept 17 1919.

9.   NA MEPO 3/1617; *Times* Sept 9 1925 9g, Sept 11 1925 9d, *IPN* Sept 17 1925.

10. NA CRIM 1/577; *DM* Nov 6 1931, *DMa* Nov 6 and 21 1931, *ET* Nov 5 and 20 1931.

11. On the Vaissiere case, see NA CRIM 1/885;*Times* Oct 22 18d, Nov 13 13g, 1936, *DM* Oct 22 and Nov 13 1936, *DE* Nov 13 1936, *Heraldton Guardian* March 23 1937.

12. On the Etheridge case, see NA CRIM 1/970 and DPP2/488; *Times* Sept 23 9d, Oct 1 7g, Oct 15 4c, Oct 20 4c, 1937, *DE* Sept 23 1937, *DMa* Sept 23 1937.

13. On the murder of Lilian Maud Chamberlain, see NA MEPO 3/1723; J. Oates, *Foul Deeds and Suspicious Deaths around Uxbridge* (Barnsley 2008), 144-5; *Times* Aug 31 7d, Sept 4 7c, Sept 14 5f, Oct 19 11d, Oct 20 11b, Nov 10 11g and Nov 19 29a, 1937, *IPN* Sept 2 and Nov 25 1937

14. *DE* Oct 20 1937.

15. NA MEPO 3/1725; *Times* Jan 18 1938 9f, *DE* Feb 8 and 10 1938, *ET* Dec 9 1937, *Aberdeen Journal* Feb 15 1938, *Dundee Courier* Nov 11 1937, *IPN* Dec 2 1937

16. NA CRIM 1/10/9; Papadimitrou, *Foul Deeds and Suspicious Deaths in Barnet, Finchley and Hendon*, 133-5; *Times* May 6 13g, May 16 21d, May 19 7e, 1938.

17. *Times* April 28 2c, May 15 2c, 1942, *DE* May 15 1942.

18. *Times* April 13 6b, April 20 20b, 1939.

19. NA MEPO 3/2223; Papadimitrou, *Foul Deeds and Suspicious Deaths in Barnet, Finchley and Hendon*, 154-7.

20. On the Horner case, see NA MEPO 3/2250; Oates, *Unsolved London Murders of the 1940s and 1950s*, 37-45; *DMa* April 6 1943.

21. *Times* June 19 2c, July 20 2g, 1943, *DM* July 20 1943, *DE* July 20 1943, *ET* June 3 and Aug 3 1943.

22. On the McCormack case, see NA MEPO 3/3015; Stratmann, *Greater London Murders*, 127-32; *Times* Sept 28 1948 2g and *DM* Sept 14 1948.

23. Downie, *Murder in London*, 161-2, Papadimitrou, *Foul Deeds and Suspicious Deaths in Barnet, Finchley and Hendon*, 168-76; *Times* Oct 12 2d, Oct 13 2b, Oct 28 6e, Nov 4 6c, Nov 23 2c, Nov 24 6e, Nov 26 2c, 1949, Jan 6 2e and Jan 7 3c 1950, *DM* Oct 11, Nov 24 and 25, 1949.

24. *DM* Dec 18 1949.

25. J. Grout & L. Fisher, *Murder without Motive* (London 2009); *This is Local London* Sept 16 2008 and *Hendon & Finchley Times* Oct 9 2009.

26. J. Williams, *Hume* (London 1960), R. Furneaux, *Famous Criminal Cases 6* (London 1960), 49-91, Shaw, *Second Companion to Murder*, 98-100; *DM* Nov 16 and Dec 7 1949, Jan 19 and 27 1950

27. *DM* Feb 2 and 3 1959

28. *DM* Feb 7 1961.

29. *DM* Aug 21 1976

30. *DMa* Oct 9 2001.

31. NA CRIM 1/2390; *Times* Dec 17 1953 3d, Jan 13 13g, March 3 3g, March 4 4e, March 5 4f, 1954, *DM* March 3 1954, *DMa* Dec 17, 18 and 19 1953, March 5 1954.

32. On the Pulfer case, see NA DPP 2/2654; Papadimitrou, *Foul Deeds and Suspicious Deaths in Barnet, Finchley and Hendon*, 177-81; *Times* March 28 10a, March 29 10d, March 30 4a, April 13 3c and May 9 6c 1957, *DM* March 27 1957, *DE* March 28 and 29 1957, *DMa* March 28 1957.

33. NA CRIM 1/3549.

34. W. Young, *Obsessive Poisoner* (London 1973) and A. Holden, *The St Albans Poisoner* (London 1974), J. Sharp on CrimeLibrary and J.B. Cavanagh (*Neuropathology and Applied Neurobiology* 17 [1991], 3-9); *DM* July 6 1962.

35. *DM* June 20 and 30 1972, Nov 25 2006.

36. *DM* Aug 3 1990.

7. EAST LONDON

1. On Charlie Brown and his tavern, see the 'Isle of Dogs Life' homepage.

2. On these four cases, see NA MEPO 20/1.

3. On Cronin, see *Times* June 22 1925 11f and July 31 1925 4d; www.eastlondonhistory.com.

4. On the Plaistow Horror, see OldBaileyOnline; *Times* Sept 17 1895 13e, Sept 18 1895 5b and 7d, *Hampshire Telegraph* Sept 21 1895, *Auckland Star* Oct 5 1895, *Poverty Bay Herald* Sept 17 1895; also N. Freeman, *1895, Drama, Disaster and Disgrace in Late Victorian Britain* (Edinburgh 2011), 156-64. On the extraordinary Cocker case, see *DM* July 31 1918, *IPN* Aug 8 1918 and *Lloyd's Sunday News* Aug 4 1918. For a full account of these cases, see J. Bondeson (*Ripperologist* 138 [2014], 42-7).

5. On these two cases, see L. Rhodes & K. Abnett, *Foul Deeds and Suspicious Deaths in Barking, Dagenham & Chadwell Heath* (Barnsley 2007), 159-70 and *DM* July 24 and 25, Dec 15 1964.

6. NA CRIM 1/29/4; P. Stubley, *1888: London Murders in the Year of the Ripper* (London 2012), 208-10, OldBaileyOnline; *Times* Feb 28 1888 10e, *Sta* Feb 22 and March 21 1888, *RN* Feb 26 and March 4 1888, *LWN* March 4 1888.

7. The main accounts of the murder of Amelia Jeffs and the West Ham

Vanishings are E. O'Donnell, *Strange Disappearances* (London 1927), 292-7 and *Rooms of Mystery* (London 1931), 86-104, R. Whittington-Egan in T. Wilmot (Ed.) *Weekend Book of Murder and Mayhem* (Leeds 1983), 43-7 and *Murder Files* (London 2006), 128-30; see also Oates, *Unsolved Murders in Victorian and Edwardian London*, 88-95. There is an interesting discussion of the case on the Casebook website.

8. Early newspaper coverage of the murder includes *Times* Feb 15 1890 7f, *MP* Feb 15 1890, *DN* Feb 17 1890, *Sta* Feb 15 1890, *IPN* Feb 8 and 15 1890, *PIP* Feb 22 and March 1 1890, *RN* Feb 16 1890.

9. On the inquest, see *Times* Feb 18 1890 12b, *DN* Feb 18 1890, *Sta* Feb 18 1890, *LWN* Feb 23 1890, *RN* Feb 23 1890.

10. *Times* March 4 1890 11a and March 11 1890 4f, *MP* March 11 1890, *DN* March 4 1890, *Sta* March 4 1890, *IPN* March 8 1890, *LWN* March 9 and 16 1890, *RN* March 16 1890.

11. On the mysterious business with the keys, see *Times* May 17 1890 13f and May 19 1890 6d, *Sta* May 17 1890, *IPN* May 24 1890.

12. M. Macnaghten, *Days of my Years* (London 1914), 123-6; *MP* Aug 5 1891.

13. E. O'Donnell, *Strange Disappearances* (London 1927), 292-7, Oates, *Unsolved Murders in Victorian and Edwardian London*, 88-95; *DN* April 3 1882 and Jan 14 1884, *PIP* Feb 4, April 15 and 22, July 24 1882, *Lloyd's News* June 3 1882, *RN* Dec 10 1882.

14. *Times* Aug 12 1892 15e, Jan 9 1893 13b, *DN* Aug 5 1892, *LWN* Aug 14 1892, *Sta* Jan 9 1893, *RN* Jan 15 1893.

15. *IPN* July 8 1893.

16. L. Rhodes & K. Abnett, *Foul Deeds and Suspicious Deaths in Barking, Dagenham & Chadwell Heath* (Barnsley 2007), *Sta* Jan 4 1899, *LWN* Jan 8 and Feb 5 1899, *Auckland Star* Feb 18 1899; *IPN* March 11 1899, *DN* March 22 1899, *PMG* Nov 14 1899, *New Zealand Herald* April 15 1899.

17. E. O'Donnell, *Rooms of Mystery* (London 1931), 86-104,

18. *Sta* May 6 1892, *Huddersfield Chronicle* May 7 1892.

19. On the Sudul case, see *Times* Dec 25 1906 4d and *IPN* Dec 29 1906.

20. On the Nadin case, see NA CRIM 1/111/8; OldBaileyOnline and FreeBMD; *DM* Nov 23 1908, *Barrier Miner* Feb 17 1909.

21. On Limpus, see NA CRIM 1/130/1; OldBaileyOnline; *DM* Feb 12 1912, *DE* Feb 12 1912, *Evening Post* March 30 1912.

22. L. Rhodes & K. Abnett, *Foul Deeds and Suspicious Deaths in Barking, Dagenham & Chadwell Heath* (Barnsley 2007), 81-4; *Times* Jan 10 6c, Jan 15 3g, 1912.

23. NA CRIM 1/150/5 and MEPO 20/1; *Times* July 18 1914 4f, *Essex Newsman* July 25 1914, *New Zealand Herald* Sept 5 1914.

24. NA MEPO 3/262A; G. Logan, *Rope, Knife and Chair* (London 1935), 111-

20; *DM* April 30, May 1, 5 and 9 1919, *DE* May 9, June 24 and 25, July 11 1919, *IPN* May 8 1919.

25. D. Grey (*Crimes and Misdemeanours* 3(2) [2009], 60-77); *Times* July 31 9c, Aug 4 5b, Aug 8 4g, Aug 14 7c, Aug 21 7e, Aug 22 7b, Sept 20 7c and Sept 22 7a, 1919, *DM* July 3, Aug 8 and 21, Sept 20 1919.

26. On the Barton case, see *Times* Feb 4 11b, Feb 27 14e, Match 17 5e and April 3 11g, 1925, *DM* Jan 27 1925, *IPN* Jan 29 1925.

27. On the Newing case, see NA MEPO 3/1686; L. Rhodes & K. Abnutt, *Foul Deeds and Suspicious Deaths in Barking, Dagenham & Chadwell Heath* (Barnsley 2007), 143-50; TrueCrime Library; *Times* July 22 7e, Sept 22 14c, 1933.

28. On the Bauckham case, see NA CRIM 1/872; *DE* Sept 15 and 22, Oct 15 1936, *Gloucester Citizen* Oct 15 1936.

29. On Frank Hart, see NA MEPO 3/1719; *Times* April 27 16f, April 30 18c, May 1 13b, May 8 8g, May 29 11b, June 22 4f, June 28 11d, 1937, *DM* April 29 and 30 1937, *DE* April 30 1937.

30. On the Marden case, see NA CRIM 1/1178 and *Times* March 20 1940 6b and April 26 1940 8c.

31. On William Henry Davies, see NA MEPO 3/2274 and *DM* April 22 1944.

32. On the Kilbey case, see NA CRIM 1/1622; also *DM* Aug 16 1944, *Derby Evening Telegraph* Aug 1 1944.

33. On the Sedgwick case, see NA MEPO 3/2286; *Times* Feb 7 1945 2e, Feb 26 1945 2c, *DM* Jan 10 1945, *ET* Feb 6 1945.

34. On the Kemp/Senefft case, see NA CRIM 1/2707 and DPP 2/2508; *Times* Feb 20 3e, Feb 21 5b, Feb 28 5a, March 14 6f, April 28 4a, May 14 6c, 1956, *DE* Feb20 and April 28 1956, *DMa* Feb 20 and April 28 1956..

35. NA CRIM 1/2952 and DPP 2/2798; *DM* March 8 1956.

36. NA MEPO 2/11145 and CRIM 1/5032; *Times* Dec 17 1968 3c.

37. *Times* May 5 1971, G. Miller (*Modern Law Review* 35 [1972]. 426-30].

DISCUSSION

1. J. Bondeson, *The London Monster* (Stroud 2005).

2. G. Logan, *Masters of Crime* (London 1928), 144-60, P.D. James & T.A. Critchley, *The Maul and the Pear Tree* (London 1987).

3. D. Severs (*Journal of Architecture* 15 [2010], 449-497).

4. Like it does in Paris; see D. Kalifa (*French Historical Studies* 27 [2004], 175-194).